Hawai'i Days

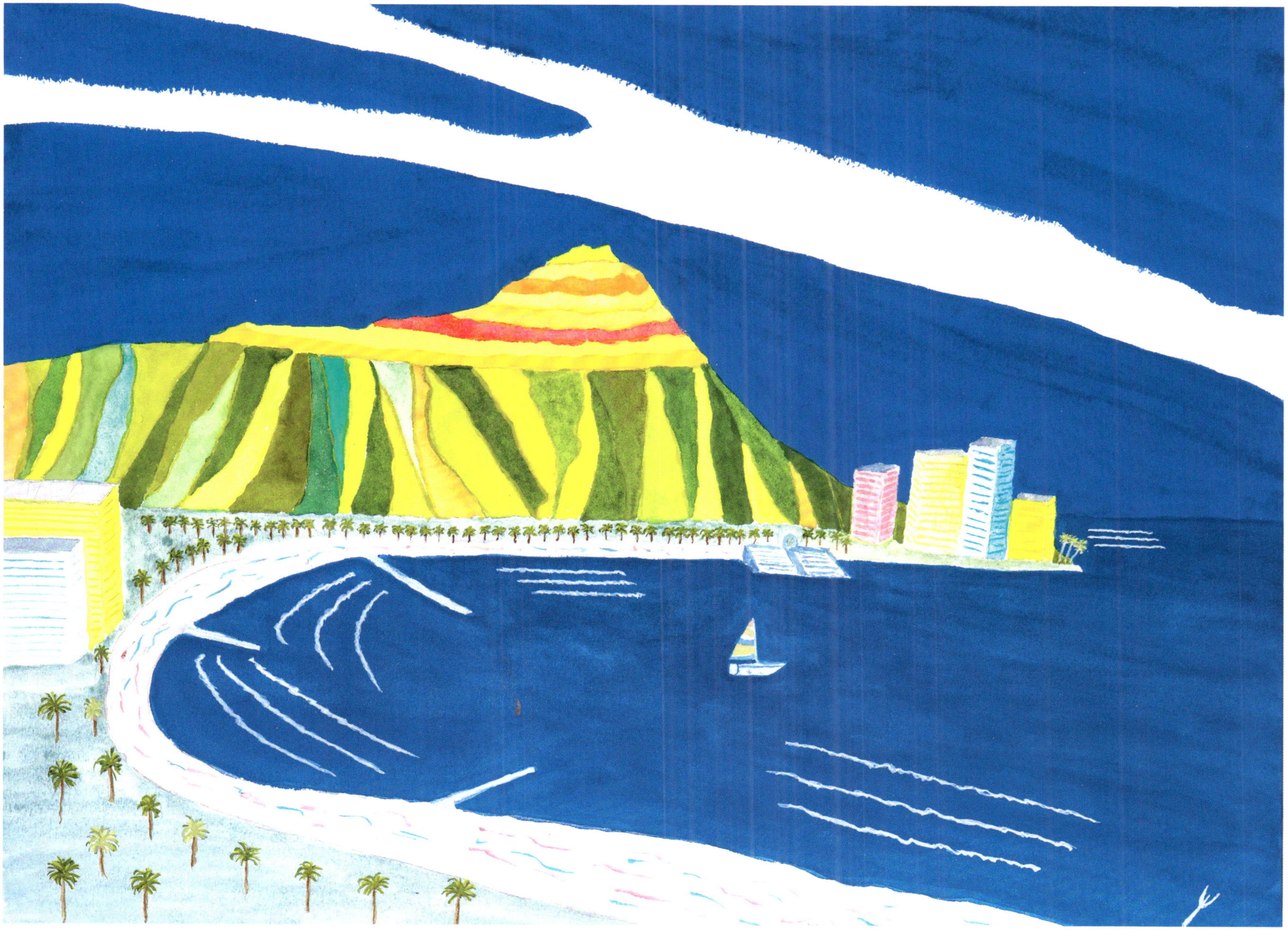

Written and Illustrated by Bro Halff

Hawai'i Days

Hawai'i Days

Written & Illustrated
by
Bro Halff

Simpler Gifts Press, LLC
San Diego

Published in 2025 by Simpler Gifts Press, LLC
and Bro Halff Gallery Hawai'i, LLC

For information, address the publishers:

Simpler Gifts Press, LLC
1050 Rosecrans Street, Suite D
San Diego, California 92106

Bro Halff Gallery Hawai'i, LLC
1706 Keoniloa Place
Koloa, Hawai'i 96756

Library of Congress Card Catalog Number
ISBN 978-1-885238-18-4

This book is dedicated to
the people of Hawai'i.

Hawai'i has been my home for nineteen years. I first visited it forty years ago. It has changed a great deal in those decades. Nevertheless, it remains at heart a surprising miracle.

The state of Hawai'i is an island archipelago in the eastern Pacific Ocean. It stretches for almost 1600 miles and includes 132 islands, reefs, and shoals, with eight principal islands, seven of which are permanently inhabited.

Part of the miracle of Hawai'i is its geology. The state is the southeastern tip of an undersea volcanic mountain range, primarily underwater, that stretches 3800 miles, from southeast of the Big Island of Hawai'i to the Meiji Seamount, east of the Kamchatka Peninsula in eastern Russia. This long volcanic mountain range began to form about 82 million years ago, as lava from the Hawaiian Hot Spot, under the surface of the earth, began to spew lava into the ocean and raise underwater mountains, or seamounts. The resulting Hawaiian Emperor Volcanic Mountain Chain exists because the Pacific Tectonic Plate has been migrating to the north and northwest, at about 3.4 inches per year, for over eighty million years.

Thus, while the Hawaiian Hotspot has remained in approximately the same location for all these years, the surface of the earth, on a tectonic plate, has been moving. About 47 million years ago, the plate veered from a northward to a more northwestward direction. Its speed has varied considerably over the ages, from about 3.9 inches per year to 2.05 inches per year.

The land mass that comprises most of what we call Hawai'i started forming about 5.1 million years ago, as the volume of magma produced by the Hawaiian Hotspot increased, and the most recently formed seamounts rose higher above the ocean than had earlier seamounts in the chain. Therefore, the two highest mountains in the archipelago, Mauna Kea and Mauna Loa, rise to an altitude of almost 14,000 feet above sea level. Mauna Kea was once over 15,000 feet above sea level, but all the Hawaiian volcanic mountains gradually subside under their own weight. It is exciting to realize that these mountains, while rising only 14,000 feet above sea level, have bases that lie over 16,000 feet below sea level. That is, these are mountains that are over thirty thousand feet high, from their bases to their summits.

The magma, rising through the earth's mantle from its lower crust through its upper crust, accounts for the existence of the Hawaiian Islands. Southeast of Kīlauea, the most active volcano on the Big Island, is a seamount, Lō'ihi, which eventually will break the surface of the ocean to become a new island, or an extension of the Big Island.

I mention all this geological history to lend perspective to the Hawai'i that we experience today. The archipelago is the southeastern tip of a mountain range that the earth has been fashioning, and transporting northwest, for over eighty million years. Further, increased magma flow in the last five million years has precipitated the emergence of the eight principal islands in the chain.

What is perhaps most remarkable is that this archipelago is the most isolated inhabited island chain in the world, in terms of its distance from any major island mass or continent. It is almost 2500 miles from the West Coast of the United States. When you fly to Hawai'i, this geographical reality strikes you forcefully. In a flight lasting at least five to six hours, you see nothing except ocean and clouds. When the Hawaiian Islands finally appear, they appear so diminutive from the air that it is hard to believe that airplanes successfully navigate to them. They are needles in the haystack.

This book and its companion volume, *Hawai'i Visions,* are my efforts to convey some of the awe, surprise, and delight that Hawai'i has inspired in me over the last forty years. Living here, I have discovered that Hawai'i is a world unto itself, geographically isolated, historically unparalleled in its range of events and influences, and culturally unique.

However, even a thorough introduction to Hawai'i's history and geological saga could not portray Hawai'i's truest gift to those who settle here. What Hawai'i bestows on many who visit and live here is a deep and abiding love, or *aloha,* for these islands, and for the people who give them a culture all its own. Hawai'i is no longer isolated, in terms of travel to and from other destinations, but its way of being, of seeing the world, and of relating to others makes it unique and priceless. It will always remain for me a surprising miracle, even though it is one that many hands and minds have helped to forge. They have done so under the steady influence of the land and ocean that constitute Hawai'i's "āina," meaning the land and manifestations of nature that sustain all life in Hawai'i.

This, then, is a personal story for me. I hope that as I tell it, in art, prose and poetry, I can give you a glimpse into the elusive spirit of Hawai'i, which changes but somehow remains constant, on islands that comprise worlds in their own universe.

A Warm Blessing

An orange
smudge
on the lips
of the horizon
kisses
a driveway
and three palm trees,
reminding them
that the bright-winged light,
dressed in purple,
rose, gold,
and lavender robes,
has blazed
a trail home,
and now
will leave them
to share
a long chat
with a neighborhood
of farsighted
stars.

Late Light, Po'ipū, Kaua'i

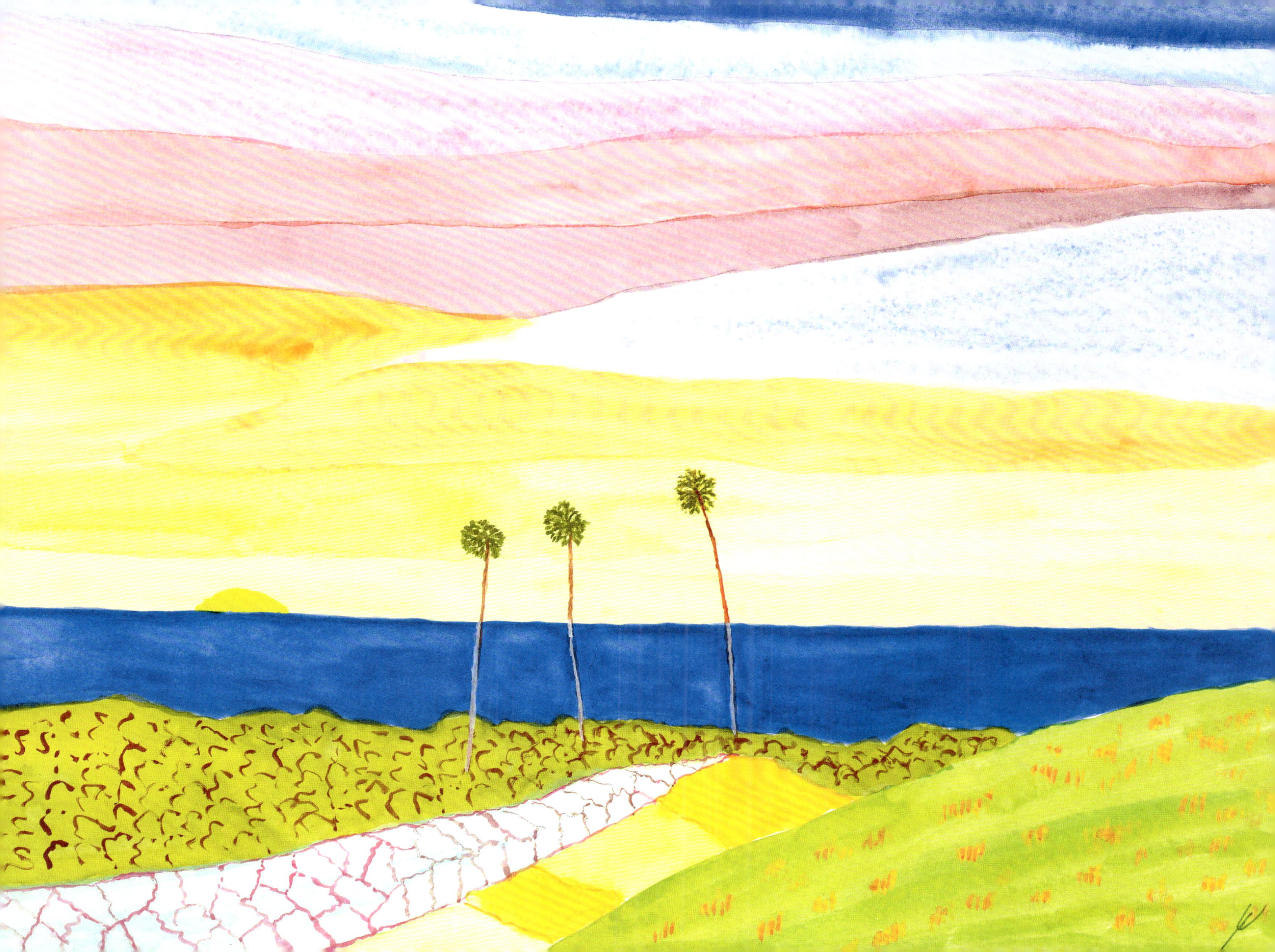

A Stranger Coming Home

When I need it,
the quiet red cottage
rests
in sunlight,
and when shadows
overtake it,
while the forest,
and the mountain,
and the twisted road
loom
about it,
I open my eyes
to its untroubled gaze,
which spots
the green lawn
that sits waiting for me,
before its always
happy-to-open
front door.

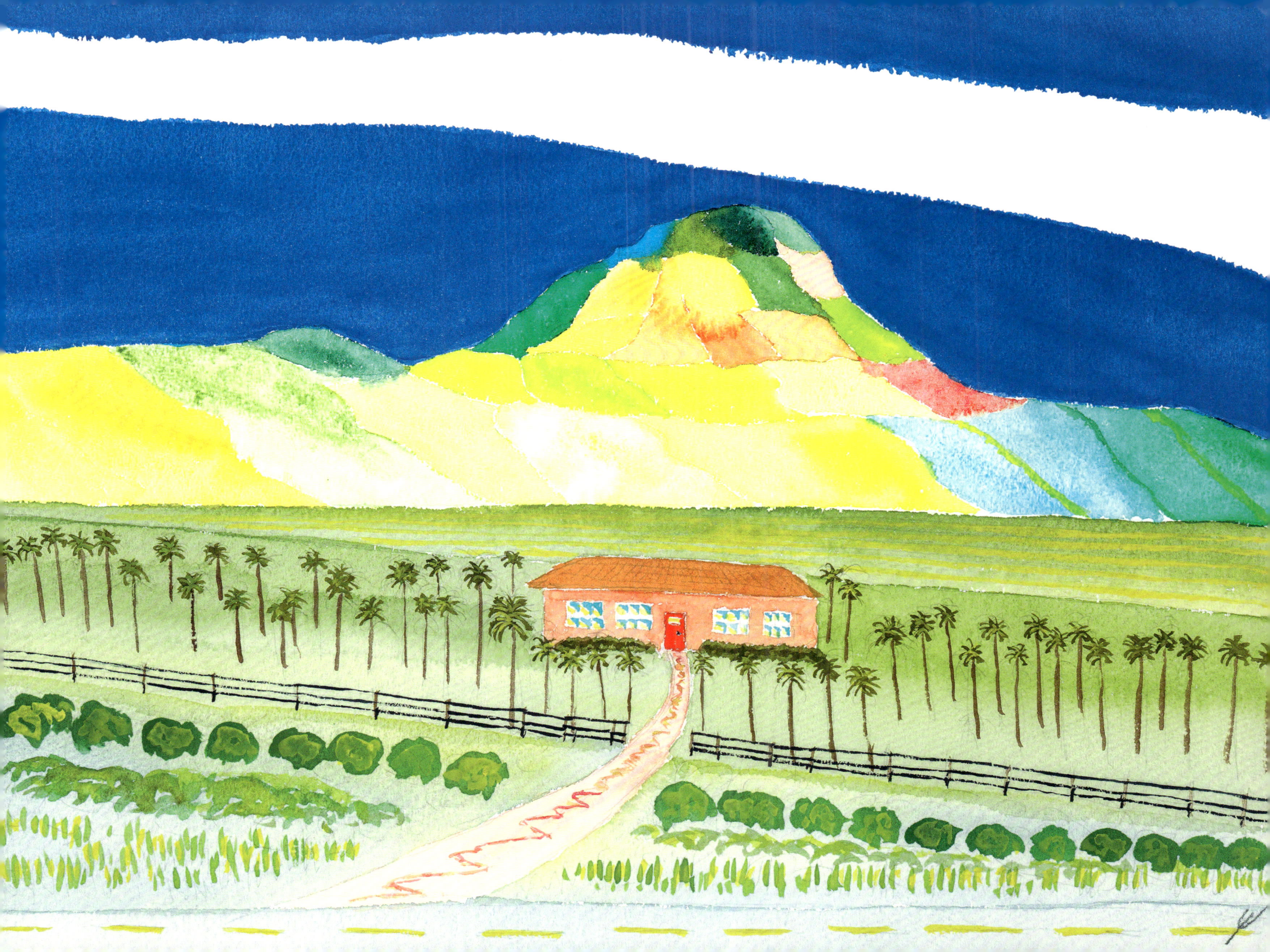

Autumn Pilgrims

High mountains,
running their way
to the ocean,
bump into clouds
that cling to the summits,
casting
their tears
and their shadows
on the broad shoulders
of peaks,
which have enough sense
to let everything,
even sunlight,
slide off their backs.

Kālepa Ridge, Kaua'i

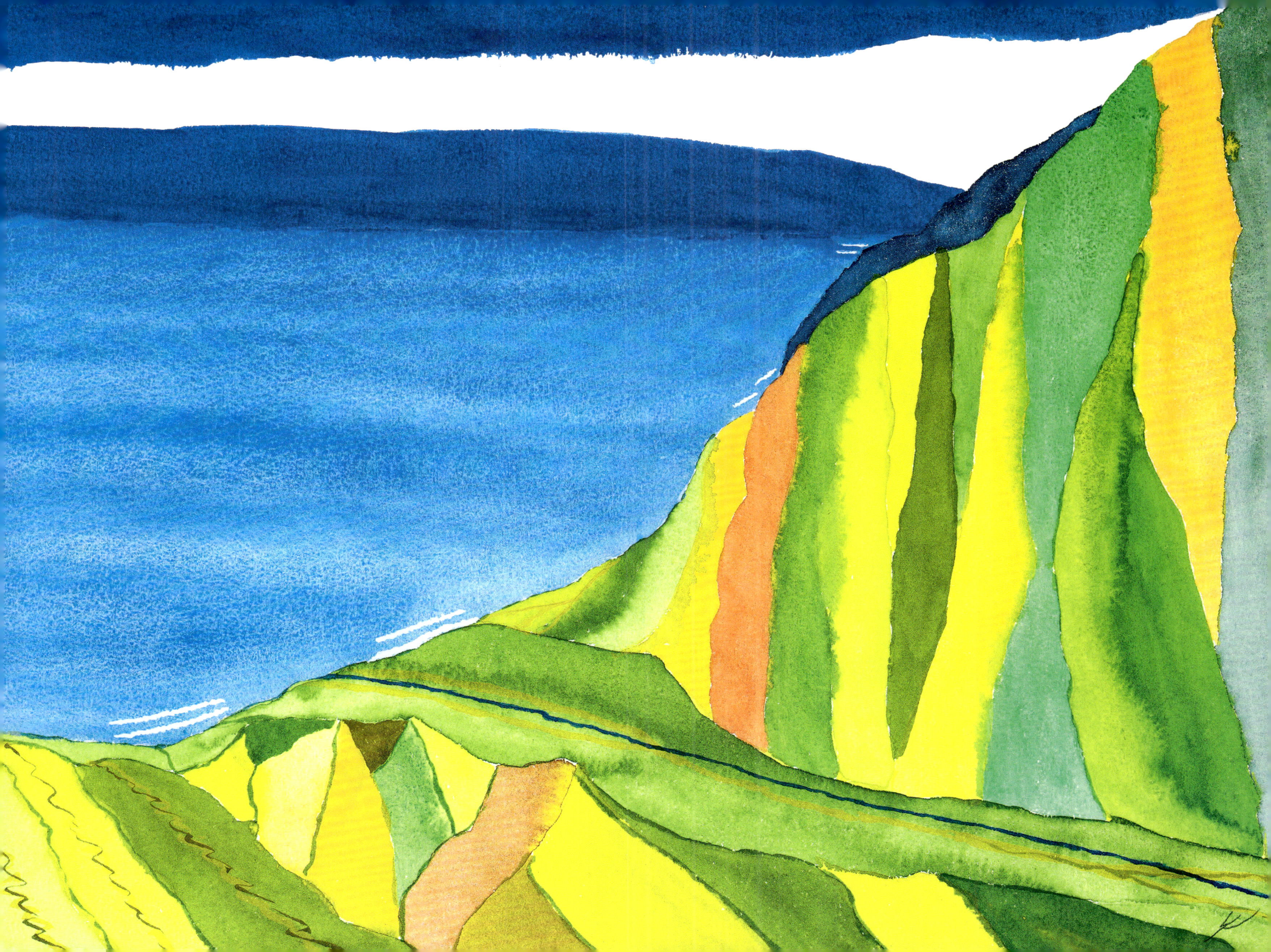

An Unplanned Vacation

The green coast
blossoms
in the early afternoon,
unfolding its foliage
in the extravagant sunlight,
as it climbs
pudgy hills,
to get a glimpse
of the ocean,
before stretching out
for a peaceful nap,
while distant waves
raise their heads,
to tell stories
of islands,
and the green coast
daydreams
of sand
between its toes.

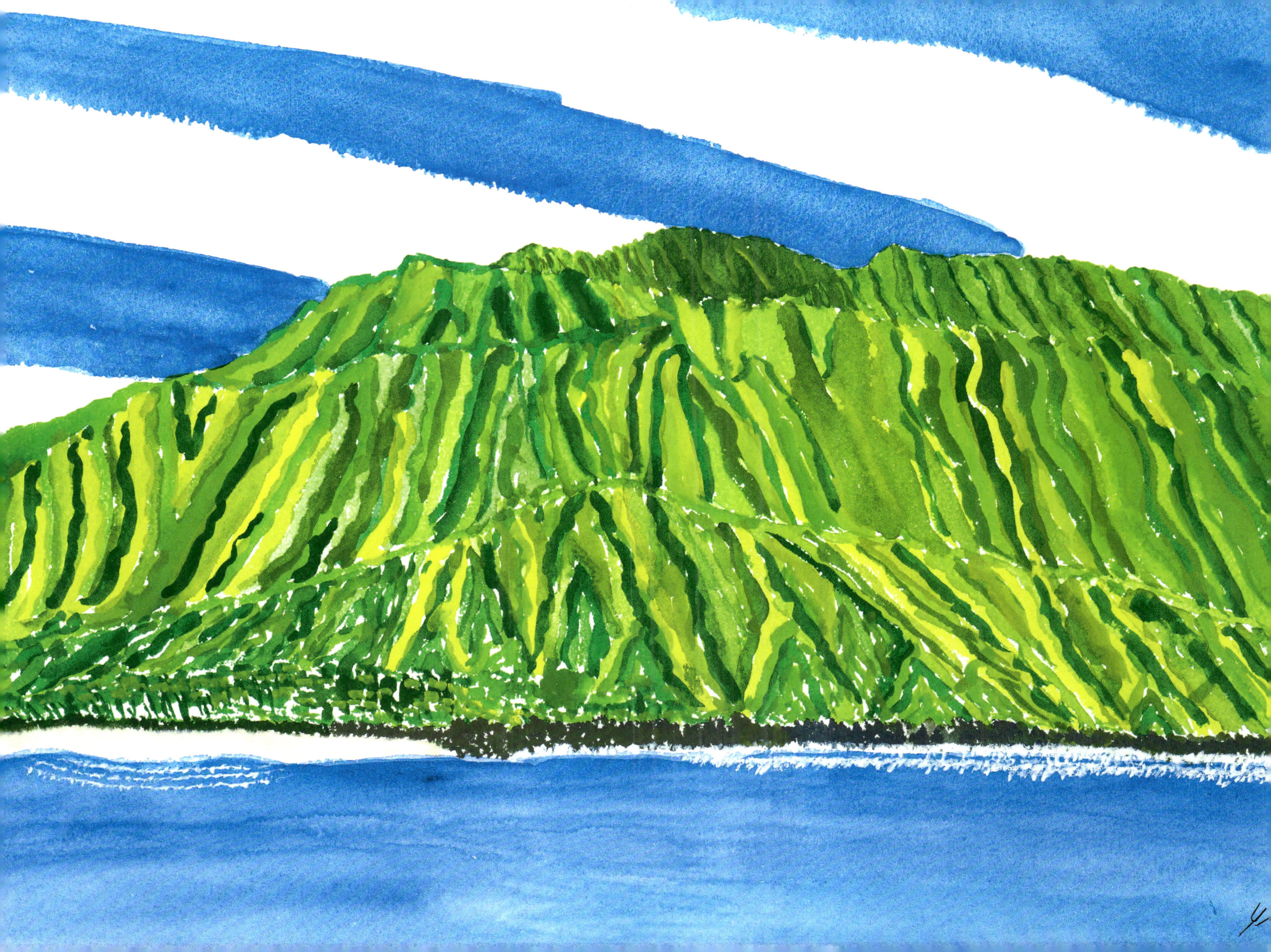

Partners

A wind
off the ocean,
tugging
at palm trees,
dances
across the island,
twisting
in and out
of the arms
of hibiscus bushes,
until it leaps
up the side
of a mountain,
where it finds
a bevy of clouds,
waiting,
with unfurled petticoats,
to trip the light fantastic
across a sky
that welcomes
the first breath
of spring.

South Shore of Kaua'i in Spring

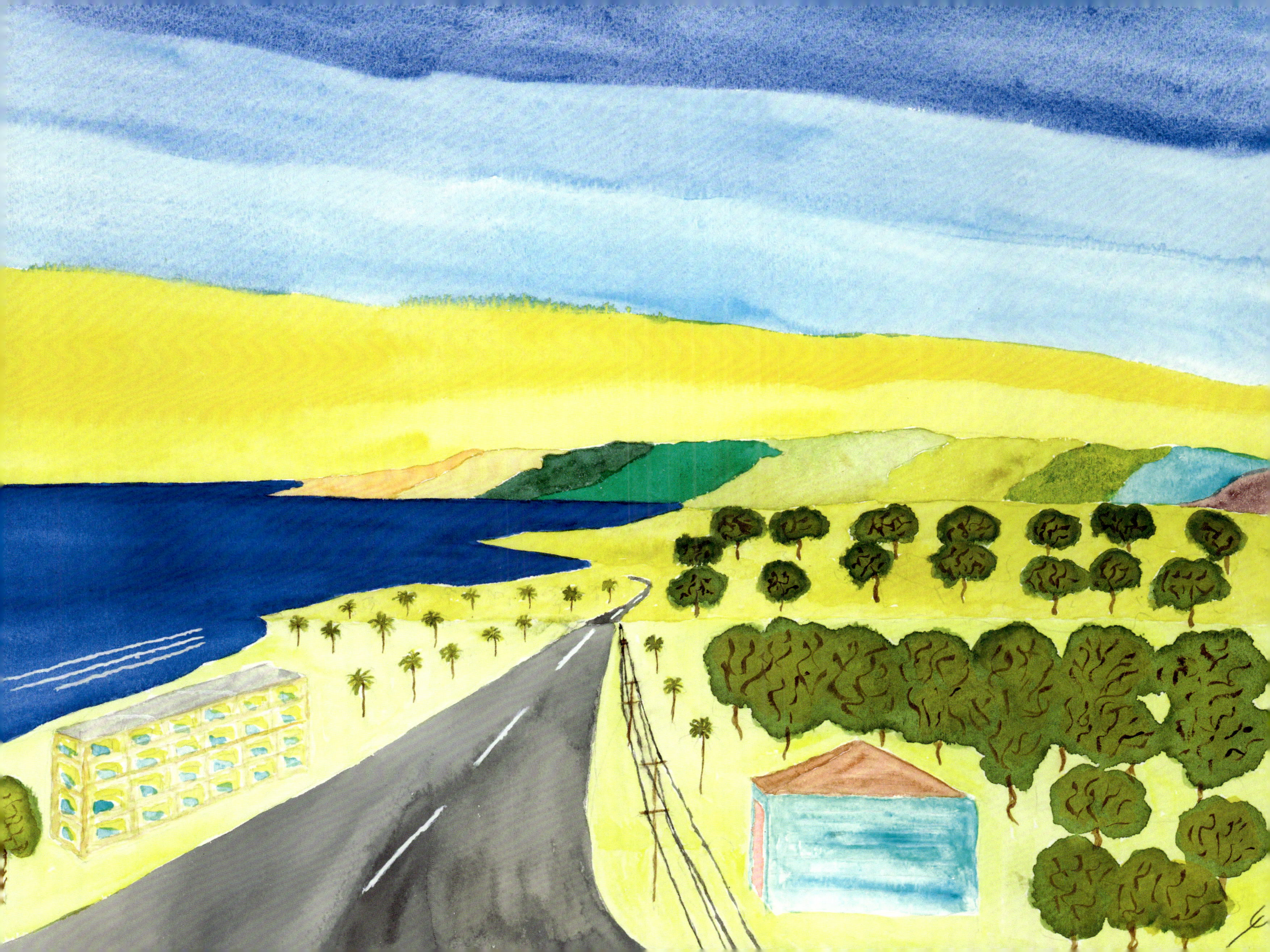

Facing Out

An old mountain,
with its wrinkled brow,
beams
in late light,
watching the ocean
unfurl its aproned lap,
which unseen hands
wrinkle and straighten,
while the mountain
gazes at a sailboat,
floating
at the horizon,
and high-hatted clouds
set afloat
a fleet
of calm-faced shadows.

A Soft Caress

A hula dancer
in a red and white dress,
a slow-growing
hibiscus garden,
lifts her arms
and sways her body –
glancing skyward,
she signals
a forest of stars,
which answer her
with a wayward smile,
as she draws
into her embrace
the shadow
of a graceful
kiawe tree.

A Cool Suitor

The tradewinds
return,
blessed messengers,
promising
a second spring,
before summer's fever
banishes
all kisses
from the soft-spoken
north.

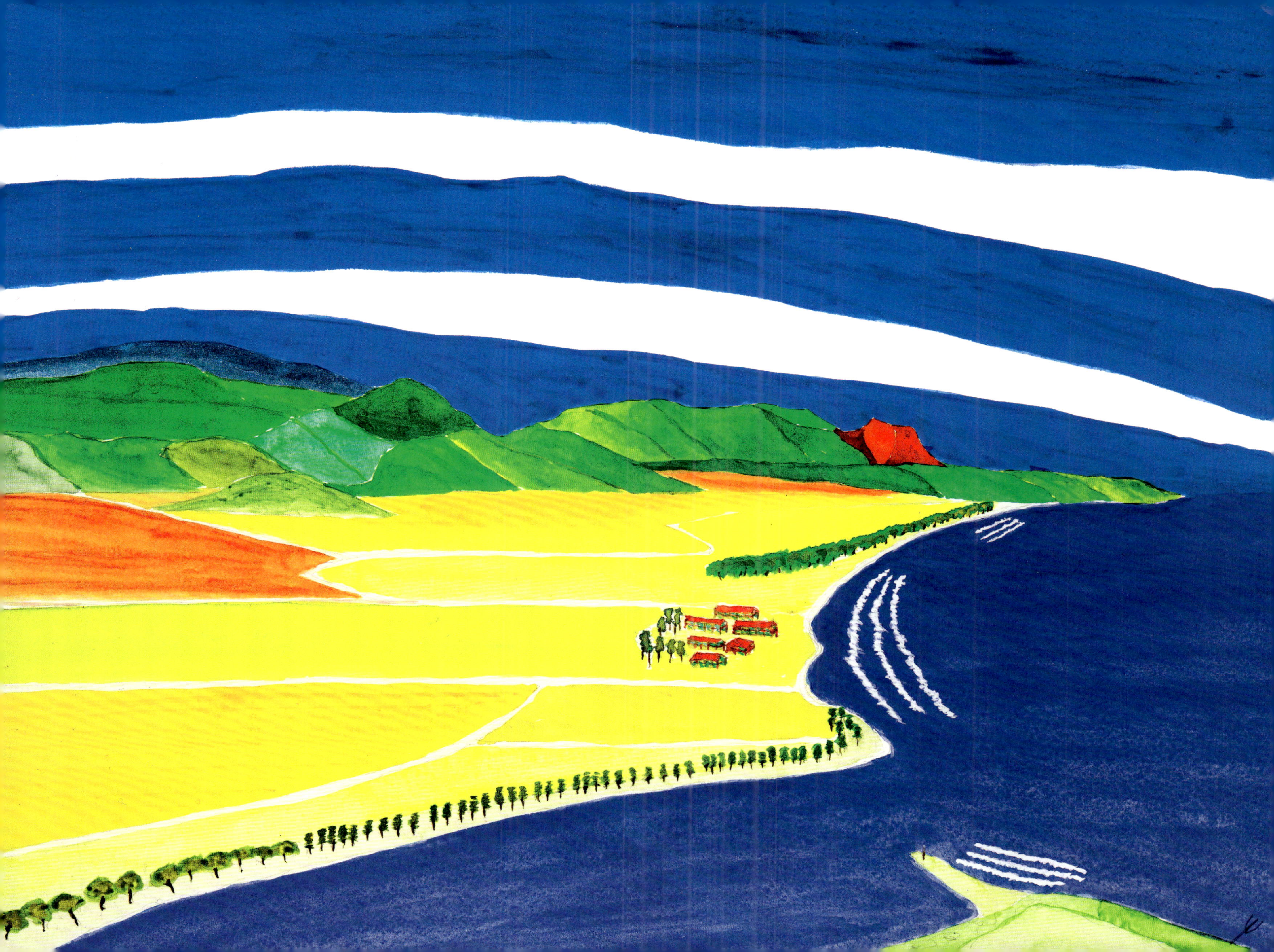

Sheltering the Past

Children grow up
when you least expect it,
running away
from their old photographs –
seeing them
perched there
in timeless sunlight,
sitting on an old car,
bestowing their smiles,
you cannot imagine
that now, on distant roads,
they step on accelerators
and head
for the horizon,
their faces serious,
worrying about
tomorrow.

Old Kōloa House, Kaua'i

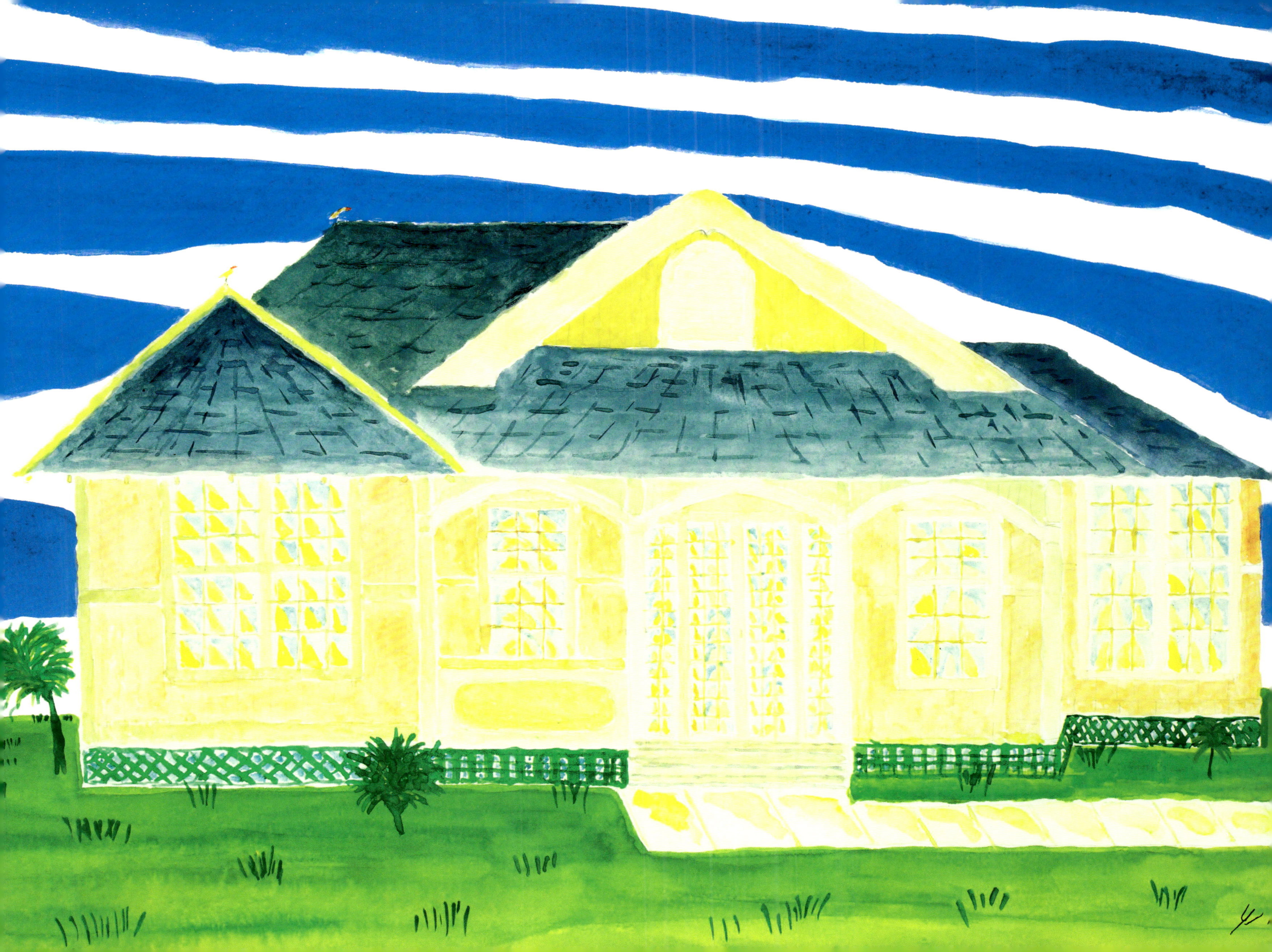

Day and Night

A rose sky
at dusk
settles down
for a nap
on the horizon's broad shoulders,
until, dozing off,
it dreams
of awakening,
under a downpour
of silver
confetti.

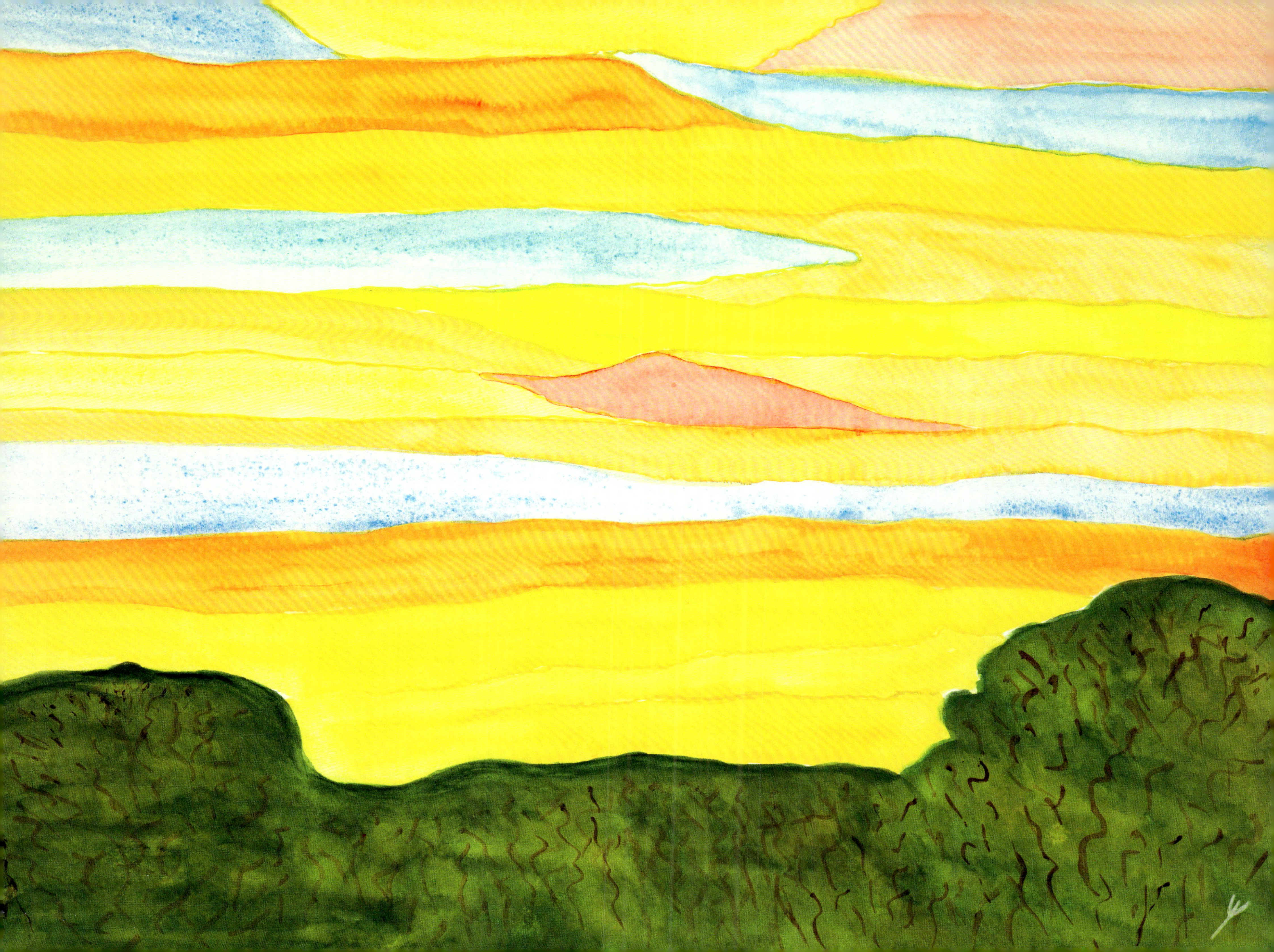

A Fond Welcome

An old fisherman
sits
on a park bench,
healing his nets –
listening
to the waves,
somersaulting
over one another,
as they cheer
in the subdued light,
he lets his fingers
dance
with translucent strands,
which greet
each other
and entwine,
holding hands,
while the old man
lets a sea breeze
comb out his beard,
as he,
with calm hands,
builds a home
for wayfaring
fish.

Reef Fishing, Po'ipū, Kaua'i

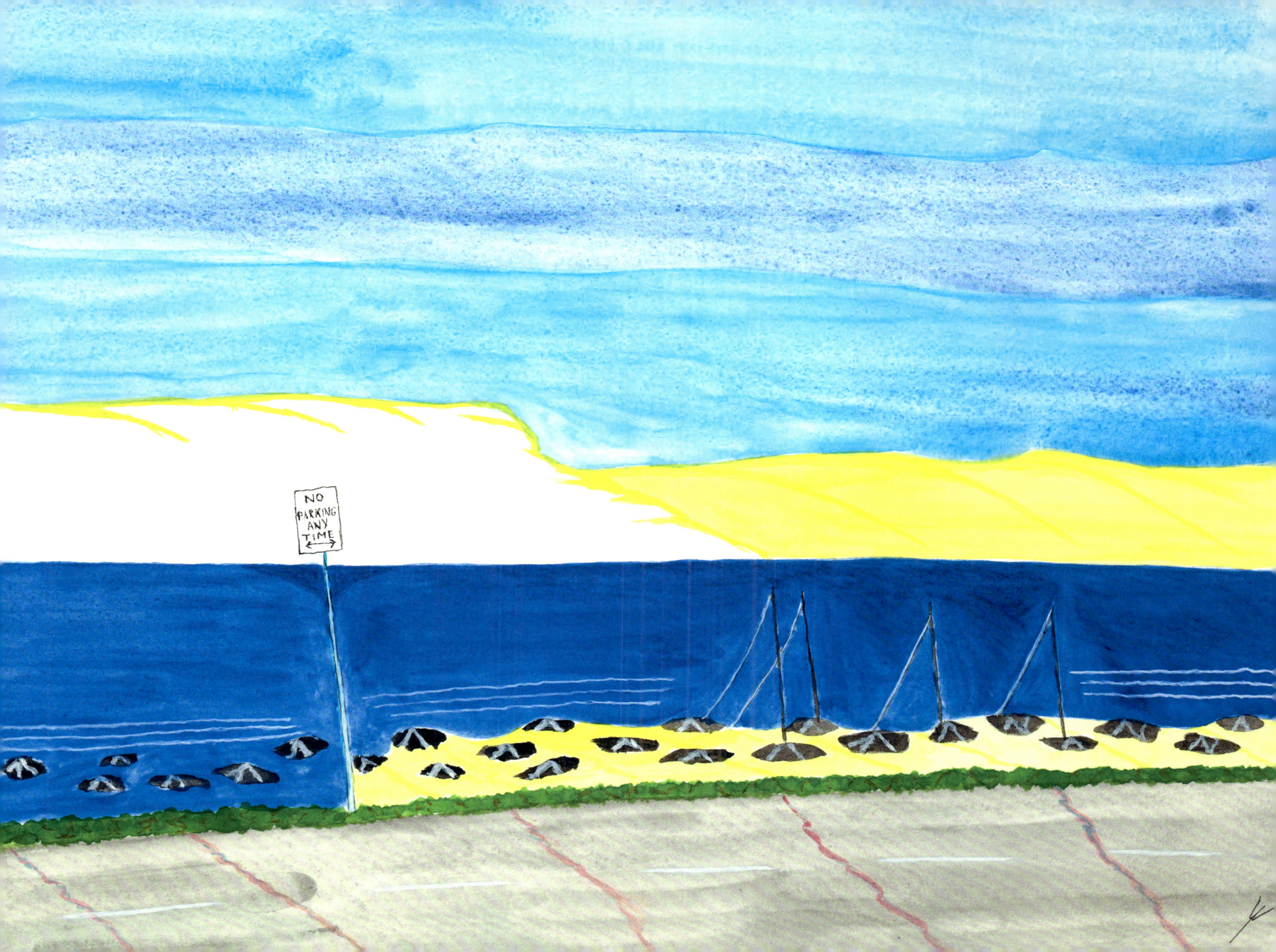
NO
PARKING
ANY
TIME

Enchanting Kaua'i

Magic
island,
asleep
in the afternoon,
you raise
your mountaintops
to rainbows,
and populate
grassy fields
with the grazing
shadows
of clouds.

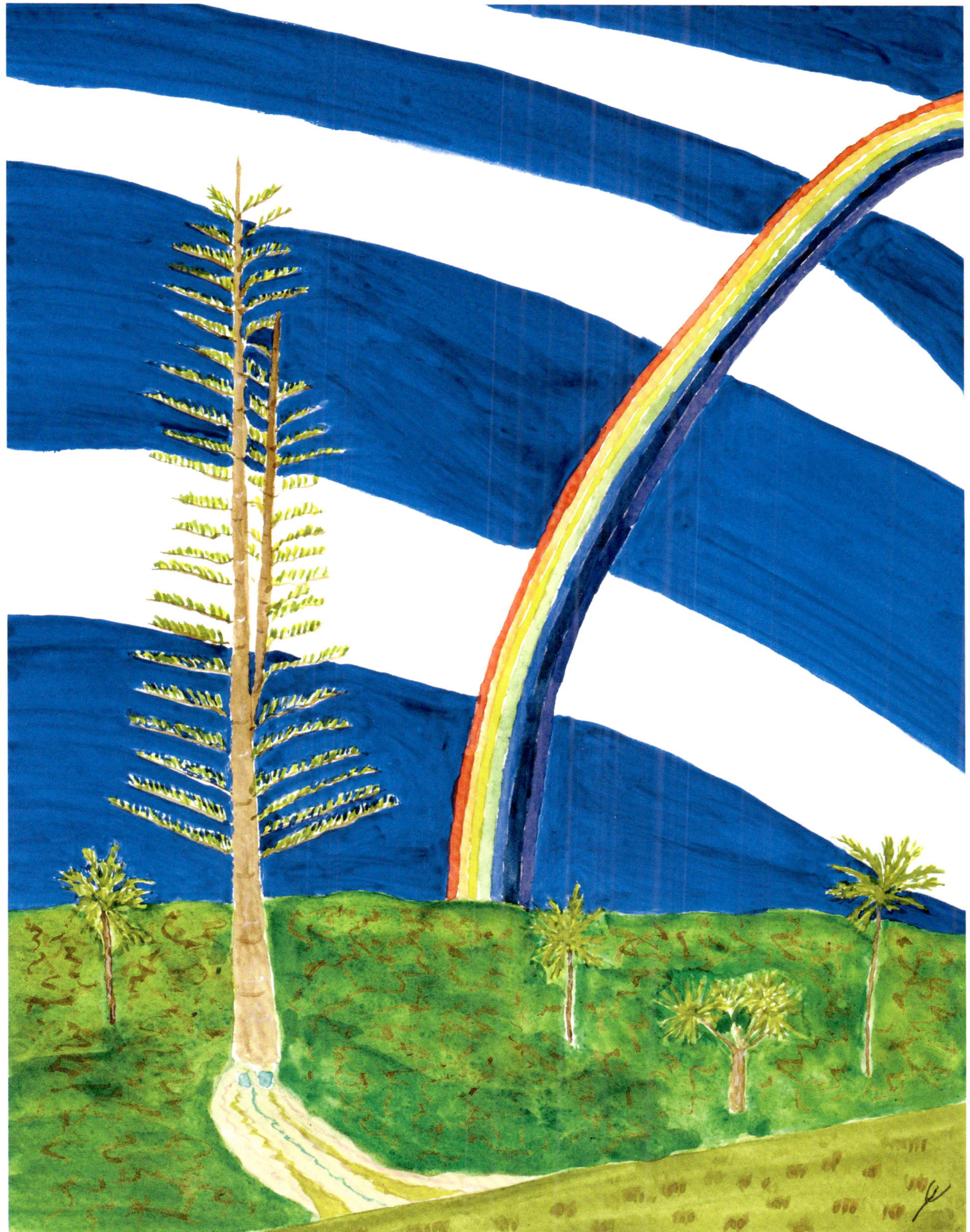

Before the Harvest

Cane whispers
to the wind,
while streams
in sluices
gurgle
and gasp,
leaving a wanderer
to tramp down the path,
listening
to unseen companions,
in fields
that outstretch their hands,
to wayfarers
who welcome
the news of bounty
that a flock
of egrets,
feasting on grasshoppers,
announce
to the sky.

Old Cane Road, Kōloa, Kaua'i

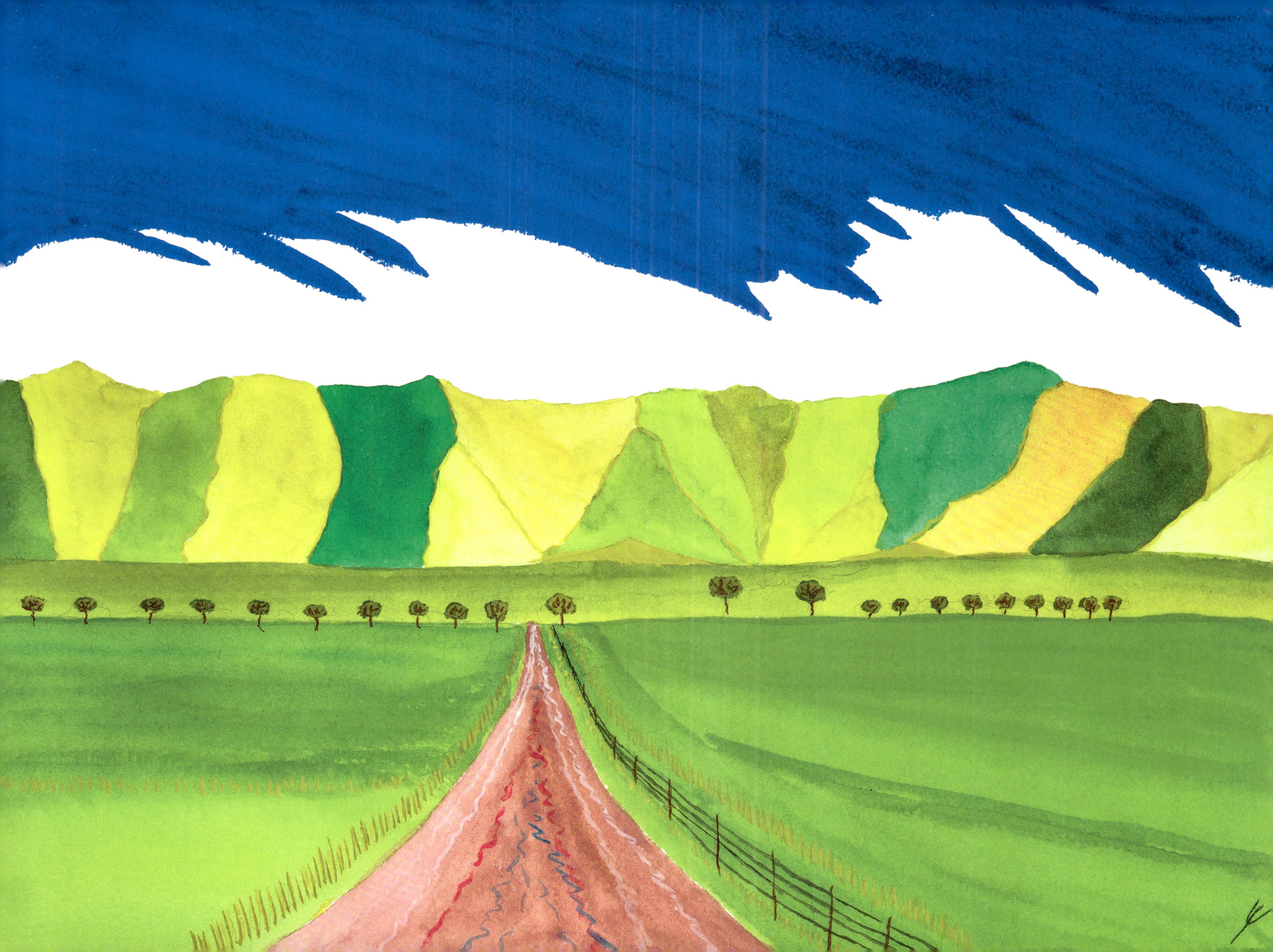

A Hanging Garden

Wisteria
blossoms
climb down a fence,
dangling their lavender flowers,
tier upon tier,
on a blustery day
in April –
shaking their ringlets,
the vines
relax
in the sunlight,
flirting
with a sidewalk
that has been following
the same gray course
for decades,
but welcomes today
the touch
of a wild-eyed
beauty,
who is tempted
to run away
with the wind.

On Vacation

The womp-womp lady
sits
on the beach,
sipping a Mai Tai,
as she chuckles
to herself –
all around her,
tidy families
play ball,
or dip their toes
in the menacing waves,
while she,
under her hibiscus-emblazoned umbrella,
lets her makeup
run,
as the sunlight,
creeping
under her wide-brimmed straw hat,
steals a kiss
from her volcano-red
lips.

Headliners

A blue sky
above the high clouds
dances
for journeying
strangers –
the big top
of the heavens
makes room
for a circus
of trapeze-artist
islands,
and whales
that welcome
the sunlight's
applause.

Southeastern Coast, Kaua'i

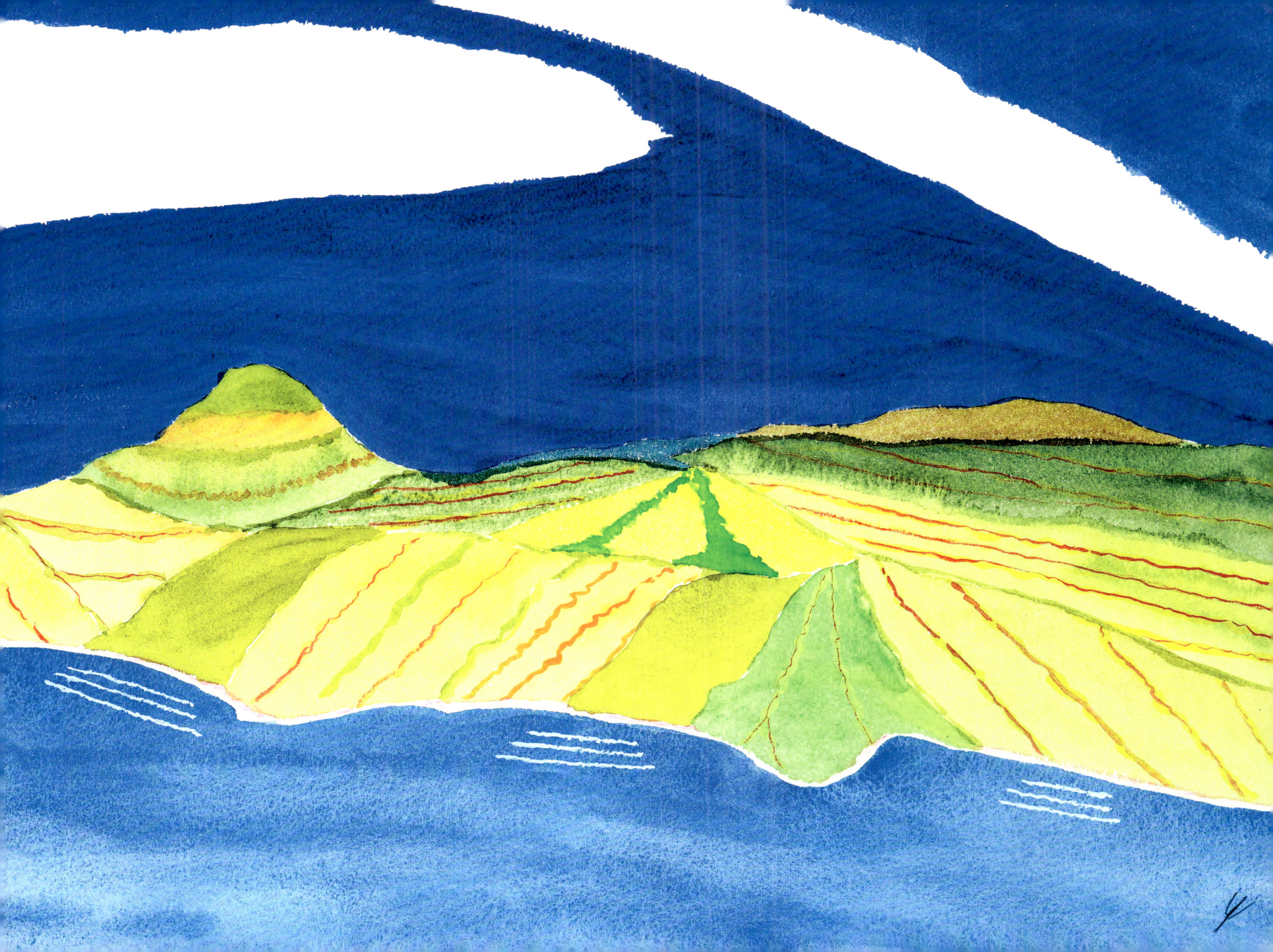

Castaways

On a calm day,
the waves
swim ashore
on their backs,
gazing up
at a porcelain sky,
where an artist
has painted
a blue and white
portrait
of a princess
who smiles
at the tawny flanks
of washed-ashore
beaches.

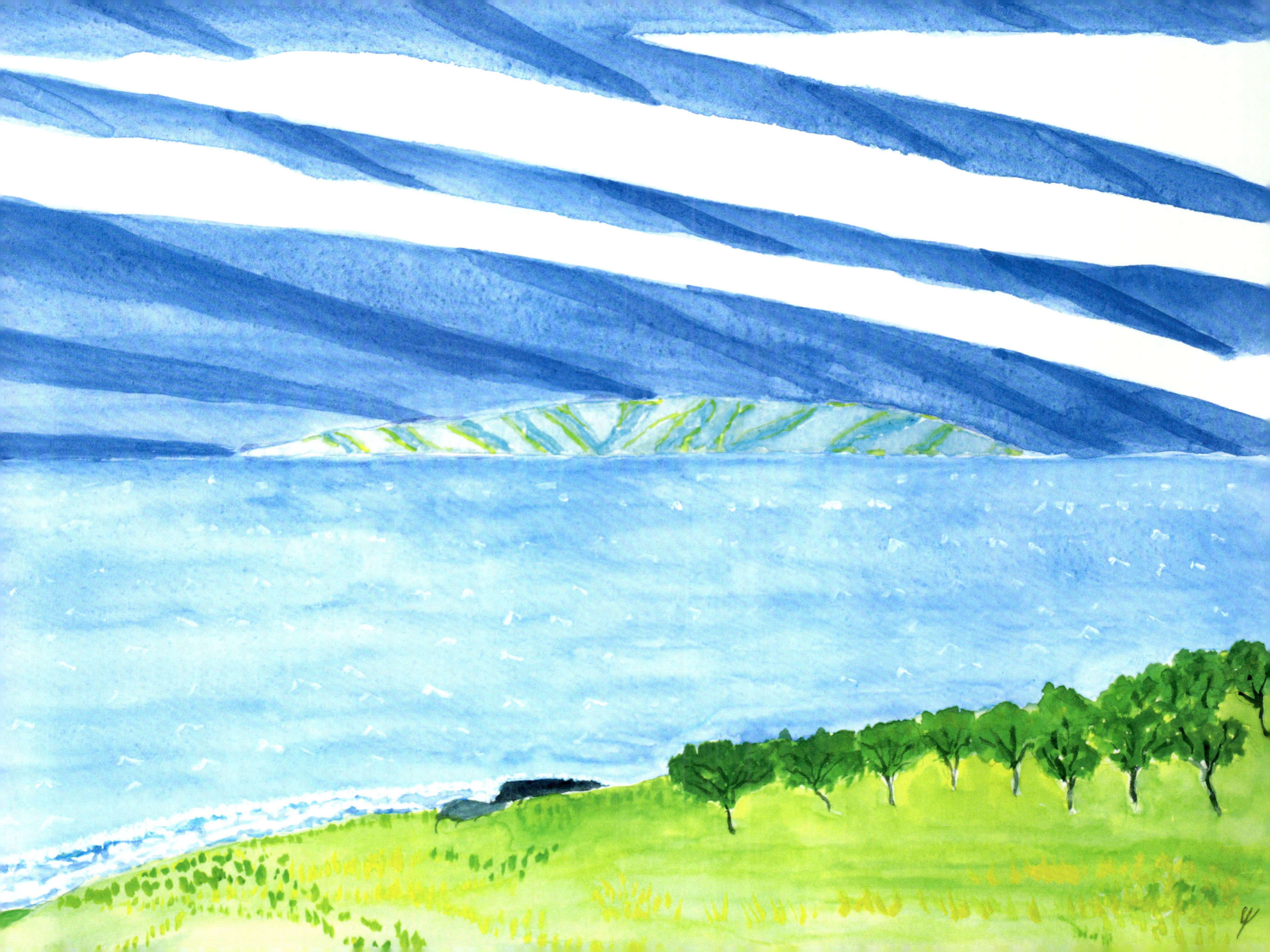

Shaky Believers

All day,
purple
bougainvillea blossoms
blow in
through the window –
resting on the carpet,
they brighten
its gray terrain –
lavender kites
that have tagged
the ground,
they wait
for a friendly breeze
to launch them again,
among gusts
that scatter
their blessings,
rewarding the grateful
and those
who are surprised
to find heaven
bestowed on them
in pieces.

Bougainvillea and Mount Hāʻupu, Kauaʻi

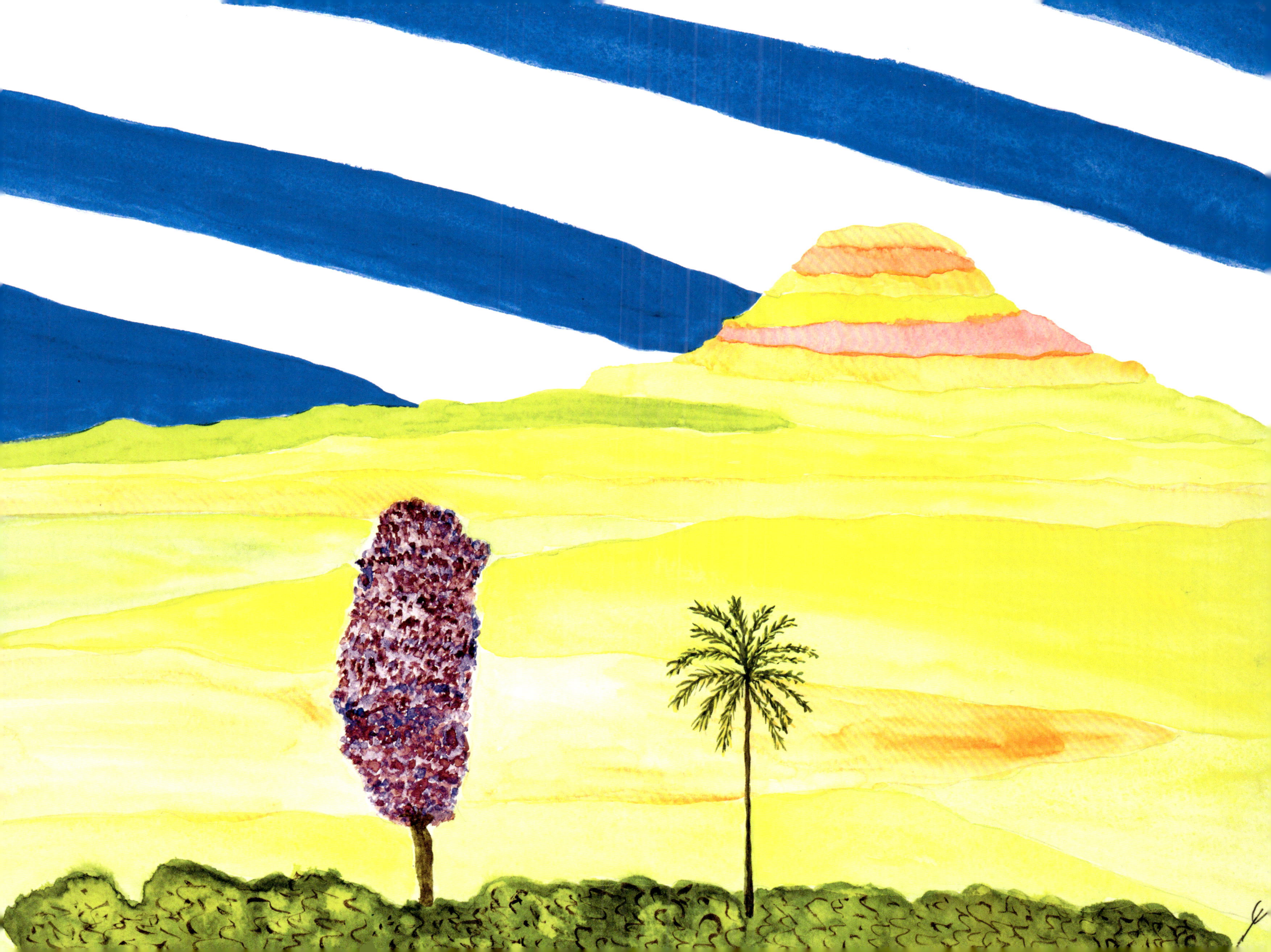

Kupuna

The well-creased face
of a Hawaiian elder
does not dole out
bright-eyed smiles,
but rests
in the shade
of a banyan tree –
he looks up,
as a stranger
lopes by,
and, watching
three paddle-shaped
leaves
float to earth,
cracks a smile
in clear sight
of his ancestors.

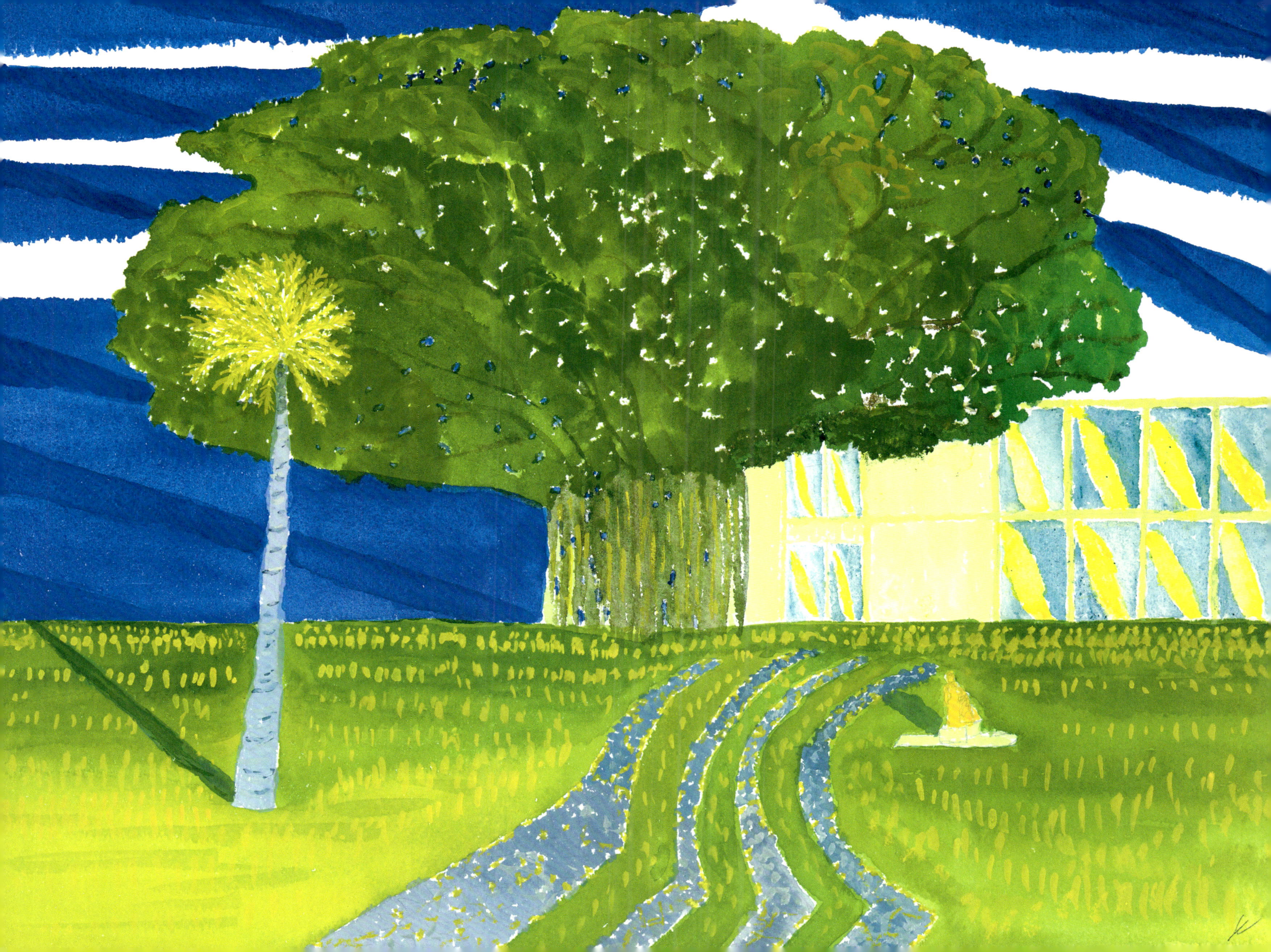

Coronation

A statue
of a Hawaiian queen,
bedecked
with white leis,
outstretches
its arms
to sunlight
and shadows,
as it gazes
toward the ocean,
where a reef
slows the waves,
until they bow
before her bronze skirt,
embroidered
with a rainbow
that a shower
has bestowed
upon her shoulders.

Rainbow Over the Ocean, Poʻipū, Kauaʻi

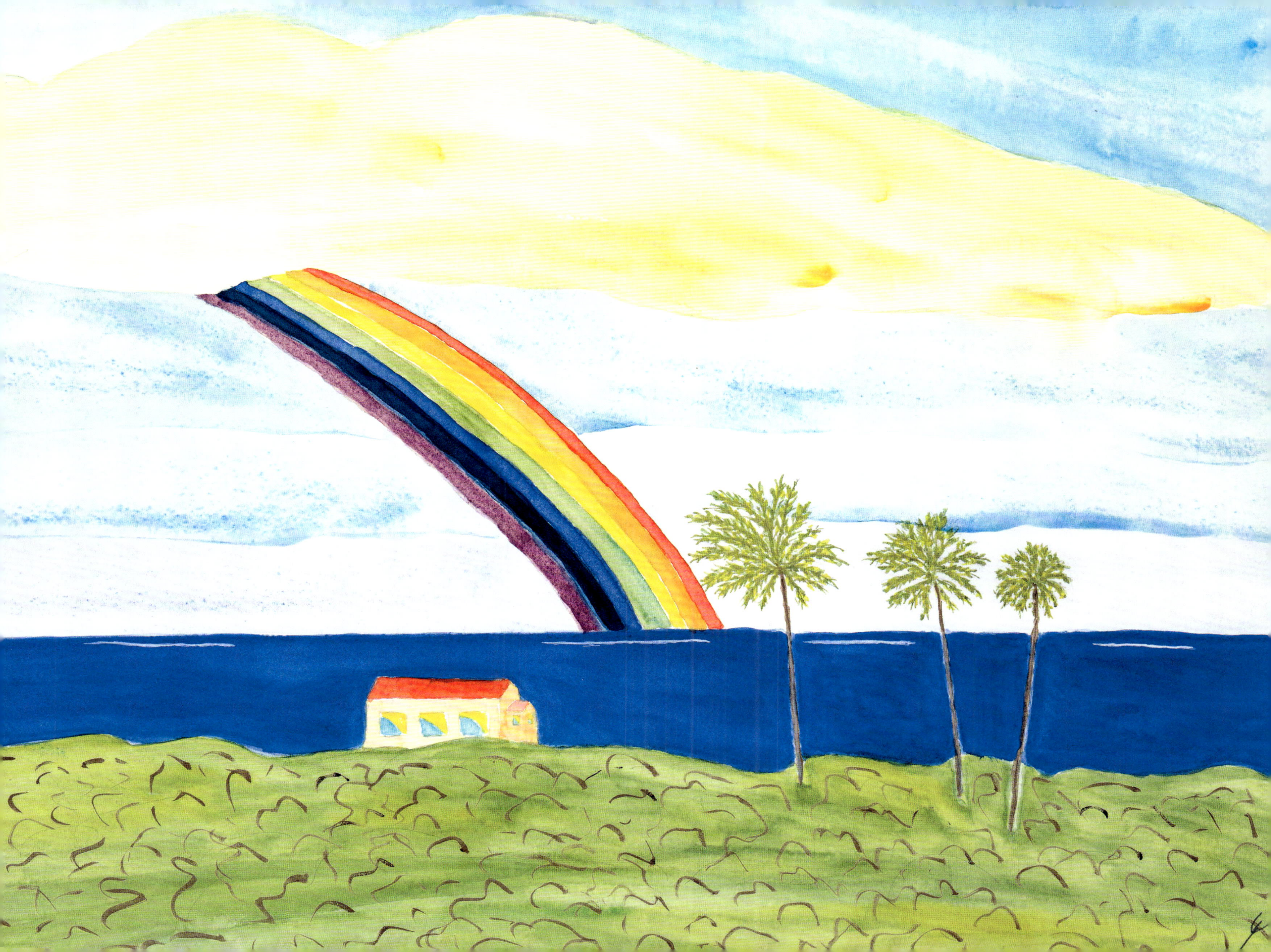

A Homecoming

A cool breeze
springs up
out of nowhere,
bearing
the scent of the ocean
on its wings –
feeling its embrace,
you lean back
and watch,
as the palm trees
dance hula
for a visitor
from the north.

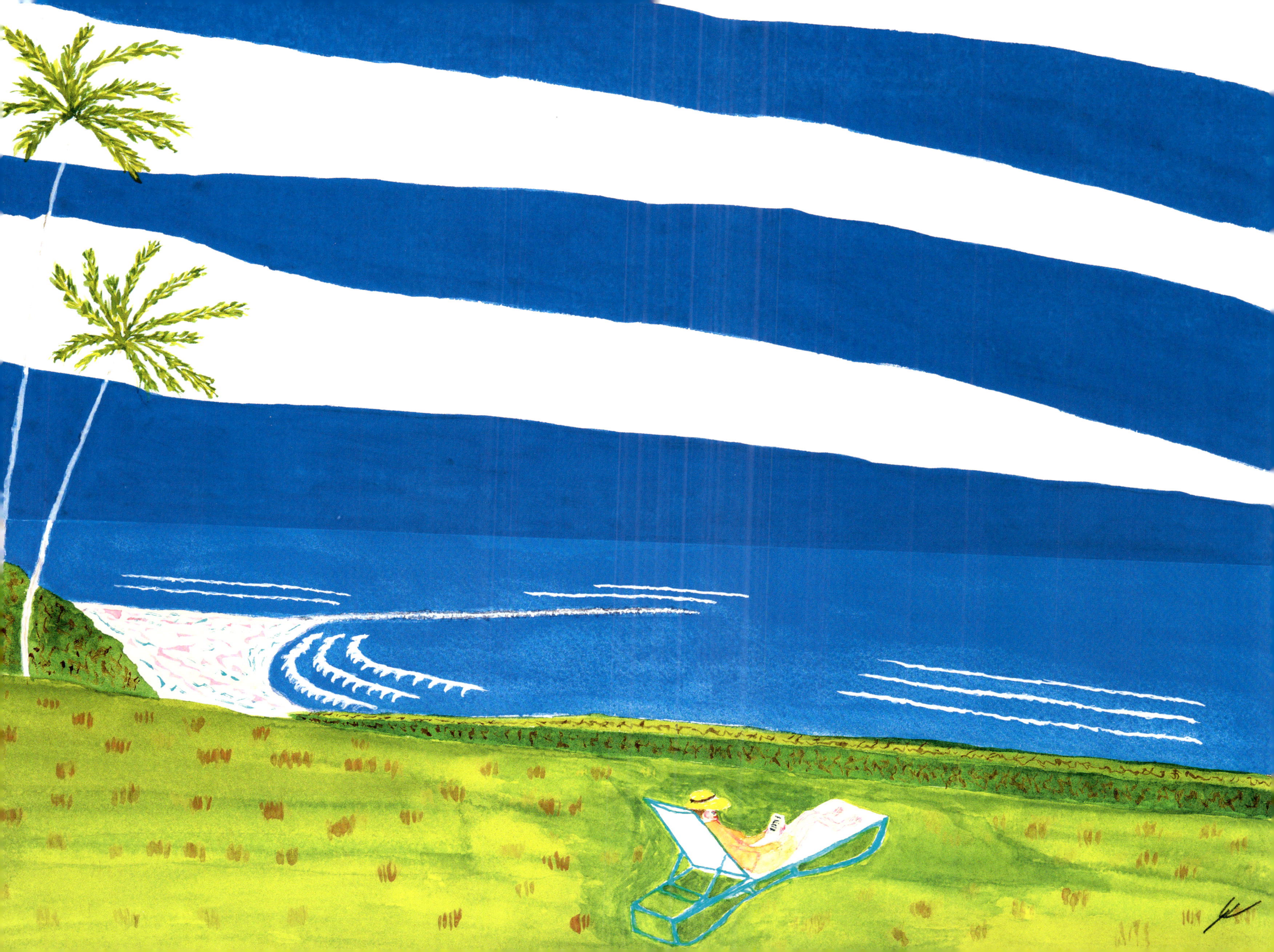

Knowing Her Way

A middle-aged Hawaiian woman
with a bright blue parasol
trudges
down the road,
while the sunlight
stretches out,
to make the grass
swelter –
her parasol
bobs,
as she sways
through a heat wave,
while a wayward palm tree
casts its shadow
onto her path,
inviting her
to dawdle
and dance.

She strides on,
surefooted,
to keep her appointment
with a broad-shouldered front porch
and a gallant tradewind.

Showing His Age

A young man
with a blue shirt
and a gray backpack
strides forward
on a sunny day,
smiling
at strangers
who lack
baseball caps
and perfect physiques –
heading
toward a hiking path
that welcomes
young legs,
he looks beyond
an old face
that beams
at the pudgy cheeks
of clouds.

A Warm Welcome

An old couple,
sauntering
down the sidewalk,
hold hands
and smile,
while sunlight
and shadows
adorn their shoulders,
and a far-flung ocean
winks
as they stroll,
leading them forward
to waves
that come ashore
on tiptoe.

Calm Day in Poʻipū, Kauaʻi

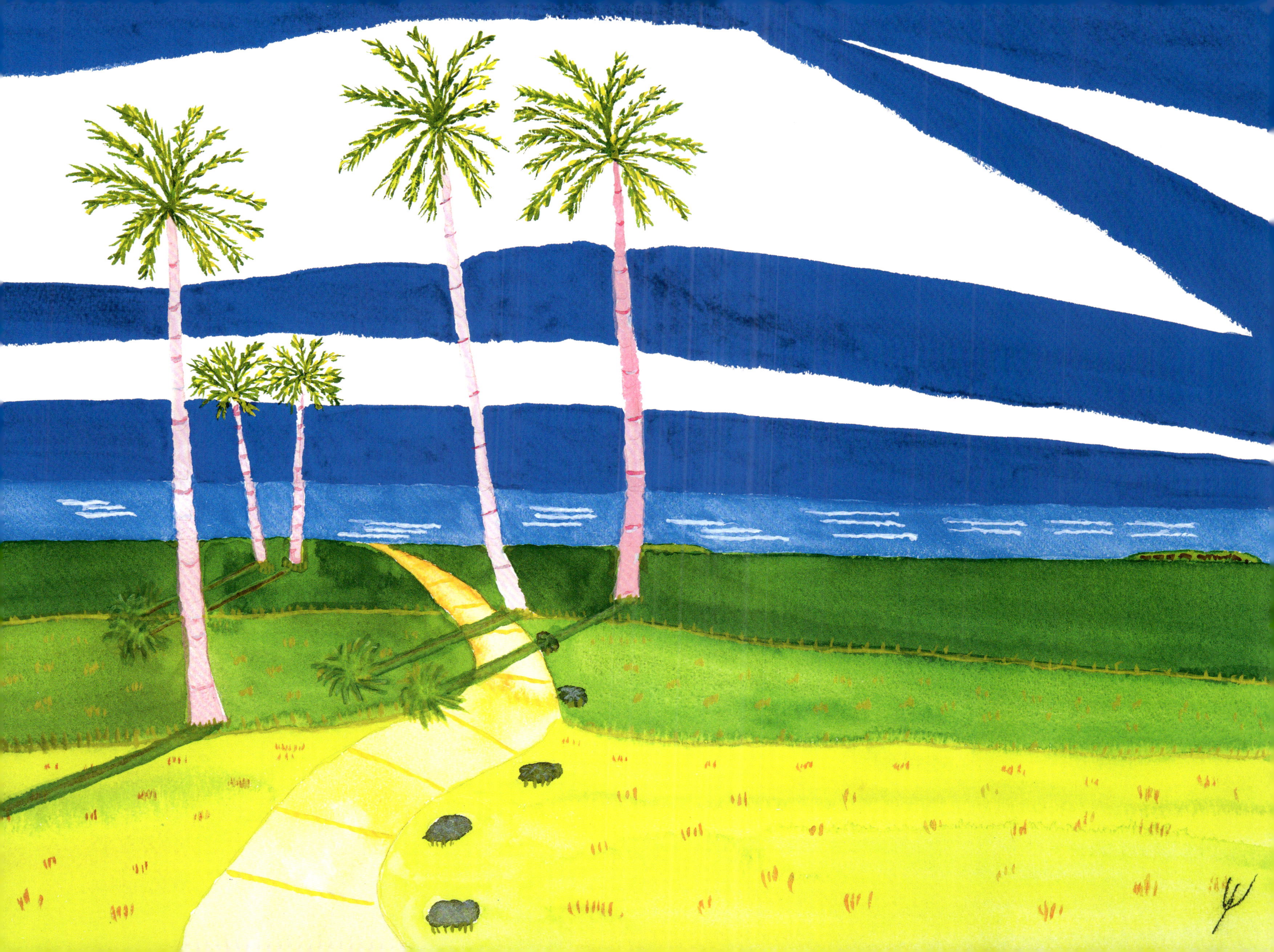

Company

The land,
reaching out
to a silver ocean,
points beyond all shadows,
and then,
remembering
a far destination,
smiles
at clouds
that follow
each other
across the neighborly
sky.

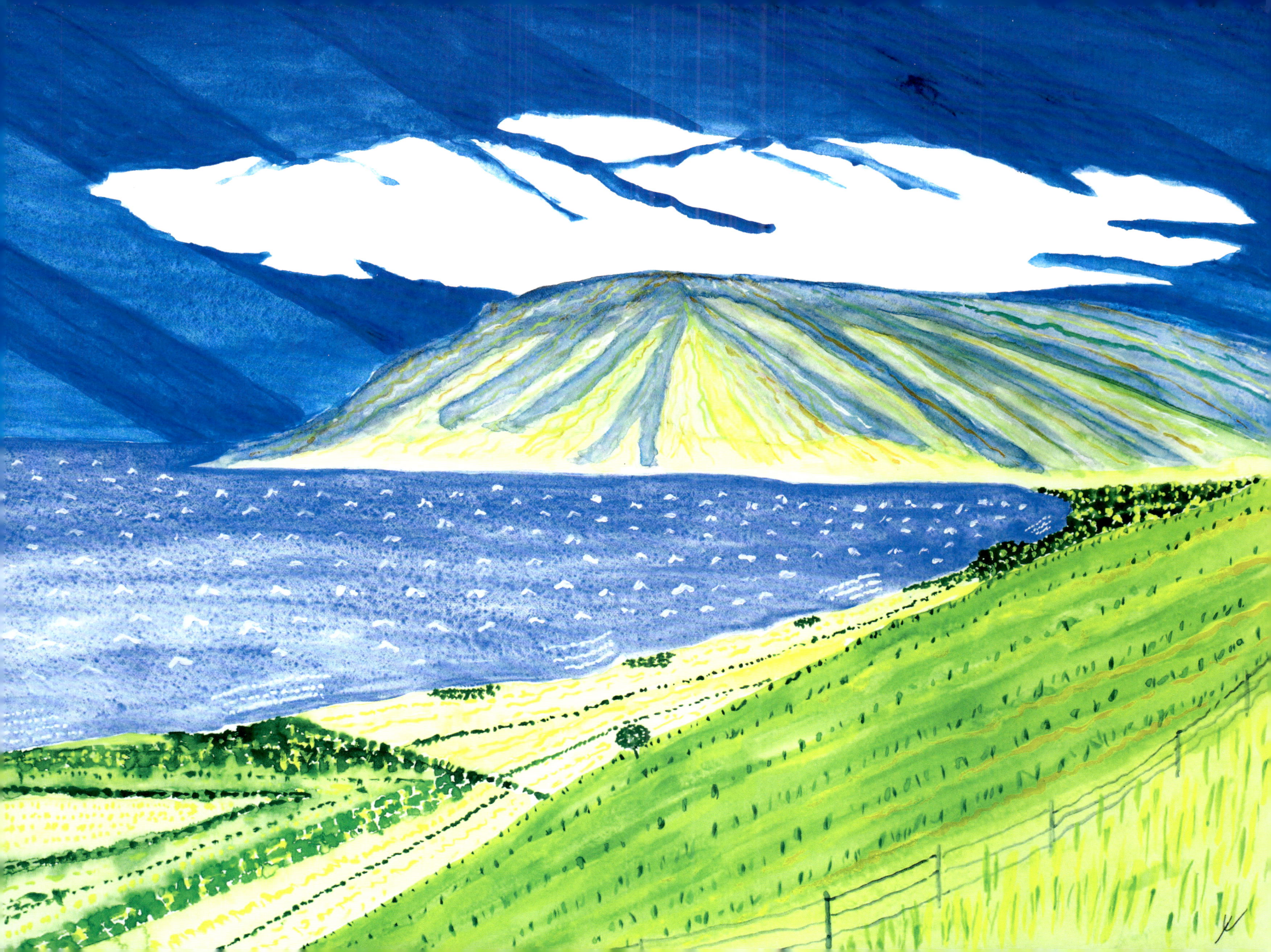

Old Hawai'i

Clouds
roll over
the solemn-faced mountains,
the ancient mountains
that long
for their gods –
the winds rise,
as the green land stretches out
its fingertips
to the ocean,
and still the mountains,
with their beards
and gray wrinkles,
sigh
in the silver rain
that veils their view
of a rainbow-crowned
heaven.

Po'ipū Rainbow, Kaua'i

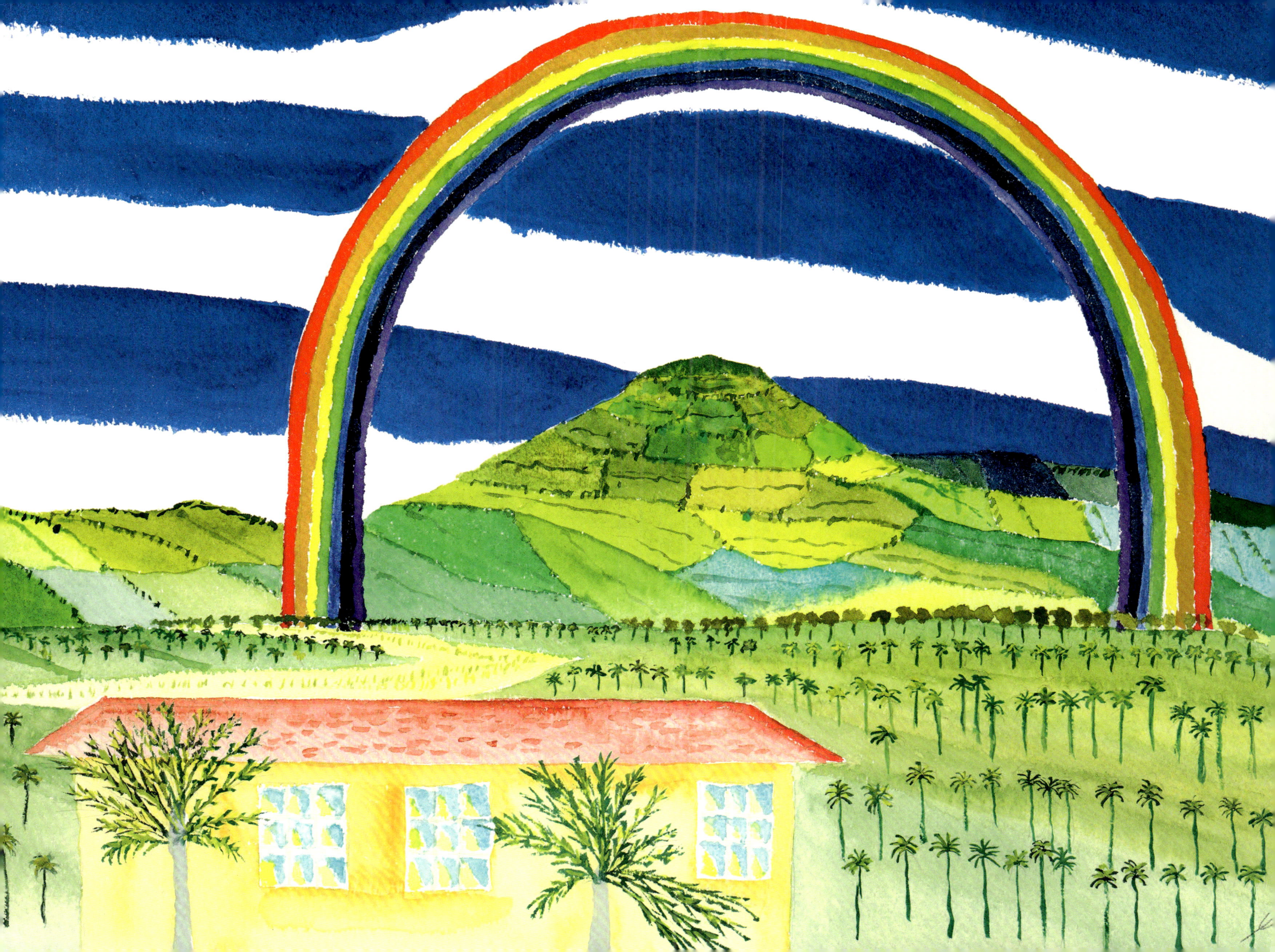

A Spring Romance

Exoctic places,
lands
that overlook
blue bays,
outstretch
their arms
to travelers
who long
to sleep
within earshot
of the whisperings
of a tireless
ocean.

High Clouds Over Mount Hā'upu, Kaua'i

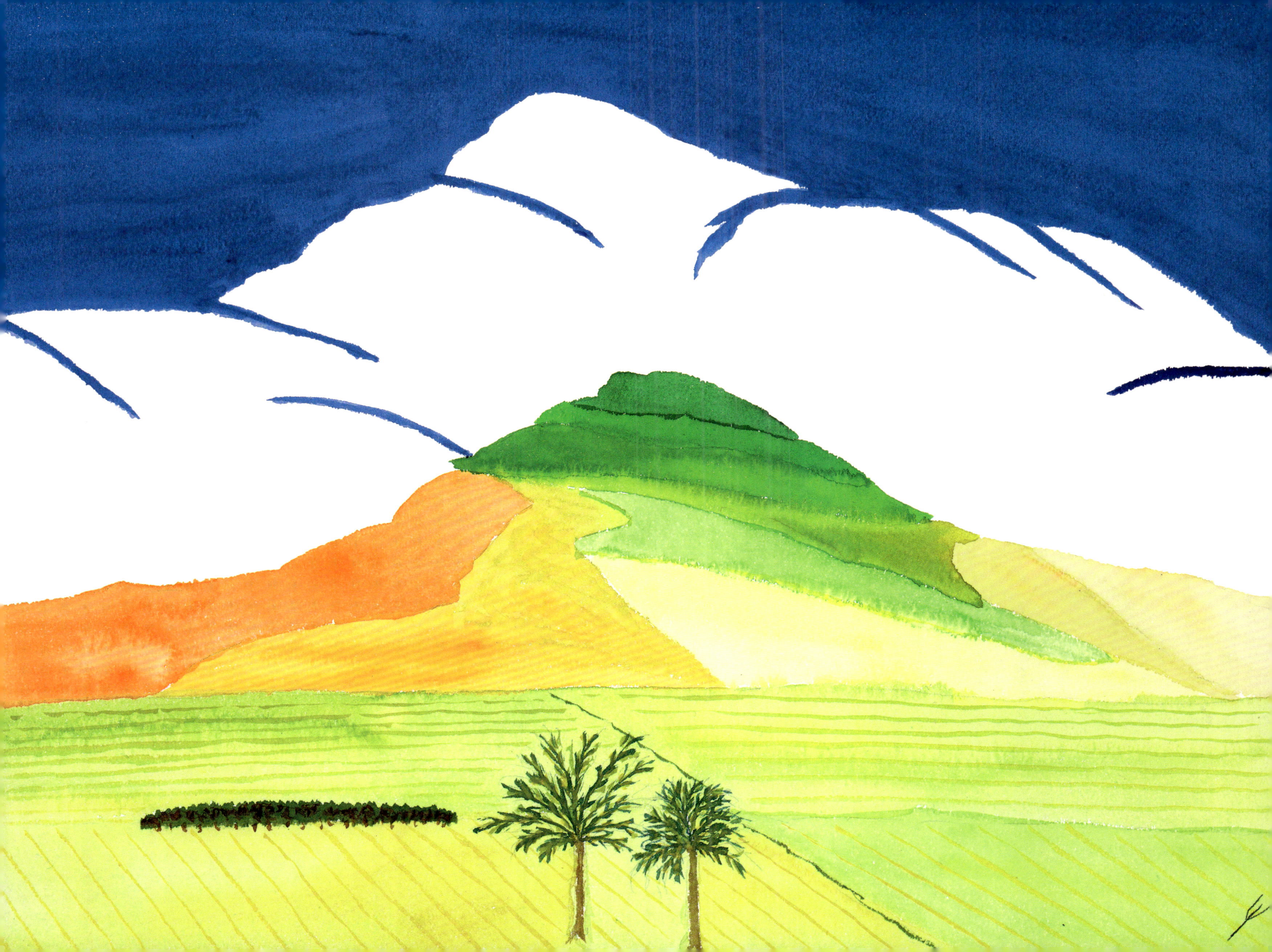

Calm Dancers

Palm trees,
waving
at strangers,
dance hula
for the sky,
and then, finding
that clouds
ignore them
and drift on,
whisper
to one another
about the fickle love
of tradewinds.

Kailua Bay, O'ahu

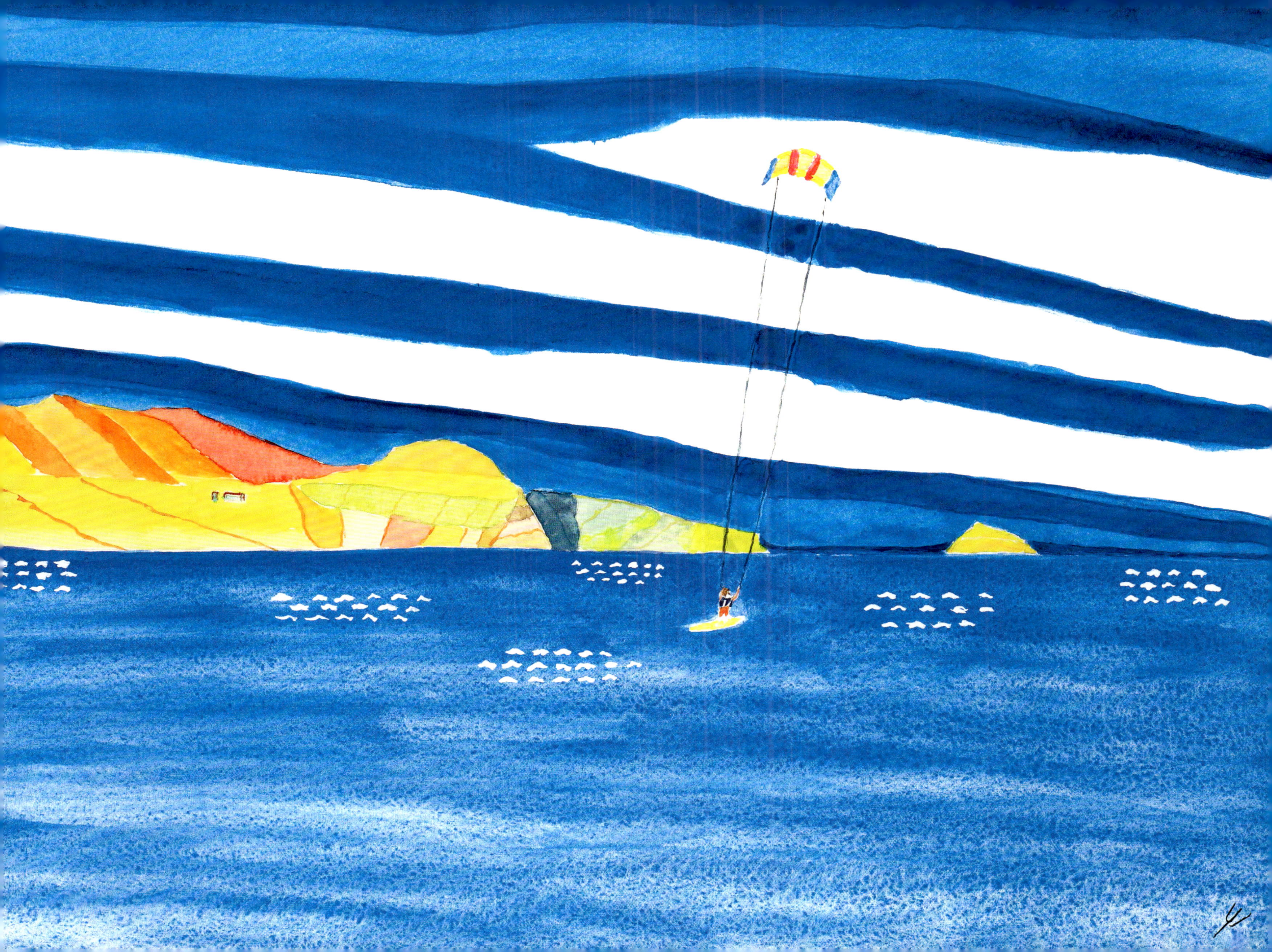

Almost Home

A young
Hawaiian girl,
holding
her ukulele,
smiles
at an unseen beach,
as she strums
the taut strings –
you awaken
to the melody,
and then gaze
at her sheltering face –
a palm tree
whispers
a few feet away,
and just
beyond the horizon,
a young island
listens
to the laughter
of the surf.

Ocean Sunrise, Po'ipū, Kaua'i

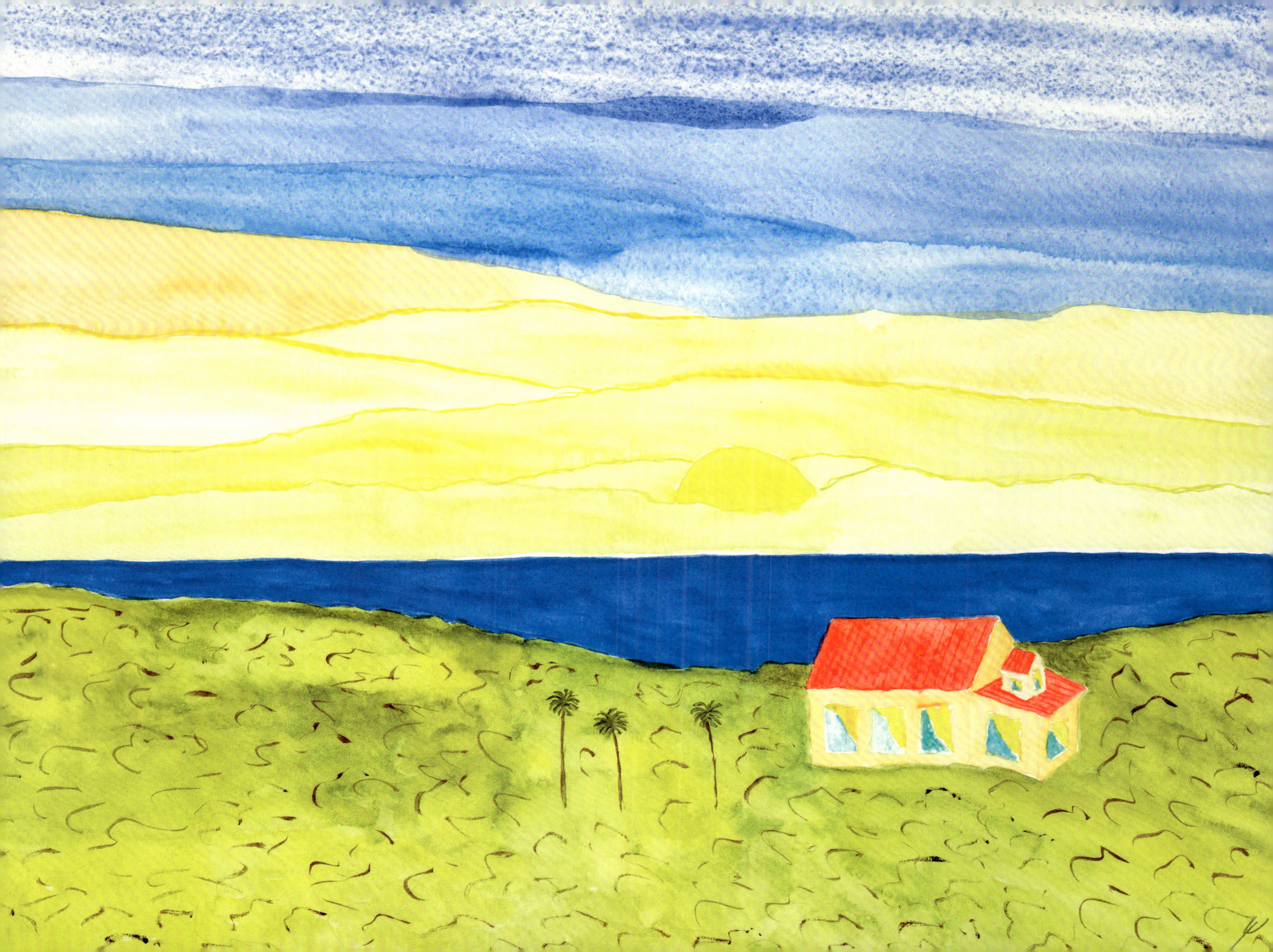

A.M.

Mistakes
and mistakes
and mistakes
pile up
from morning
to morning,
and still,
you awaken,
facing
the window's
smile,
and sigh to the bed
that you forgive it
its lumps.

A Shade Closer

A hibiscus
opens its orange petals
to the silver
moonlight,
as the long-veiled sky
clears,
and the clouds
drift away –
in the pale light,
other blossoms bob,
and their shadows
dance
on the grass –
a breeze
flirts
with a bevy
of red-hatted
beauties,
while a shy flower
with an orange bonnet
steals a smile
from the moon.

Spring Courtships

Mountains
tumble down
to the skirts
of the ocean,
then wash their feet
in the restless waves,
which whisper
of sand castles
that the land has built,
to get a view
of ships
that sigh
to the sky.

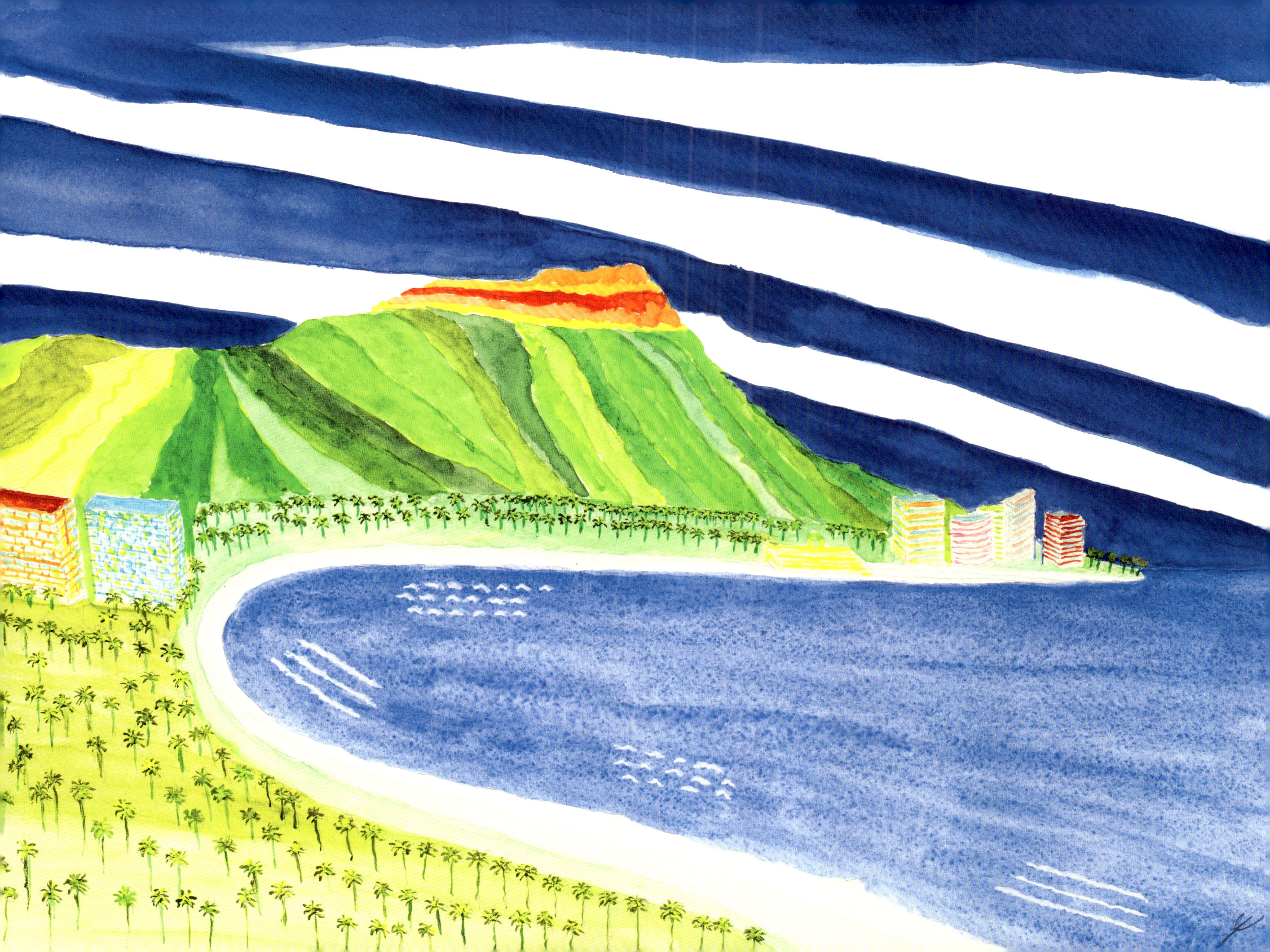

Speeding Home

A beach slipper,
deserted
in the grass,
rests
before dawn
in a mist
of gray light –
unheeded,
it lists
to one side,
with no sign
of restlessness,
and yet,
as the sun rises,
you catch sight
of it darting
toward a boy's footprint
in the forgetful
sand.

Winter Double Rainbow, Kaua'i

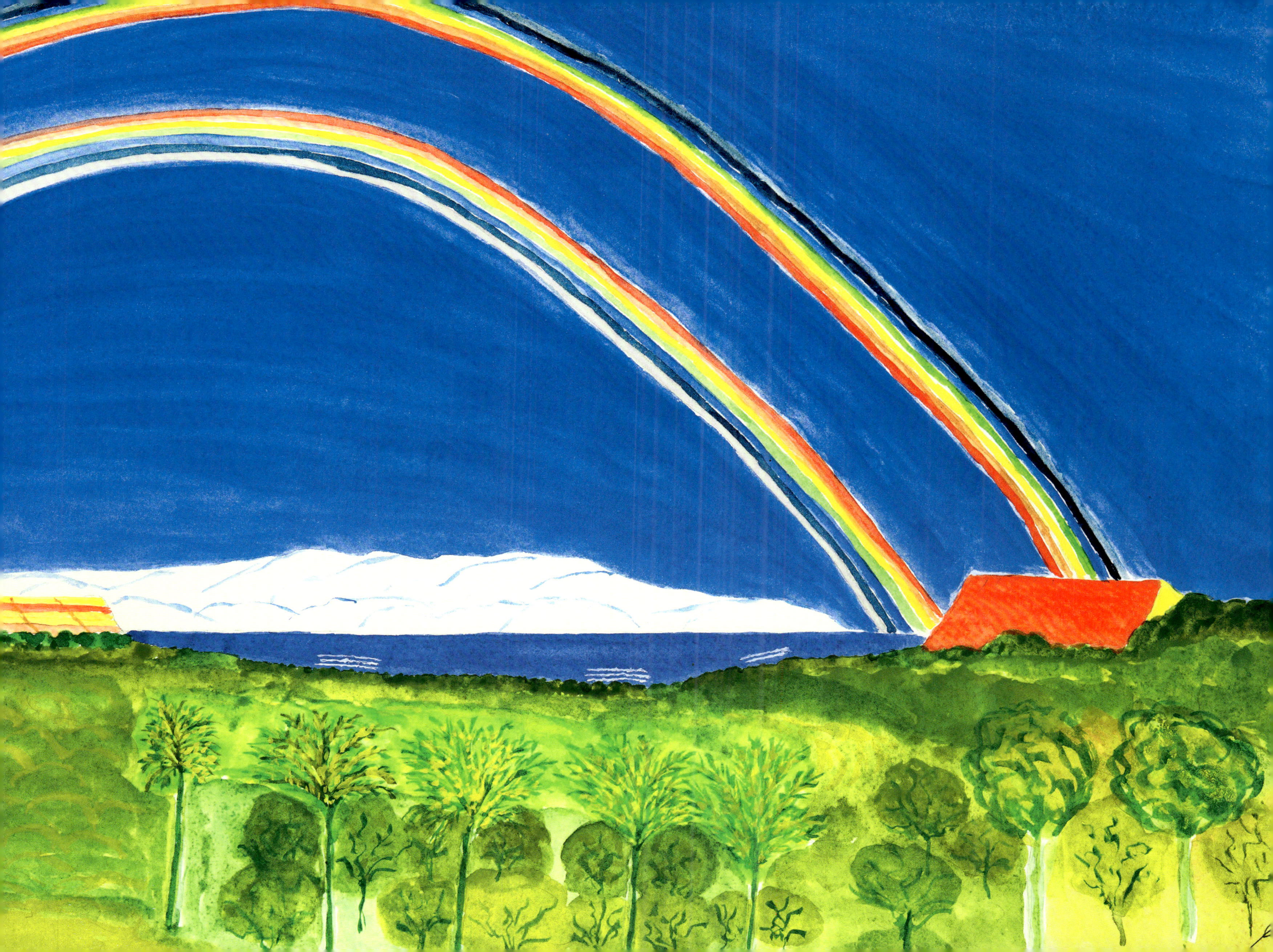

Nurturing Eden

This spring
the old man
will not see his tree
leaf out,
or his hedge
cry out
for trimming,
or the last
of his plumeria blossoms
tumble
to earth,
or the myna birds
succeed
in robbing him
of papayas,
but all
who remember him
will tap their shovels
on the ground,
and dig deeper,
to plant
a palm tree
that will grow taller
than the house
that he sheltered
with a garden.

October Sunrise, Po'ipū, Kaua'i

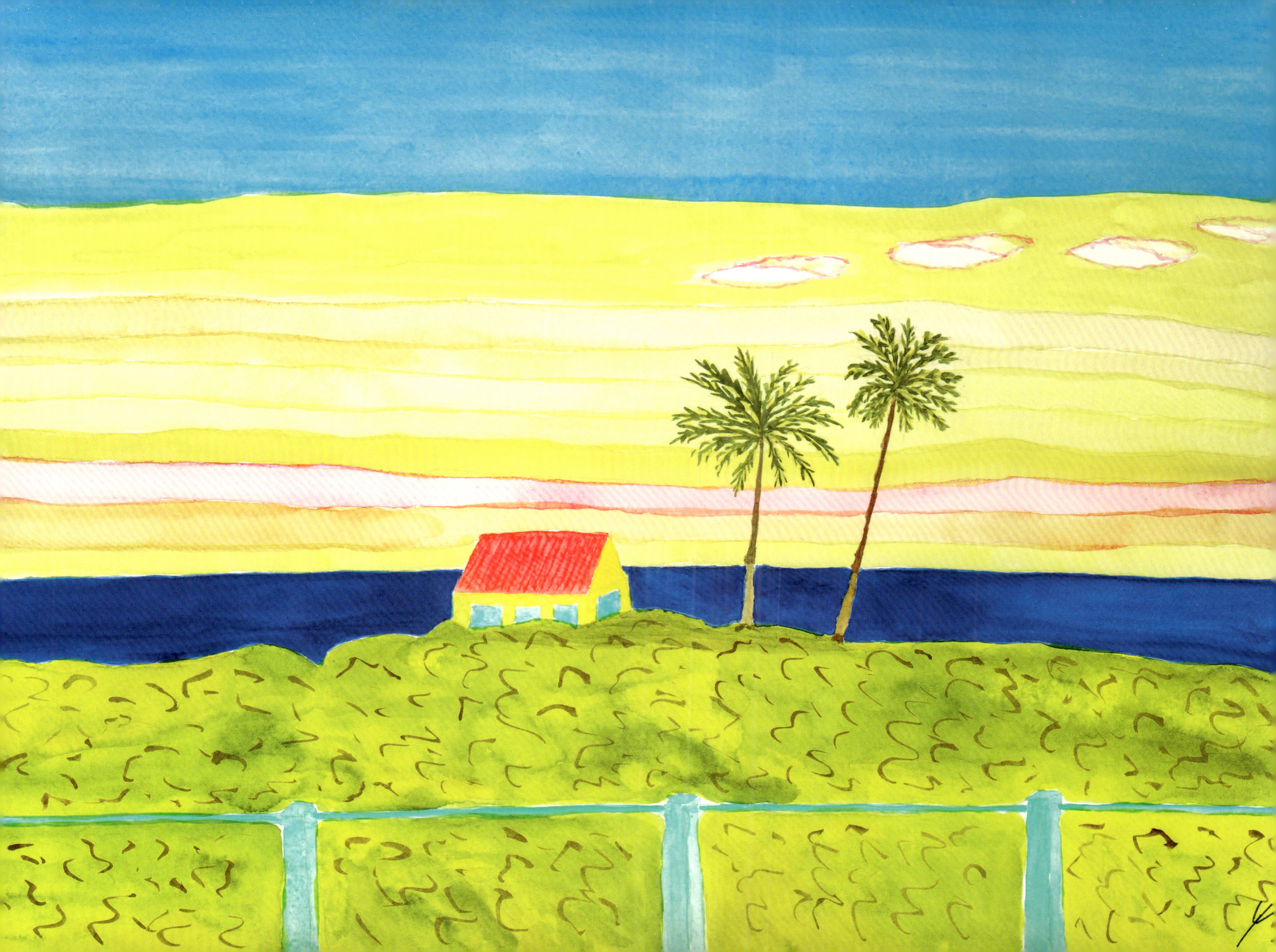

A Faithful Companion

The ocean,
tireless,
tugs at the shore,
and goes thumping
a tune
on the rocks,
while farther out,
waves
whisper
to each other,
as they unfurl
their smiles,
with white mustaches
and indigo
eyes.

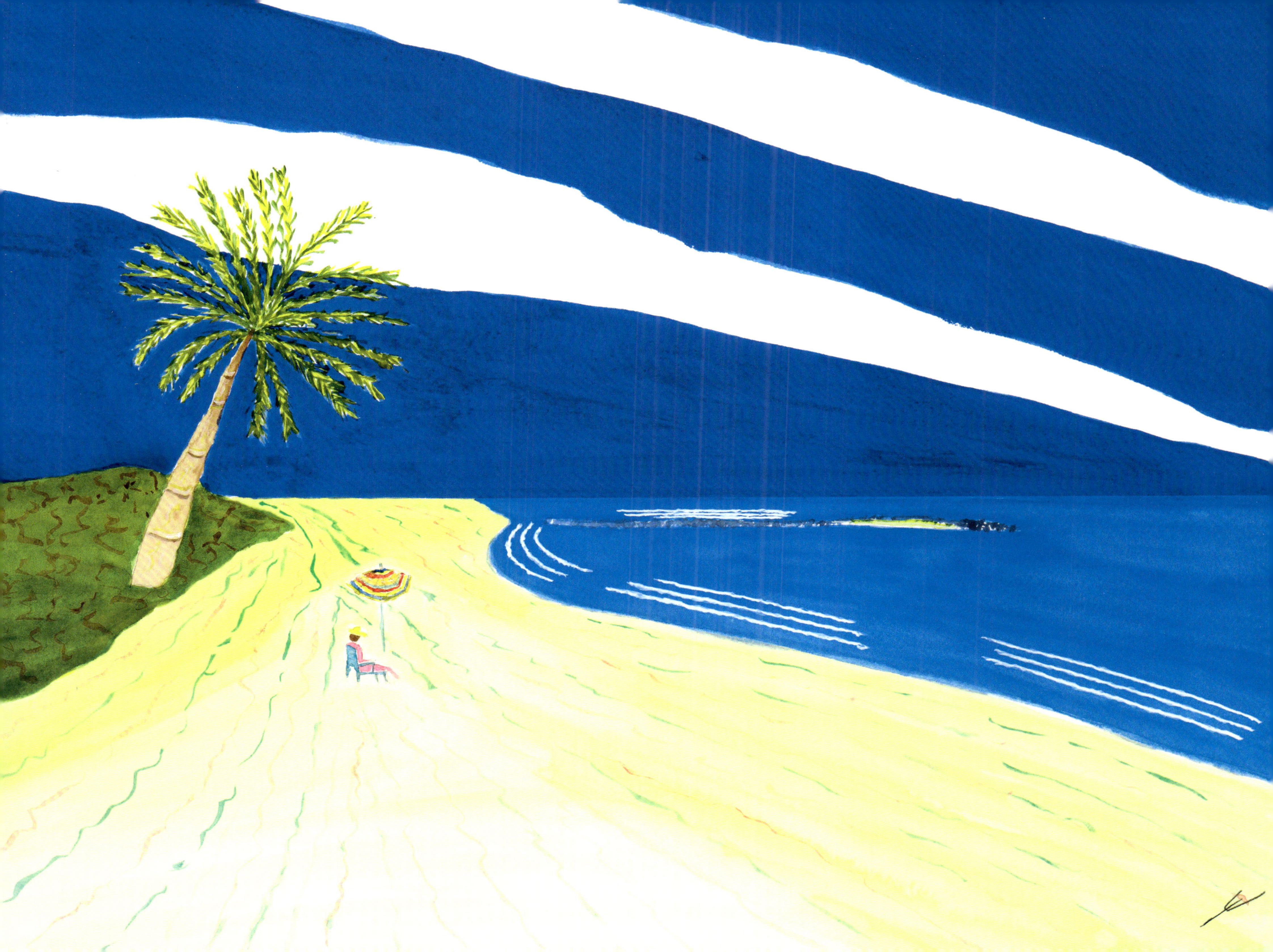

An Unsung Melody

Far-flung islands,
waiting
to be visited,
teach their palm trees
to sigh
and their beaches
to whisper –
late
in the night,
they weary
of singing,
and, resting
in the arms
of their mountains,
they dream
of other islands,
swimming
in silence,
hearing a tune
that they cannot escape.

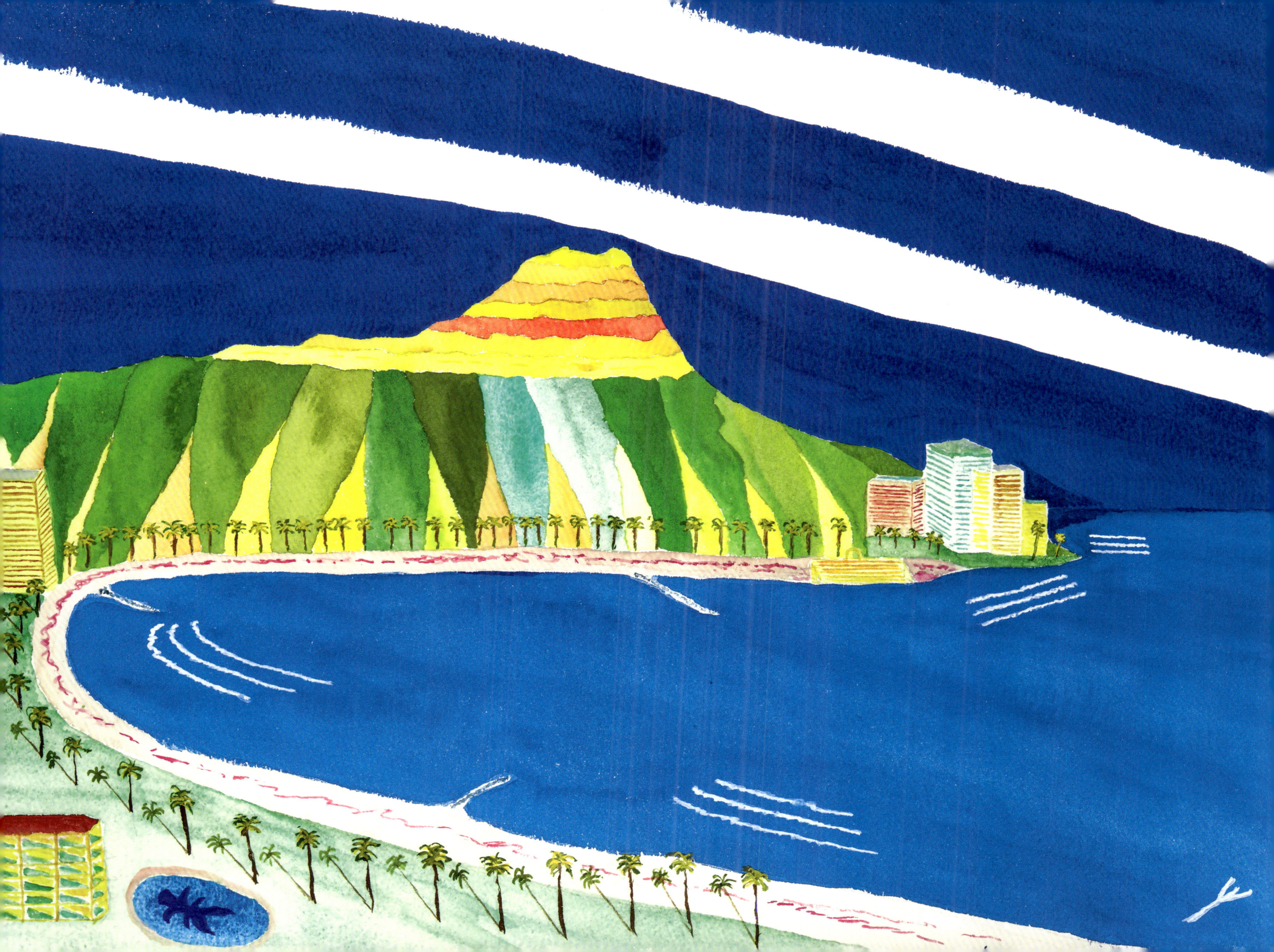

Blazing Up

The red cottage
stands,
embraced
by palm fronds
and the shadow
of a high butte,
which, bearded,
towers
above the house,
with its gray-eyed windows
and its overhanging eaves,
sheltered
by a canopy
of rock and fronds,
from which fragments
and showers
tumble,
rattling
on the tin roof
on quiet days,
while the cottage
bides its time,
welcoming
the forest's
outstretched arms,
its promise
to make room
for humble
sunlight.

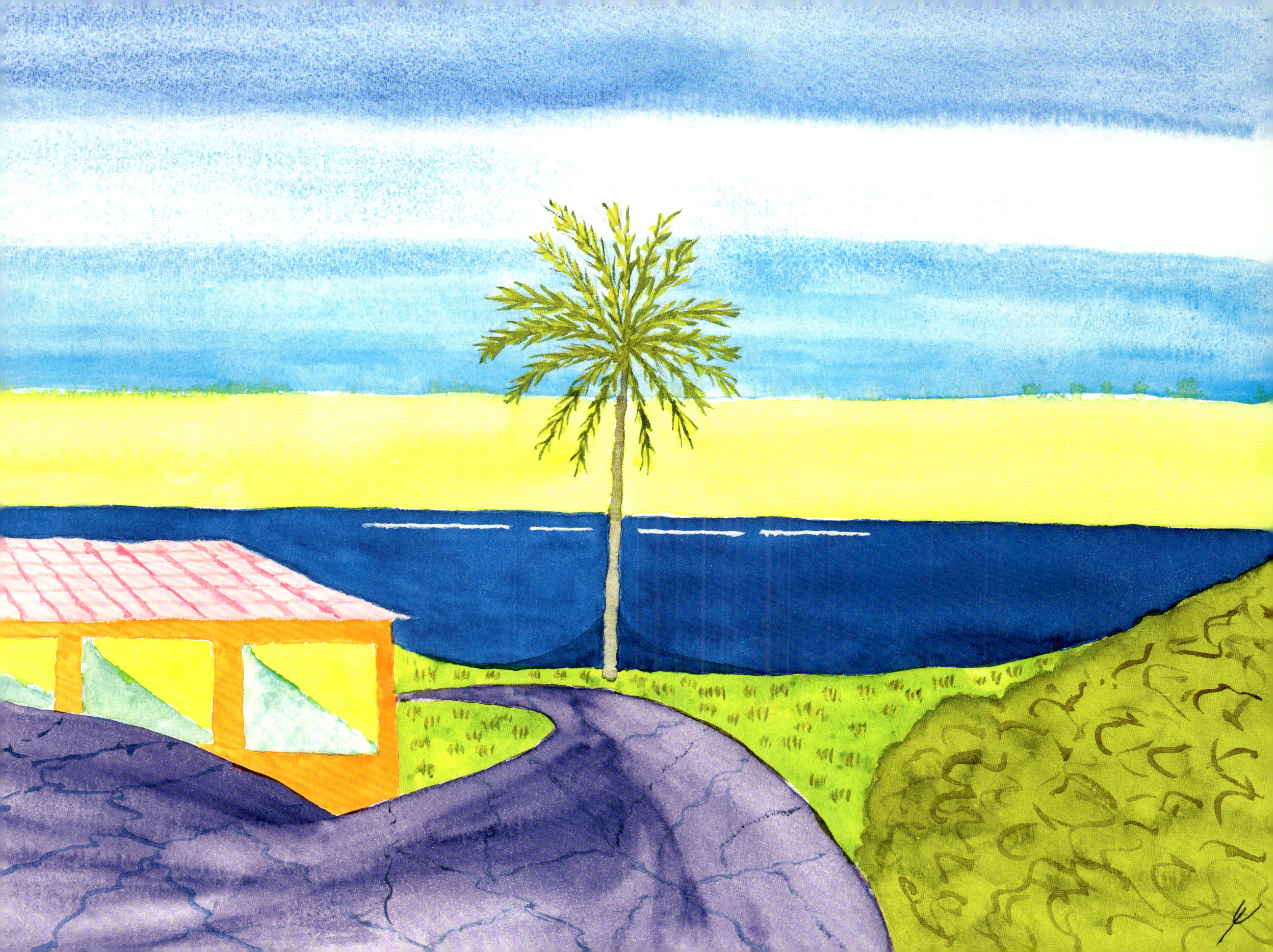

Between Chapters

Now
you know
how Mr. Wilcox
felt,
as the cool evenings,
one by one,
crept through his study windows,
and the ships
put in
and pulled out,
while he read the history
of his ancient island,
and daydreamt
of another
fiery-eyed dawn –
in the quiet night,
he could hear
the wind
crooning in the cane fields,
and listen to water
in the sluices,
giggling at its own antics –
almost dozing,
he let his book
rest in his lap,
while you,
sitting on your lanai,
lean back
in the starry-eyed night,
and calm your book
with the caress
of a wanderer
at home.

One of my favorite stories about Mount Hā'upu, which overlooks the southeastern coast of Kaua'i, concerns the legacy of noteworthy engineer and agronomist George Wilcox. Wilcox was born of New England missionaries who lived in Hanalei, on the north shore of Kaua'i. Abner and Lucy Wilcox came to Kaua'i in 1846, to staff the Wai'oli Mission. They raised five sons: Charles, George, Edward, Albert, and Samuel. George wanted to become a civil engineer. He was educated at Punahou School in Honolulu. He started his career by working in a plantation store and then digging guano, seabird dung, on Jarvis Island, 1300 miles south of Hawai'i. He eventually enrolled in Yale University's first engineering class. George returned to Hawai'i in 1863, intent on becoming an independent cane planter. He began his work as a surveyor, and then as a manager for Judge Herman Widemann, who owned cultivated land, the Grove Farm Plantation, on the east side of Kaua'i. A reliable and abundant source of water, which is required for cane cultivation, was the main need that confronted planters on the east and south sides of the island. Wilcox designed a series of irrigation ditches that brought water from the mountains to the lowland plains, where cane was grown. Widemann eventually leased, and later sold, Grove Farm Plantation to Wilcox, who became a pioneer in sugar cane cultivation, using his engineering skills and his acumen as an innovative businessman. One of his greatest obstacles was the absence of a sugar mill on Grove Farm Plantation. Paul Isenberg, owner of the adjoining Līhu'e Plantation, leased Wilcox milling services at his mill, at a substantial price and with limited milling time.

A sugar mill cost hundreds of thousands of dollars to construct, and without one, the sugar cane was worthless. By 1872, Wilcox had paid his debts to Widemann and owned Grove Farm. He turned it into a profitable company, after the Hawaiian sugar cane boom of the 1870's. Seventy years later, his nephew, Gaylord Wilcox, proposed that Grove Farm acquire the less-profitable Kōloa Plantation, south of Mount Hā'upu. Bill Moragne, his manager of operations, hiked to the top of Mount Hā'upu, from which he could survey the entirety of Kōloa Plantation and, most importantly, its mill. He could see that if a train tunnel was constructed through the mountain, cutting the transit distance from Kōloa to Grove Farm by up to ten miles, cane from Grove Farm could be milled at the Kōloa Mill. Grove Farm purchased the Kōloa Plantation and completed the tunnel in 1949. The tunnel still exists and can be traveled by ATV. The story of Mount Hā'upu's role in first separating, and eventually uniting, two of the most iconic sugar plantations in Hawai'i makes its brooding heights seem all the more momentous in the landscape and history of Kaua'i.

Wilcox's First Love

Every night,
the old man
sat reading,
upright in his wicker chair,
overlooking the ocean
in Hawai'i,
and listened
to the water
gurgling
in his sluices,
and the sugar cane
whispering
about sweet teeth
in Iowa.

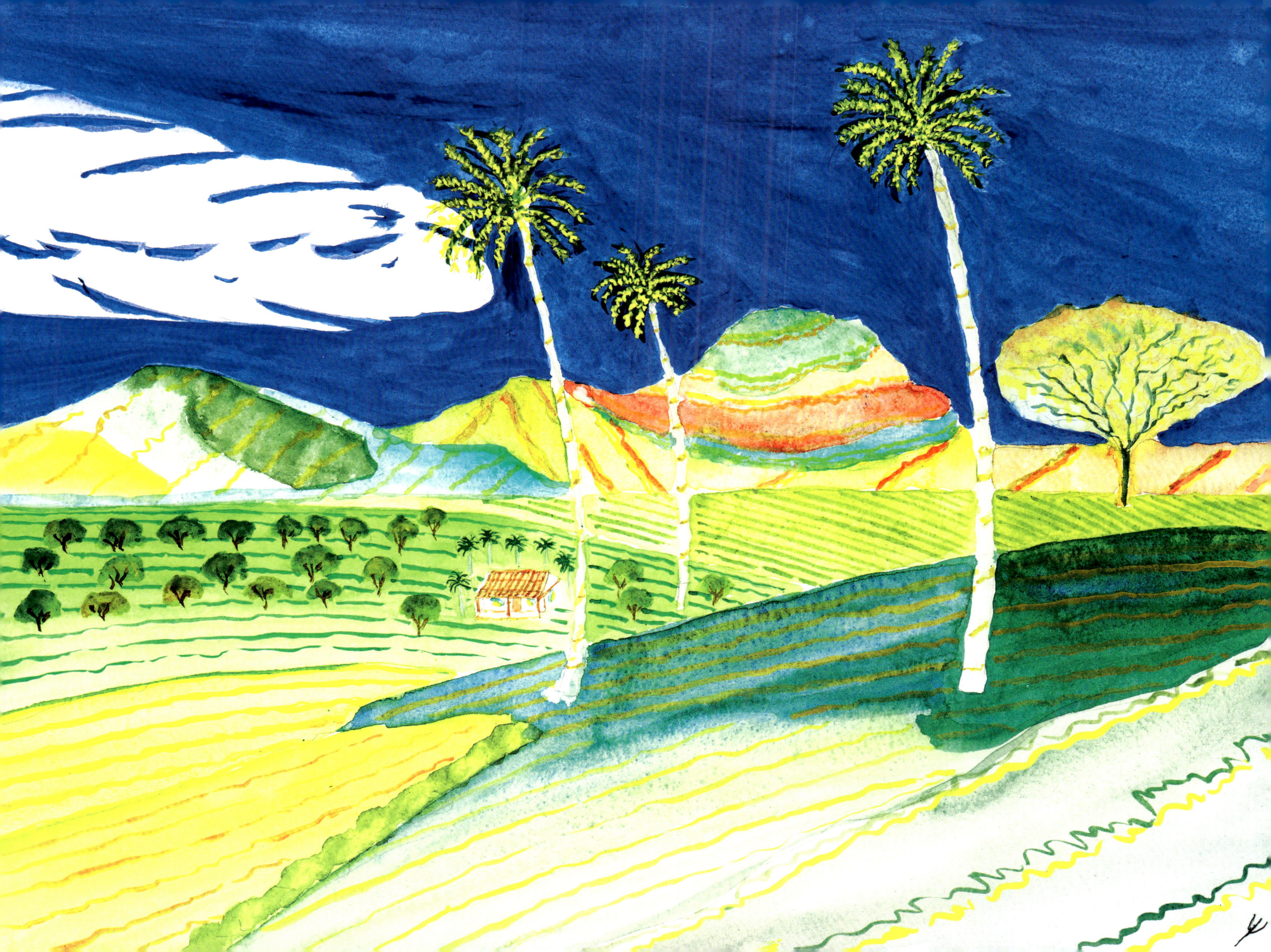

Destinations

Beaches
at the horizon
glint
and wink,
sharing
their tawny smiles
with wanderers
and stuck-at-home
daydreamers,
who glance
out their windows
at far-flung shores,
where the ocean
comes calling
on a summer day,
then decides
to settle down
among the soft skirts
of mountains.

Po'ipū House, Kaua'i

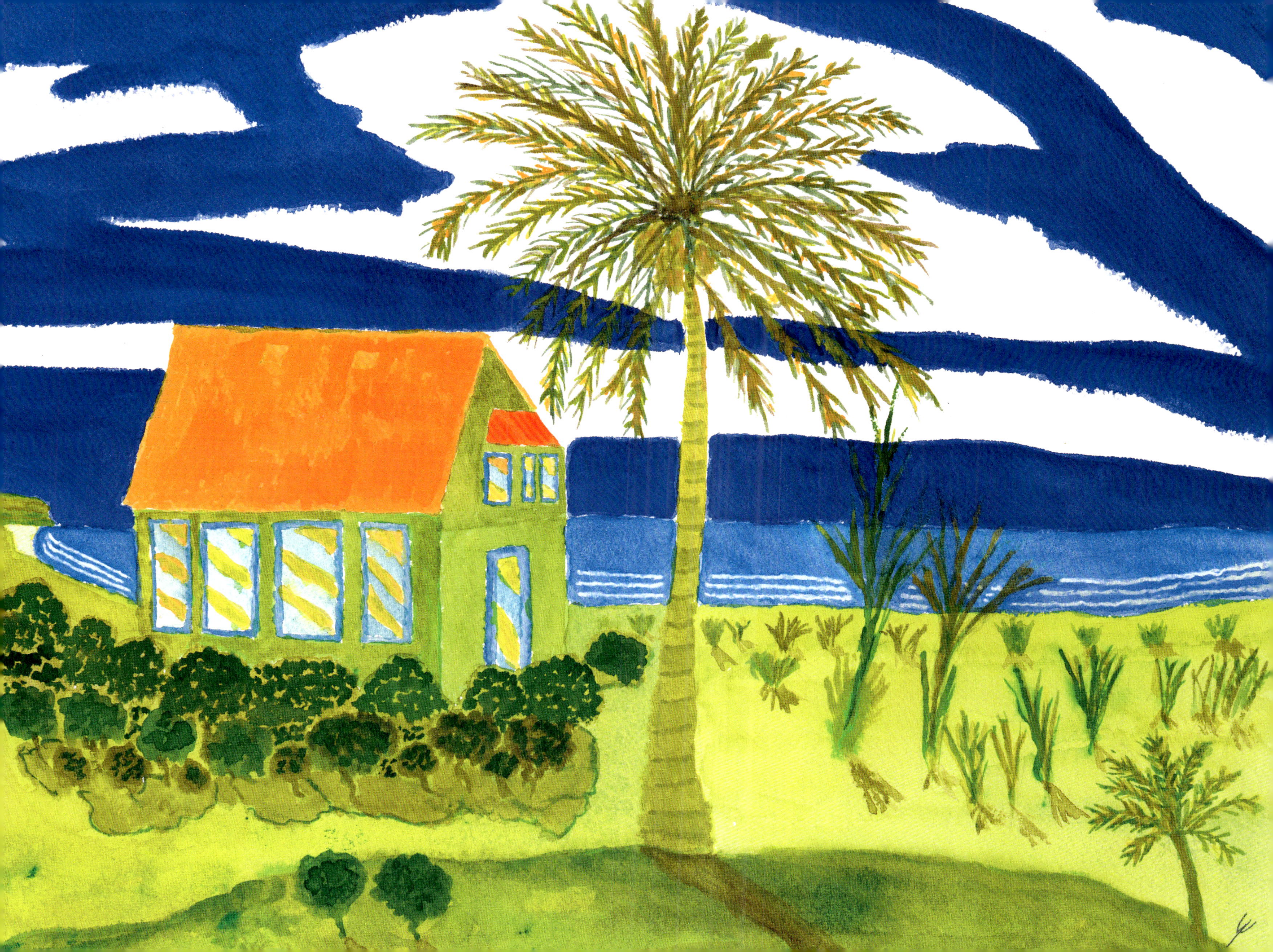

Company

Still an orange glow
crouches
on the horizon,
as you say to your father,
"See, some light is left."

Night
after night,
you welcome
its late smile,
and when at last,
it fades away,
the moon
surprises you
with its orange-lipped
grin.

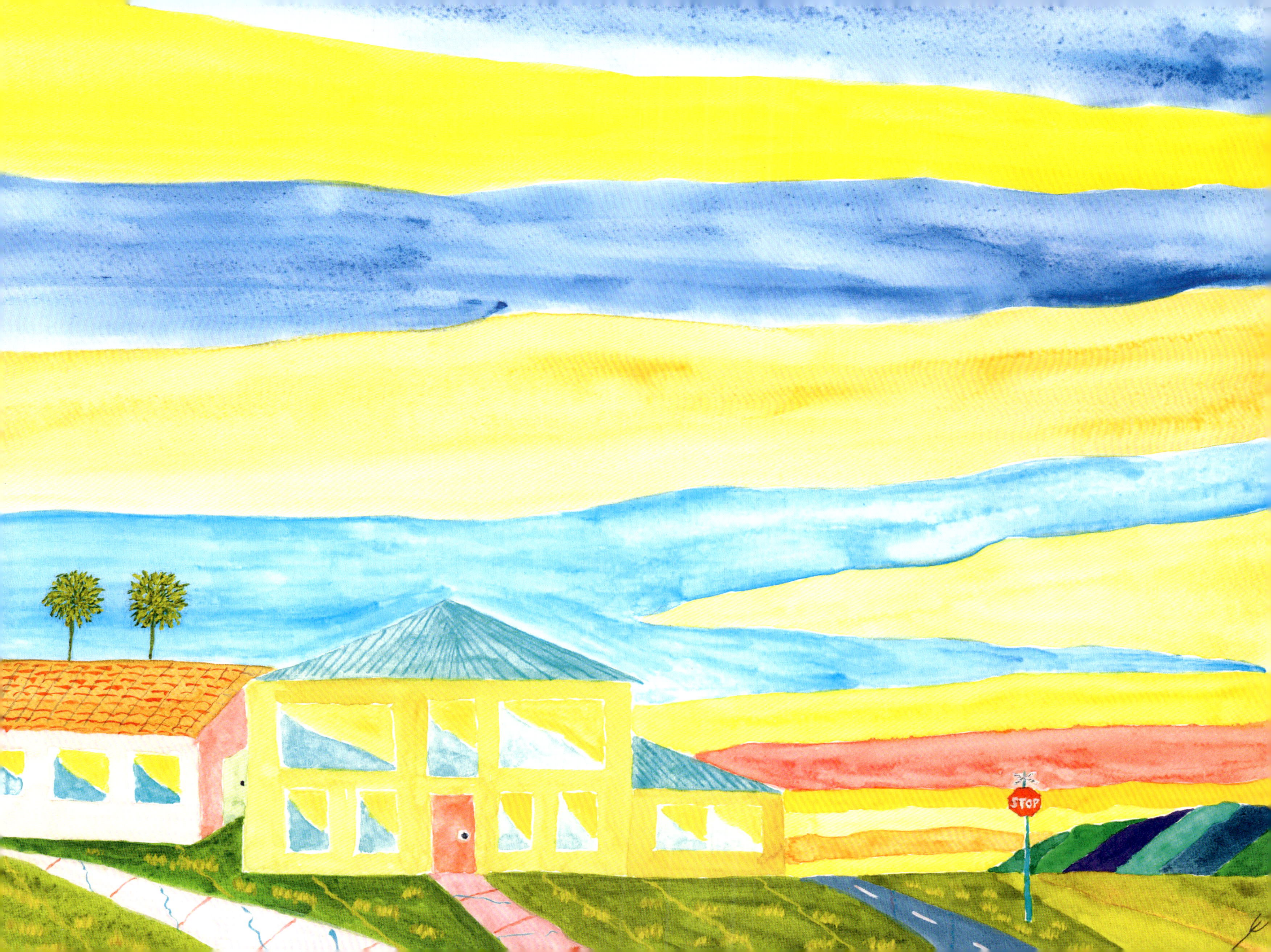
STOP

Beginnings

At dawn,
the sky
hangs up
its clothesline,
dressed with shirttails –
blue and yellow and beige
and pink,
white and lavender
and gray and tan –
all of them
dancing
in the early spring breeze,
they celebrate
dawn
with their sprightly
leaps,
while the clouds
flounce their skirts,
and the horizon
gleams,
kicking up its heels
at the sight
of a linen
rainbow.

Sunrise in Kekaha, Kaua'i

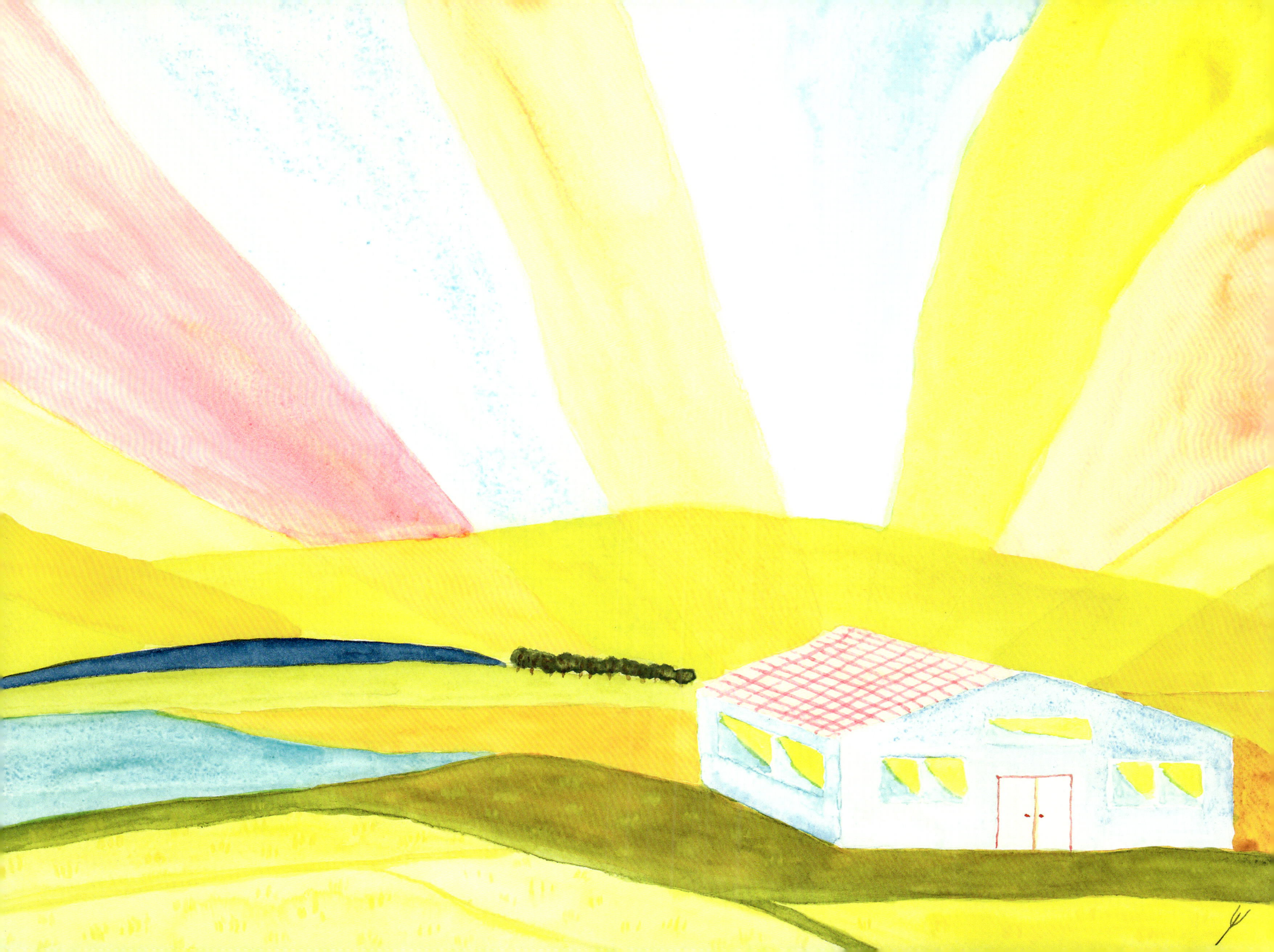

Honolulu

On the fringes
of the city,
you glimpse
the old town,
with its ragged yellow paint
and its lopsided doors,
and rooms that sag,
paying tribute
to Buddhist temples,
while wooden storefronts,
wrinkled and leaning forward,
rest their shadows
on sidewalks
that rise and fall,
lifted
on the shoulders
of monkeypod trees,
which send forth their roots
to curbs that sway,
welcoming
a harbor
where waves
dance with canoes.

Old Mission Houses, Honolulu

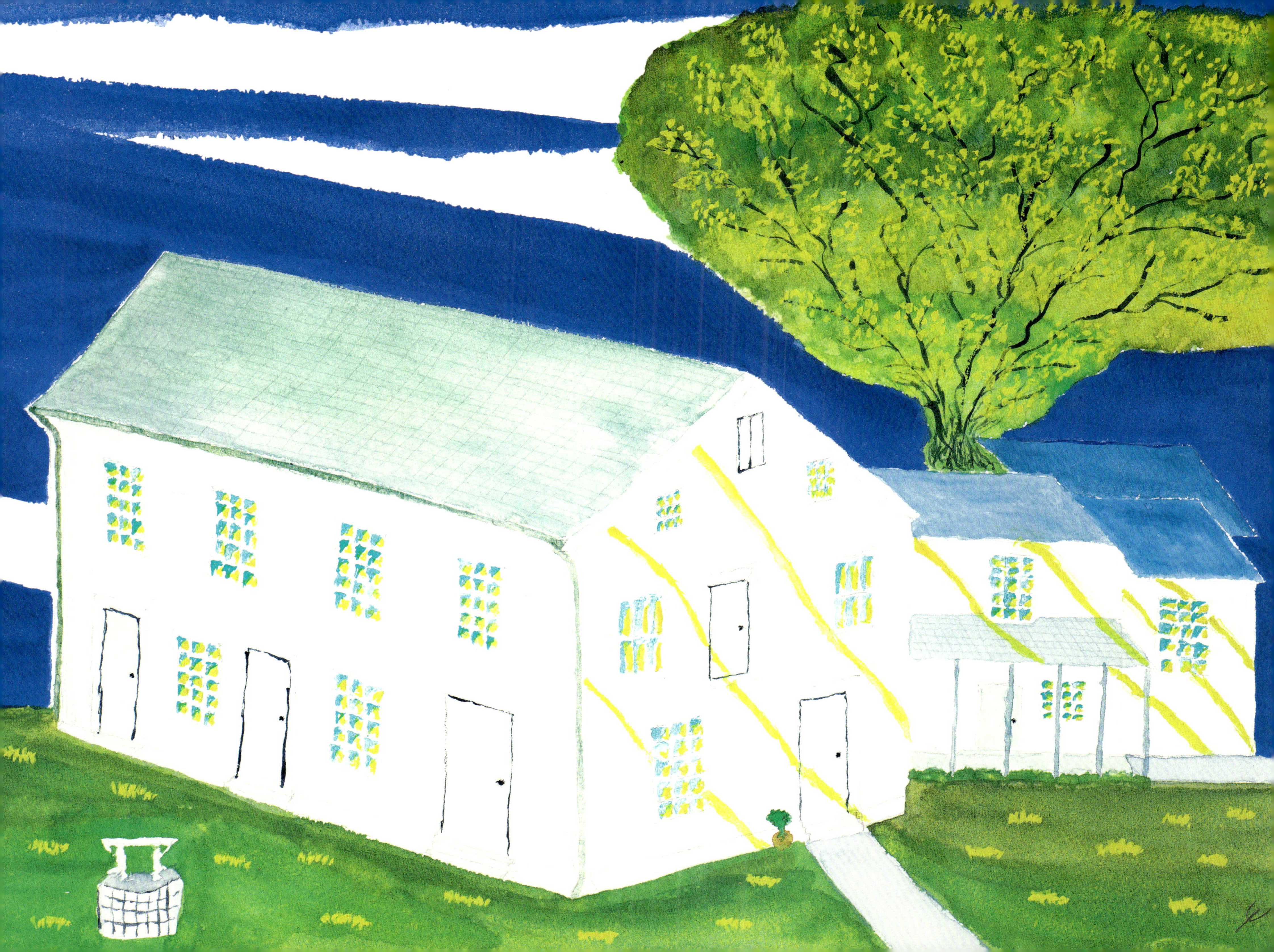

A La Mode

The young man
with a
thin
yellow
tie,
dining with his grandparents,
scowls
as he strides
through the restaurant,
leading the way,
while an old man
with gray hair
and a wrinkled
denim shirt,
and an old woman, balancing
a mauve hat
on her head,
follow the young man,
in his fitted
taupe
sports jacket,
as he brushes
past waiters,
who know
on whom
they need not
bestow
a smile
or the check.

Beach House Restaurant, Po'ipū, Kaua'i

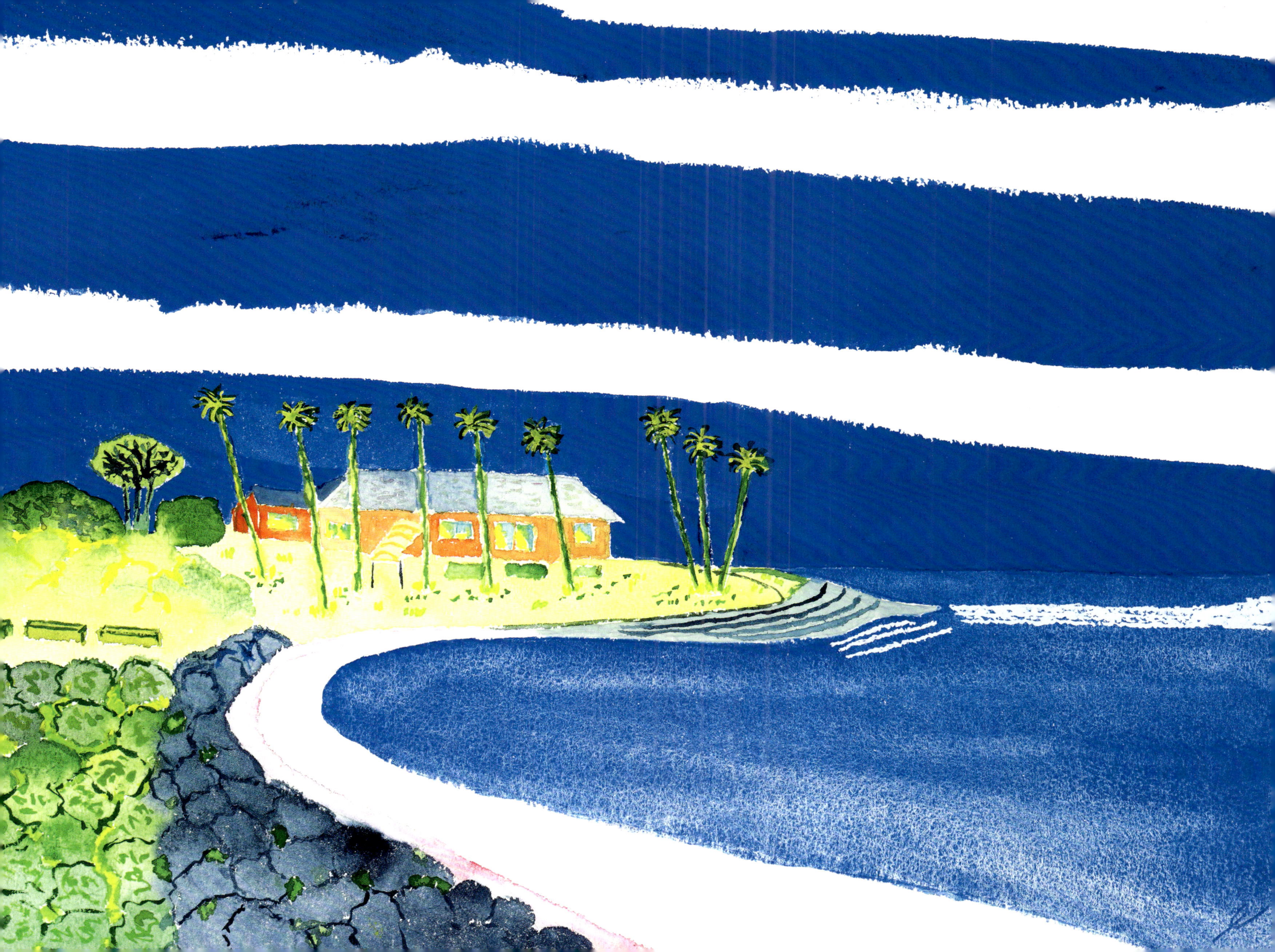

Telling Secrets

The dogs
bark at each other,
longing
to play,
then crouch down
and catapult,
taking turns
chasing
their brown and white spots
into the high grass,
which whispers
the locations
of their hide-and-seek
trails.

A Polite Awakening

A wild man
with an unbridled smile
stands on a corner,
with his ball cap askew
and his laughter
facing down the horizon,
as stylish tourists
glide by,
while the butterscotch sky
glows,
and the palm trees
hiss,
and the surf
mutters,
and the sunlight outstretches the shadows
of hibiscus blossoms,
on grass
that has dozed
all afternoon,
and now welcomes
the tickling steps
of red-crested cardinals,
who sing
to awaken
a too-long-in-paradise
calico cat.

Hawai'i on My Mind

Palm trees
shake out their
gray beards,
while beaches
glow orange
in late light –
the ocean
unfurls
its banner
of whitecaps,
and an island
that daydreams
remembers
how to swim.

A breeze
in the afternoon
settles down
by a bay,
as clouds
that are restless
let their shadows
scale mountains.

March Sunset, Po'ipū, Kaua'i

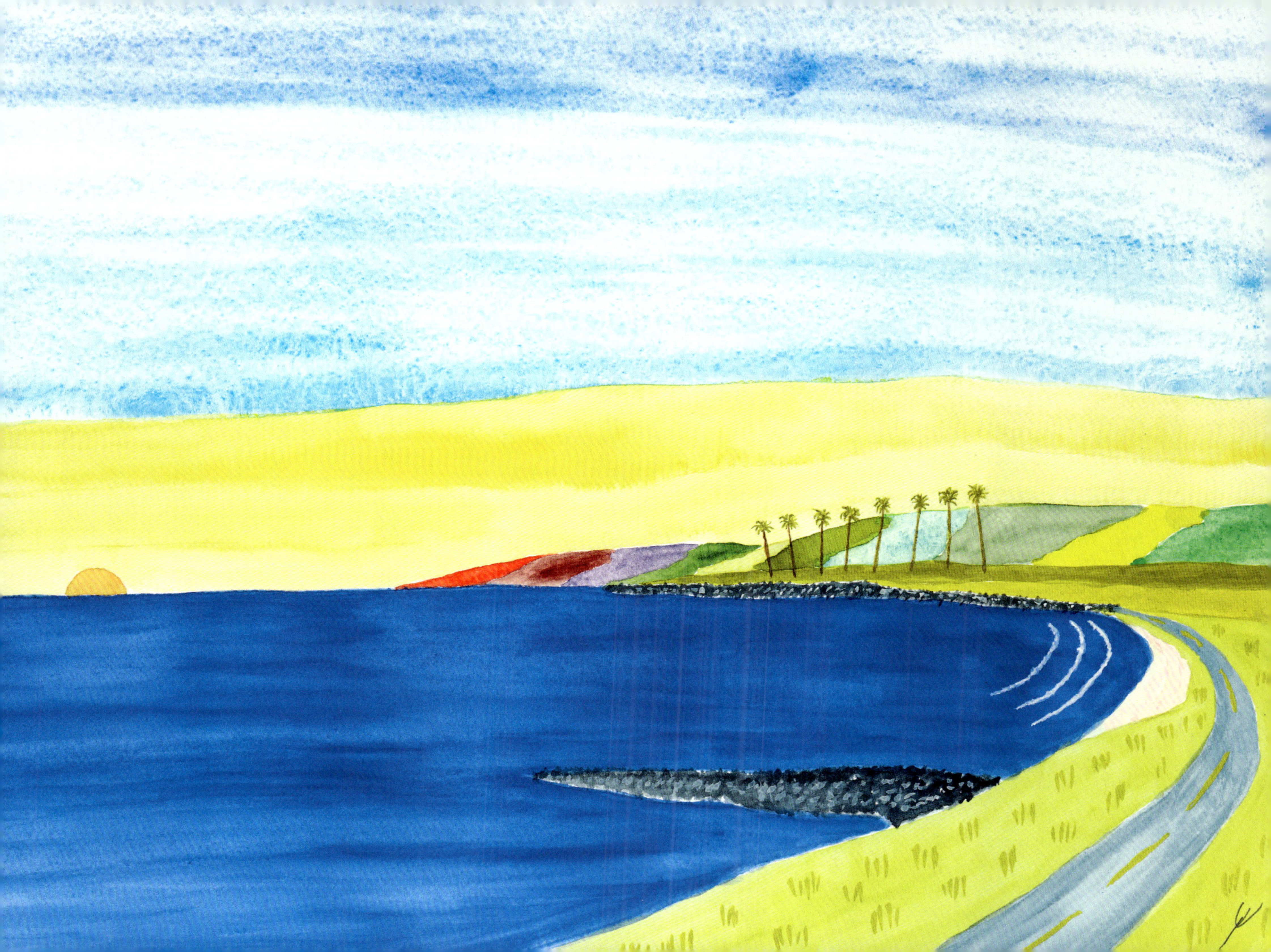

Drowsing at Home

The island
rests
on a summer
afternoon,
laughing
in dozing
sunlight,
while the waves
play leapfrog,
and the palm trees
signal
mountains,
waving their fronds
at the green summits
that lean back
against cloud pillows,
to nap
in the listless
afternoon,
which slips away,
without a thought
of swimming
to a livelier
island.

Spring Rainbow, Keoniloa Beach, Kaua'i

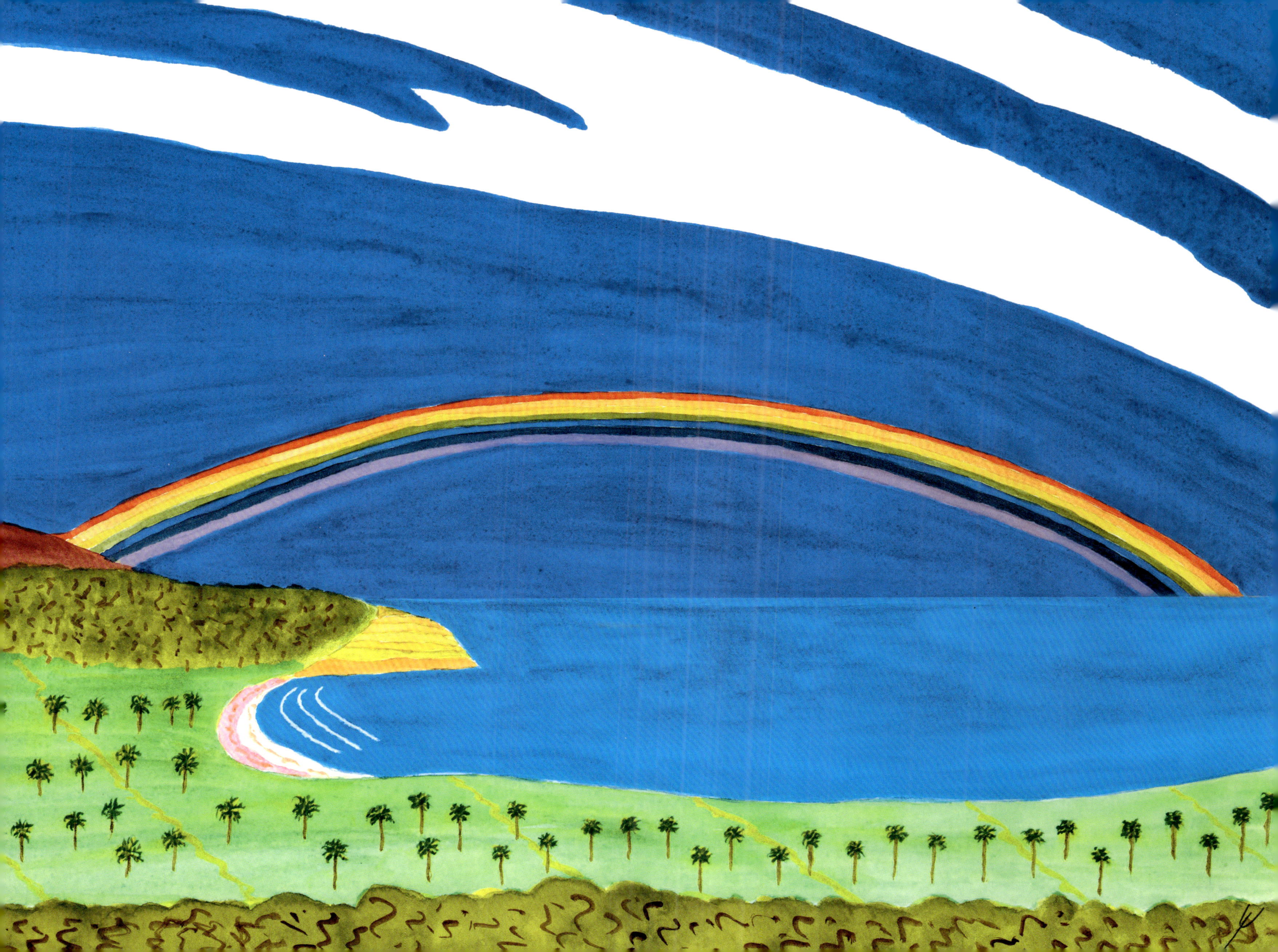

Po‘ipū Beach is the swimming beach that is closest to my home. It lies in a small bay that is protected by a reef. As a result, the beach is a favorite among tourists who want to swim or snorkel. The park that surrounds it also hosts local birthday parties and other family celebrations, as well as open-air wellness meetings and exercise classes. It is a beach for people of all ages, and for the many wild chickens who raise their families, and scavenge for food, in the park.

I love to paint this beach and its surroundings. For years I ran through the park daily. Having seen it at all times of day, in all weather, and in all seasons, I try to portray its many moods and charms. The soft light that visits the beach, the ocean, and the park gives this site an intimacy that larger and more popular beaches lack. It always strikes me as a pool of water that is cradled in the palm of the land.

Spring Sunset, Po‘ipū, Kaua‘i

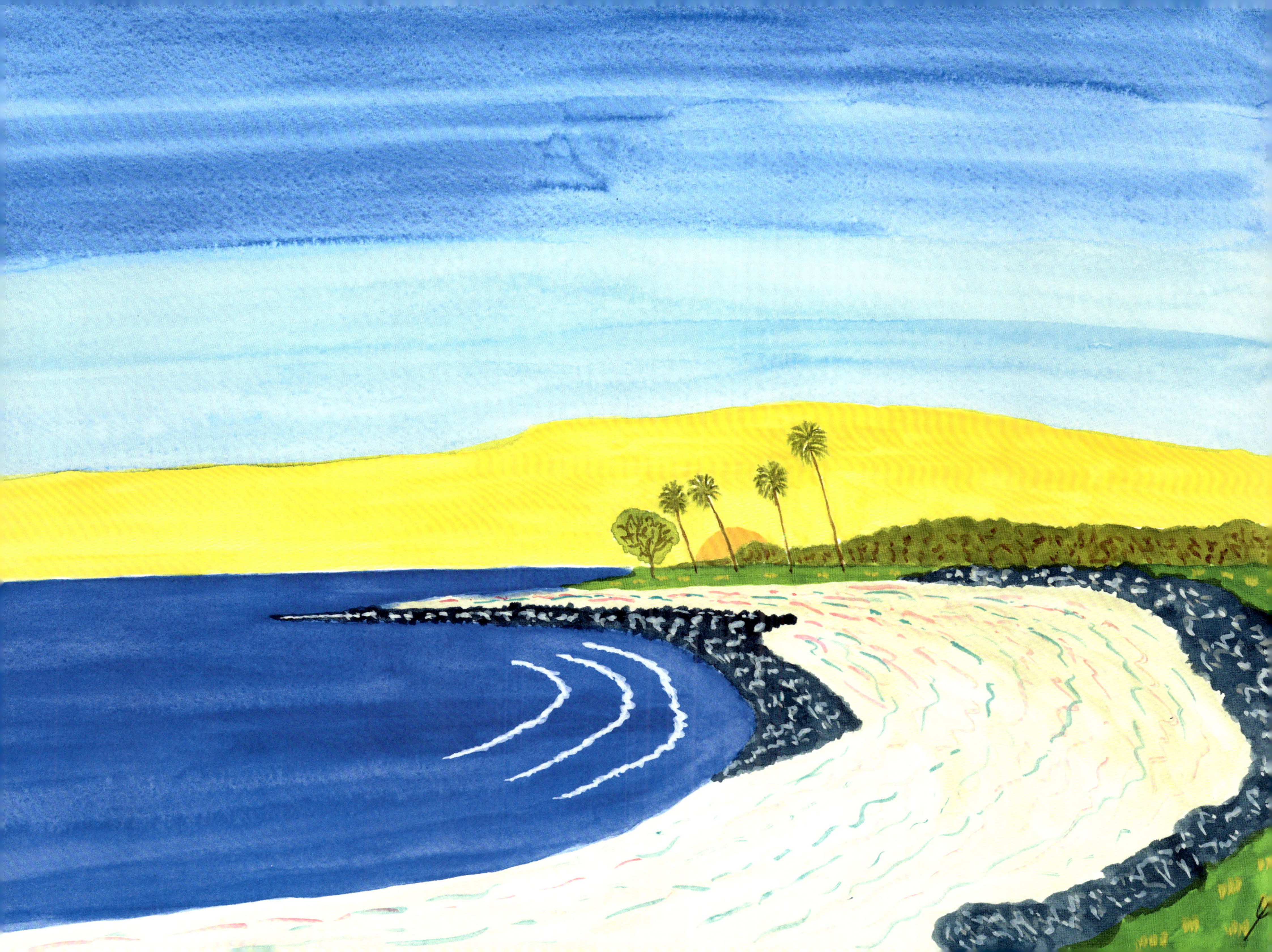

Reflections

The ocean,
a silver mirror,
welcomes
the smiles
of thin-lipped clouds,
while island mountains
cast their nets
of shadows,
and palm trees
admire themselves
in a clear-eyed
glass.

Bright Afternoon, Po'ipū, Kaua'i

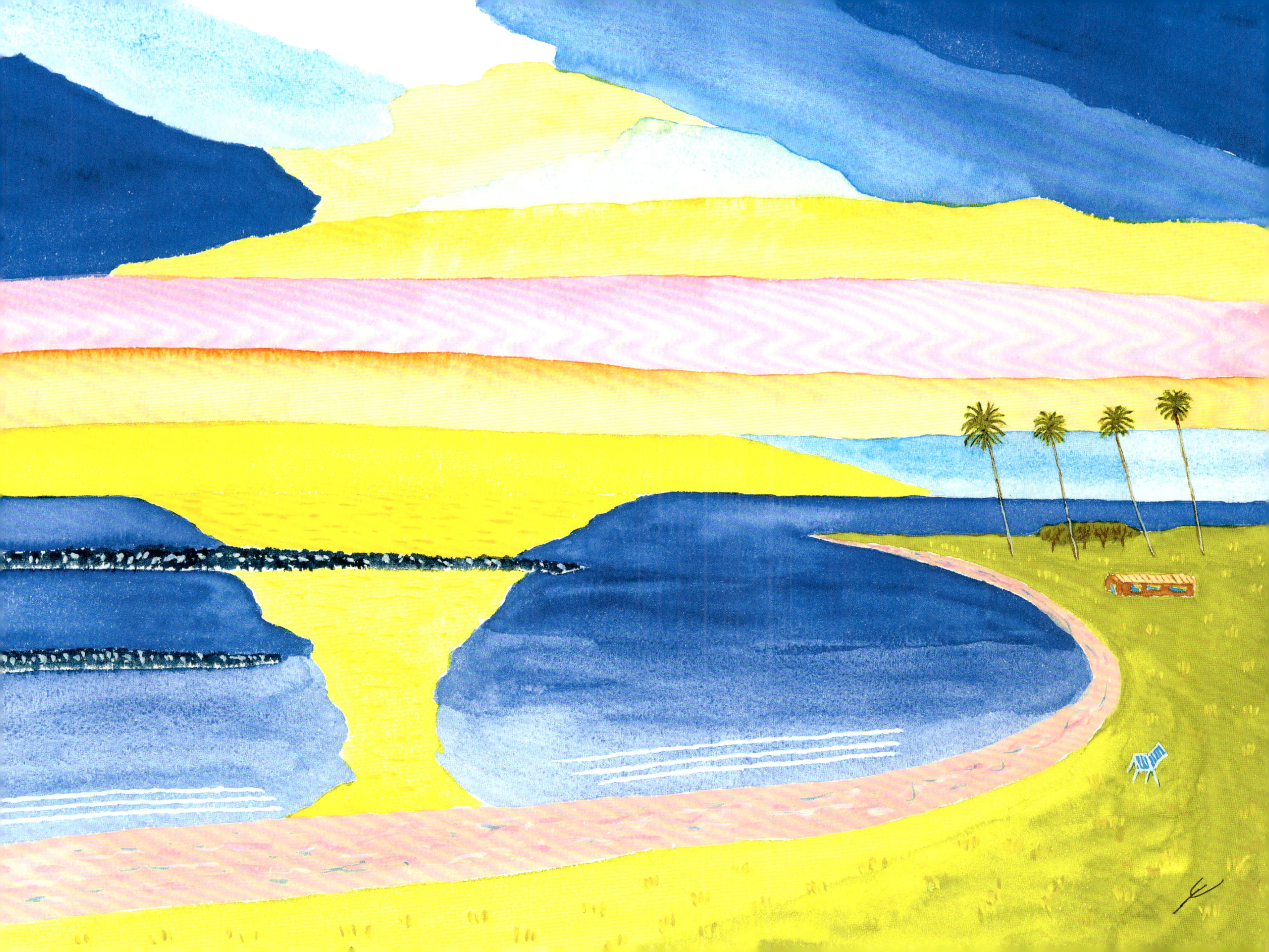

Flying High

A skirt
of orange flowers,
unfurled on the grass
around a high tree,
welcomes the sunlight
and the cool-fingered
rain,
as the flowers
open their palms,
and the light
massages
their fingertips.

The tree,
dancing with breezes,
shares its fallen smiles
with grass
that makes room
for blossoms
that beam
in their sleep.

Spring Afternoon, Po'ipū, Kaua'i

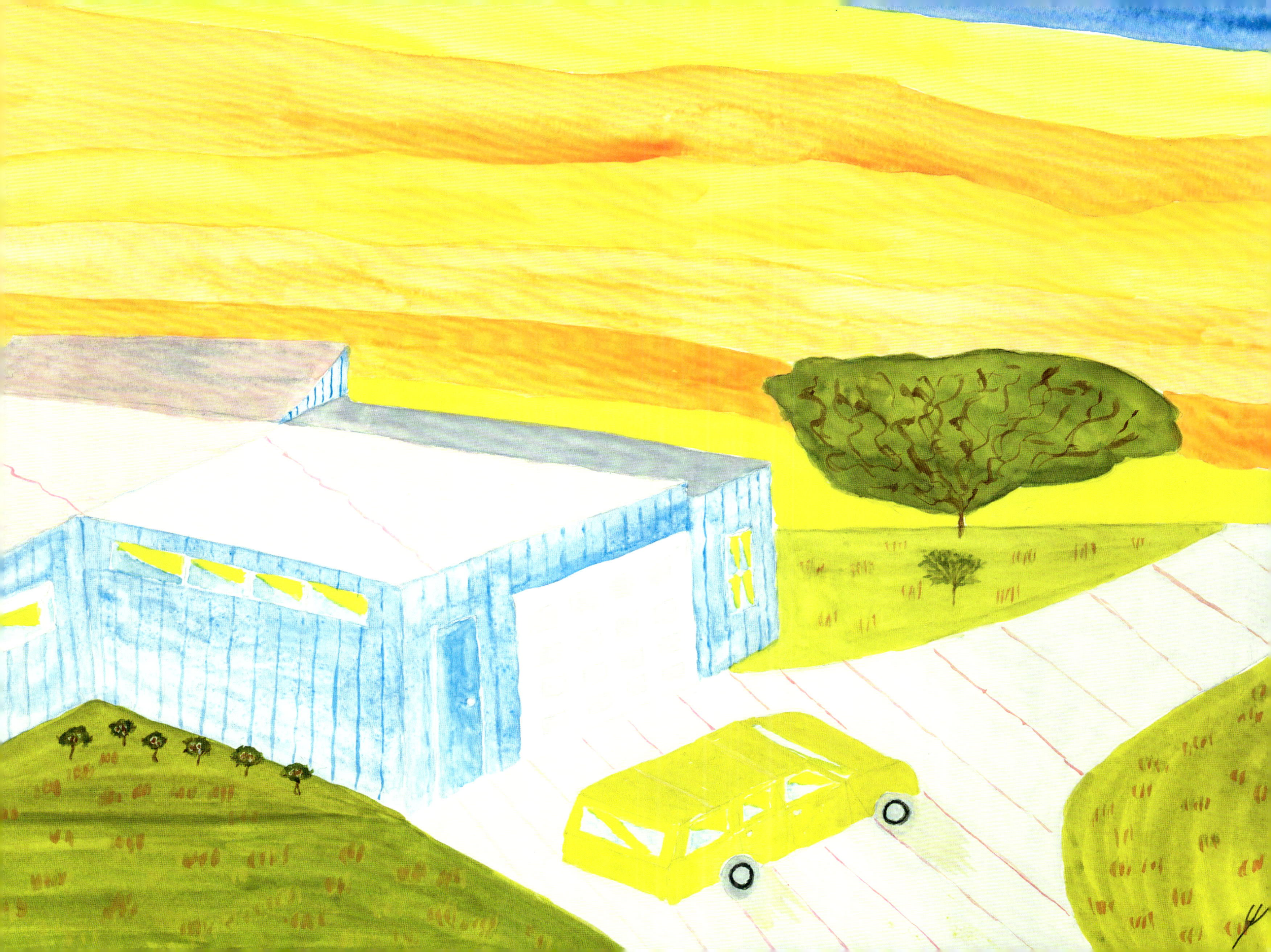

A Long Story

The ocean
embraces
the lingering shore –
a beach,
an inlet,
a peninsula –
curious visitors,
they bathe
in warm waves,
which cling
to their skirts,
inviting them
to swim
all night
under the stars.

Sunset at Ke'e Beach, Kaua'i

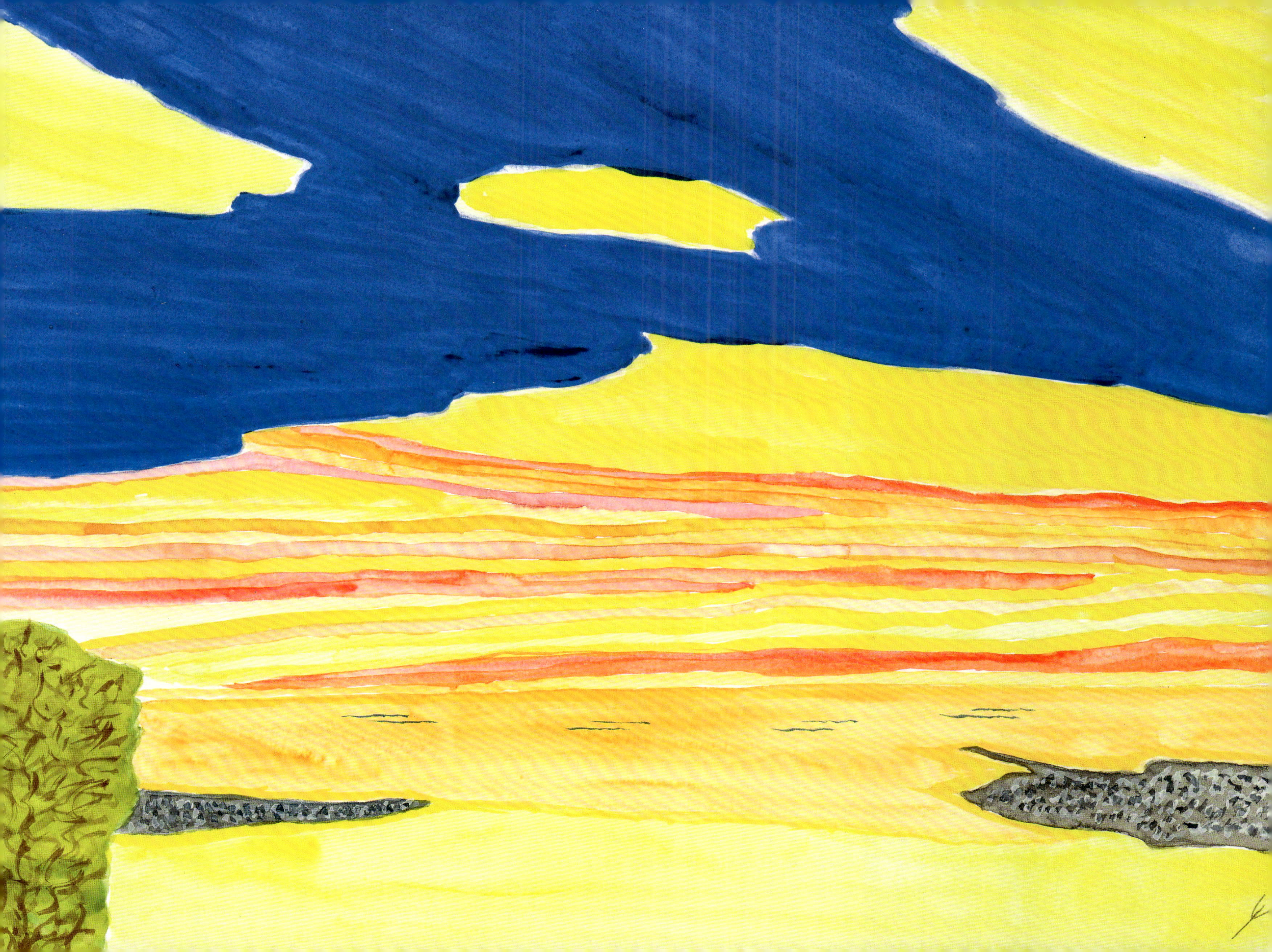

Past and Present

Who will
follow home
this shy paradise,
this land
of unsolved riddles,
with layer upon layer
of lava
and peoples?

Always
the land escapes
the names
and the feathers,
the remnants
of harvests
and conquests.

On a quiet evening,
an old man
sits smoking his pipe,
gazing out
at the harbor,
as tradewinds comb
his white hair –
watching the moon
smile
in its mirror,
he looks forward
to the morning,
when he will arise
with the dawn,
to listen
to the mountain water
giggling in sluices,
and the high cane
talking story,
passing the word
from field to field
that the true sweetness
is yet to come.

Sound and Fury

A west wind,
pushing all before it,
scatters leaves and dust
and grass and paper scraps
and plastic bottles
and left-behind feathers,
as it shakes
the trees' nervous branches,
which creak
and moan
and wave their fingertips,
while only the moon
steers a steady course,
untroubled
by a blowhard
who trumpets
his journey
from nowhere
to nowhere.

A Smiling Mirror

The moon,
a bright-eyed neighbor,
comes calling
when you least
expect her,
beaming
through the clouds
and startling
your windows –
washing clean
your lanai,
she peoples
the yard with shadows,
then beckons you
to step outside,
to dance
with a visitor
who unfurls
her silver
petticoats.

May Moonrise, Po'ipū, Kaua'i

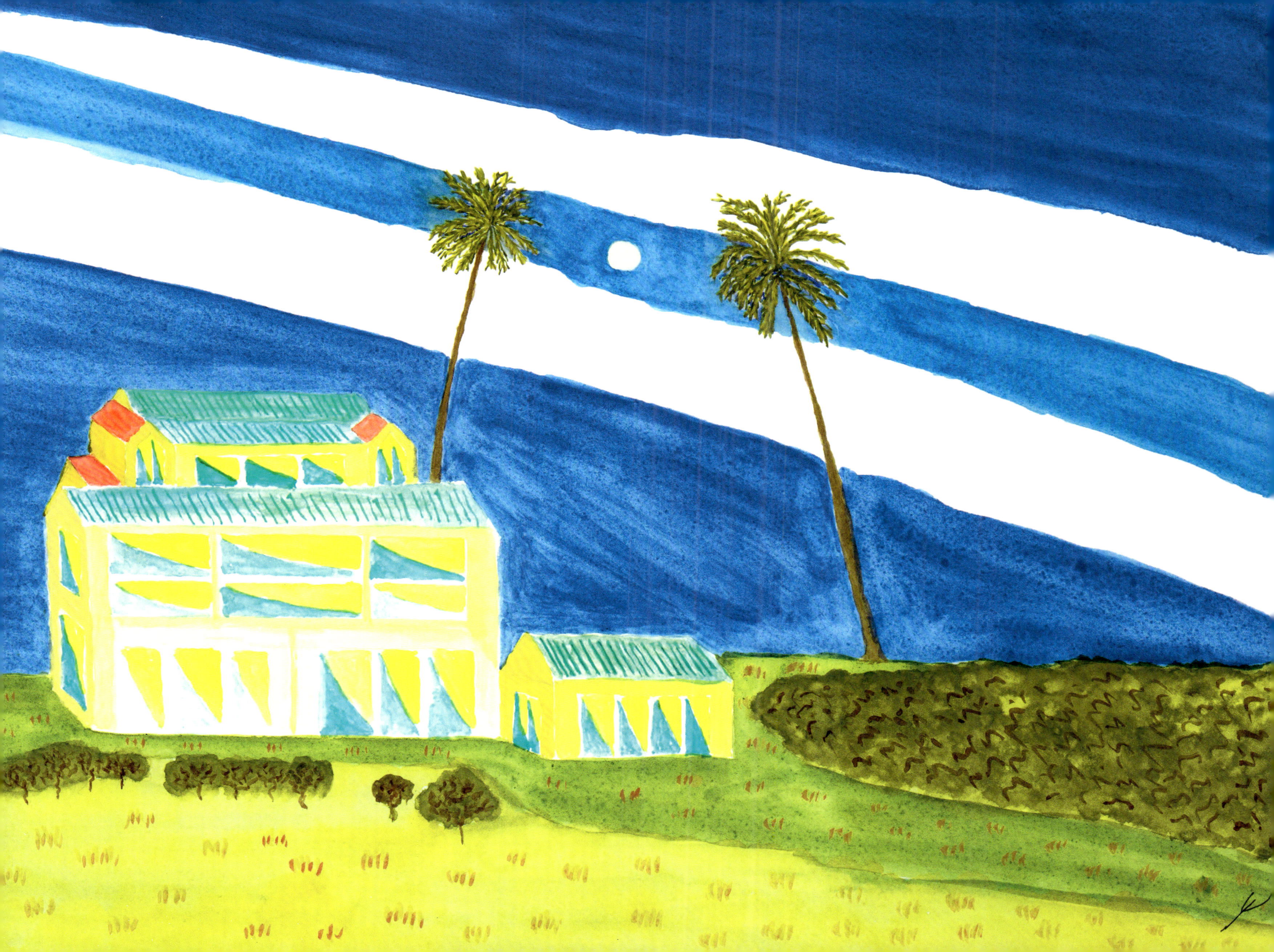

A Bright Beginning

A summer sun,
dawdling early,
lights up
an eastern cloud,
which beams
at a distant
horizon,
so modestly pale
in the lap
of the western sky,
which is happy
to awaken
to the daydreamer
of a rainbow
with wings.

Summer Sunrise, Po'ipū, Kaua'i

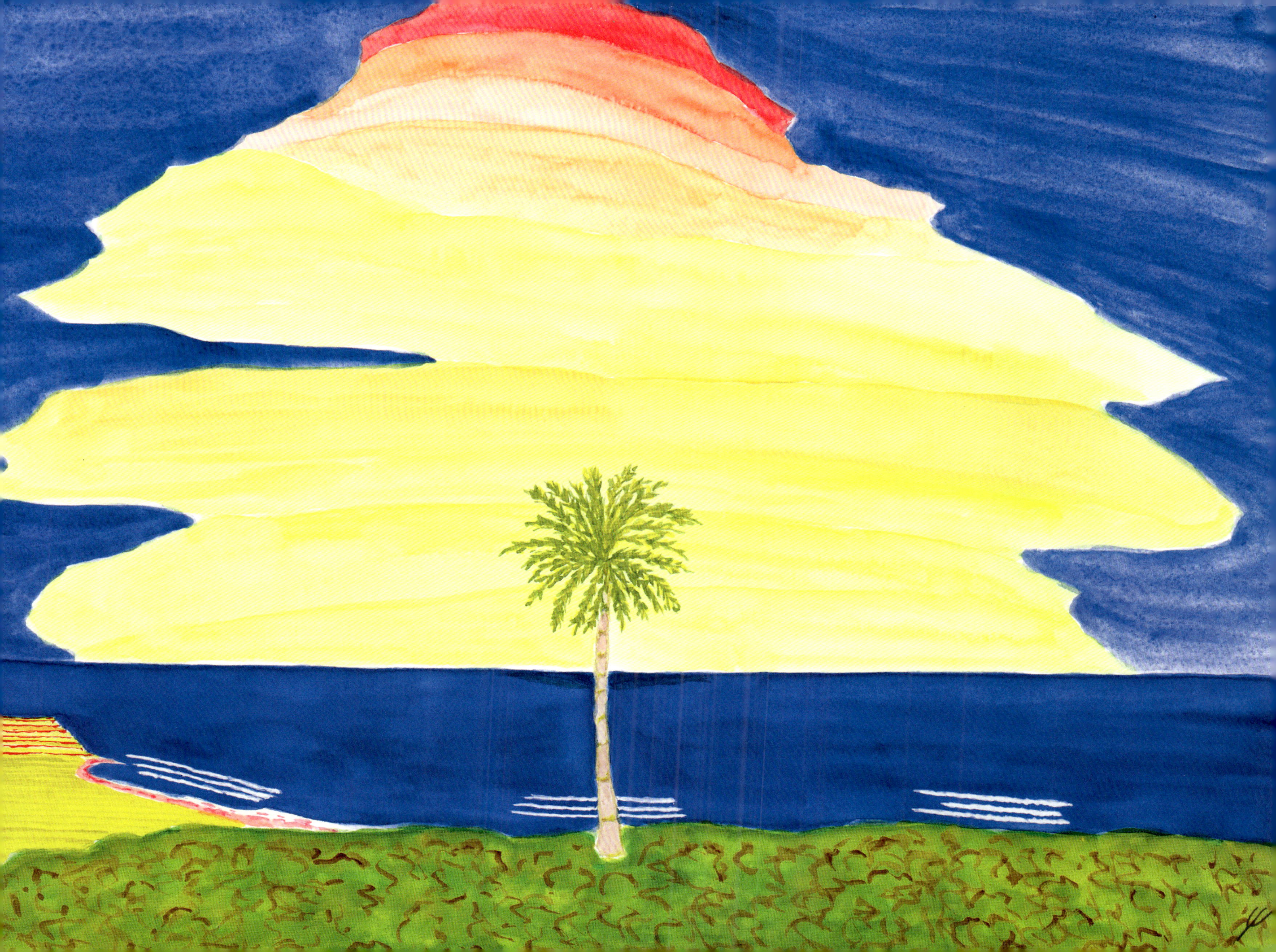

Making Peace

Clouds
weigh down
the horizon,
before blowing
away –
then the clear sky
rests
on the shoulders
of islands.

Hanalei Pier and Bay, Kaua'i

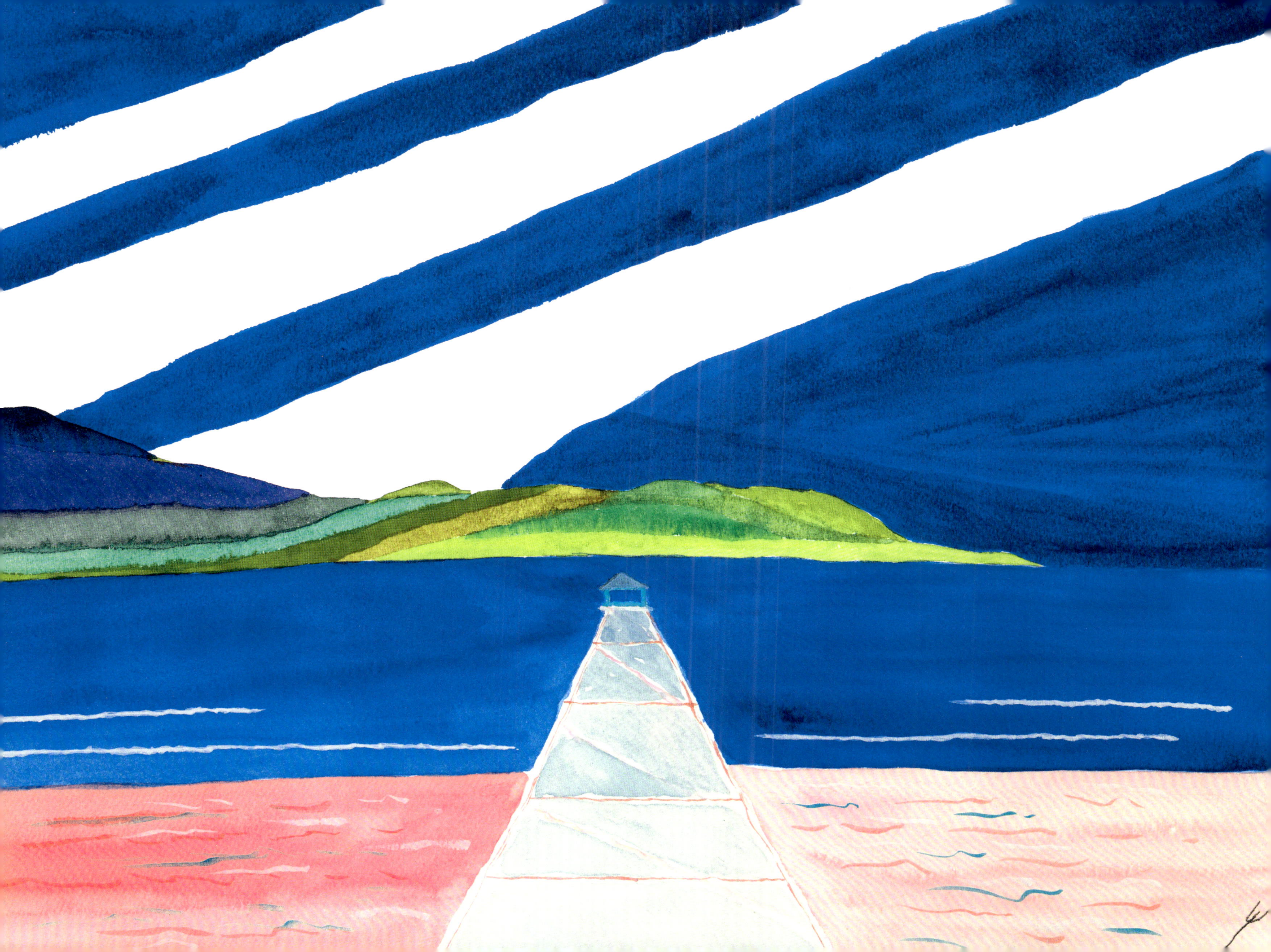

An Early Concert

A young man
strums
on his ukulele
at dawn,
picking out
a tune,
as the sun
turns shadows
into trees,
and the clouds
begin to glow,
and the grass
makes room
for wildflowers' smiles,
and the music,
floating over the ocean,
serenades
the tumbling waves,
tireless swimmers
who have heard the call
of a dreamer
who has seen the light
and taught his hands
to borrow
a song,
from a breeze
that fiddles
on palm fronds.

Spring Sunrise, Po'ipū, Kaua'i

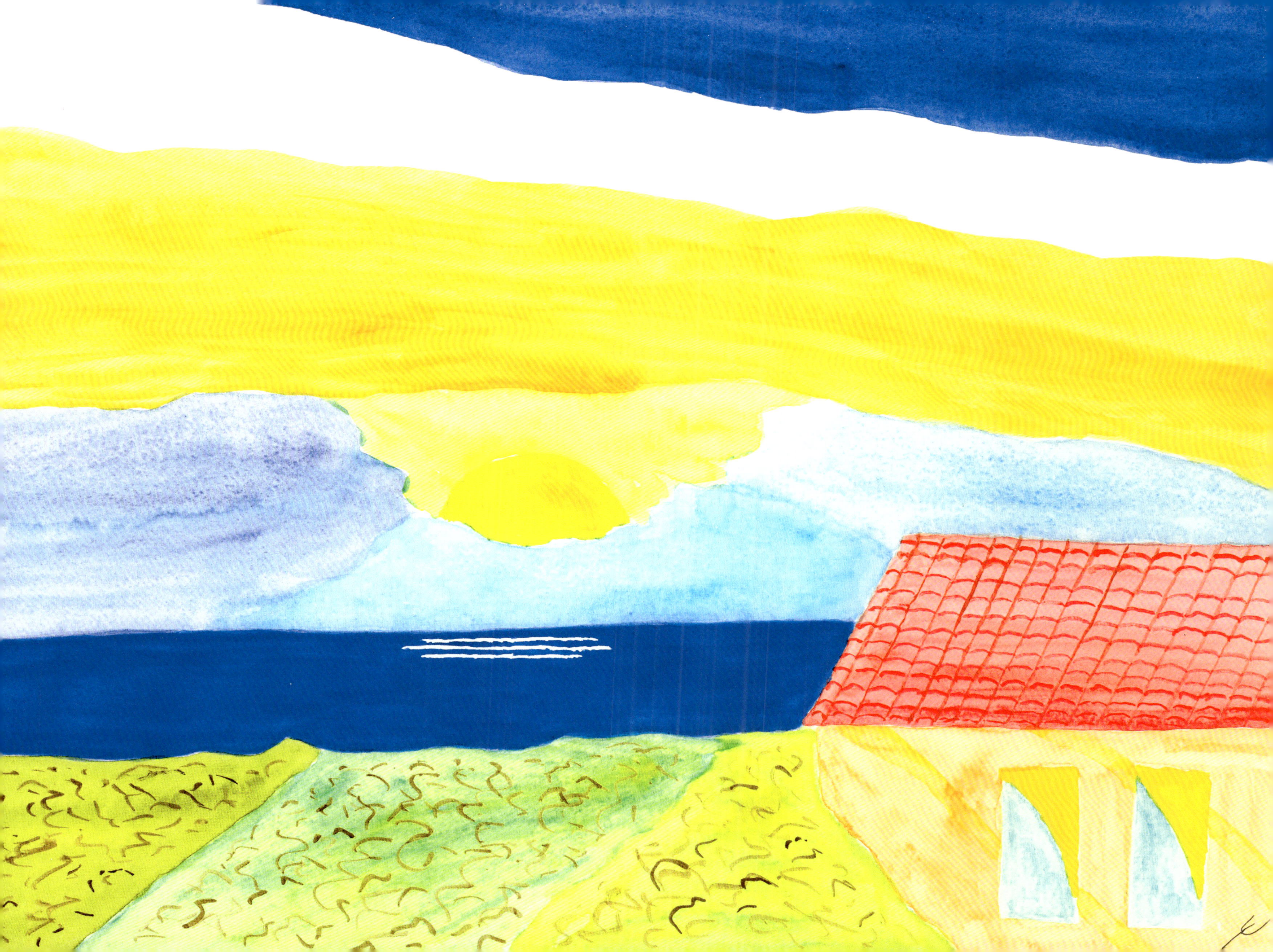

Procession

A canopy
of trees,
with a thousand
green parasols,
raises
its bower of shade
above the sunny foothills,
promising
a hidden road
that inches
toward the mountains,
which doze
beneath a mosquito net
of blue haze.

Wailua River Valley, Kaua'i

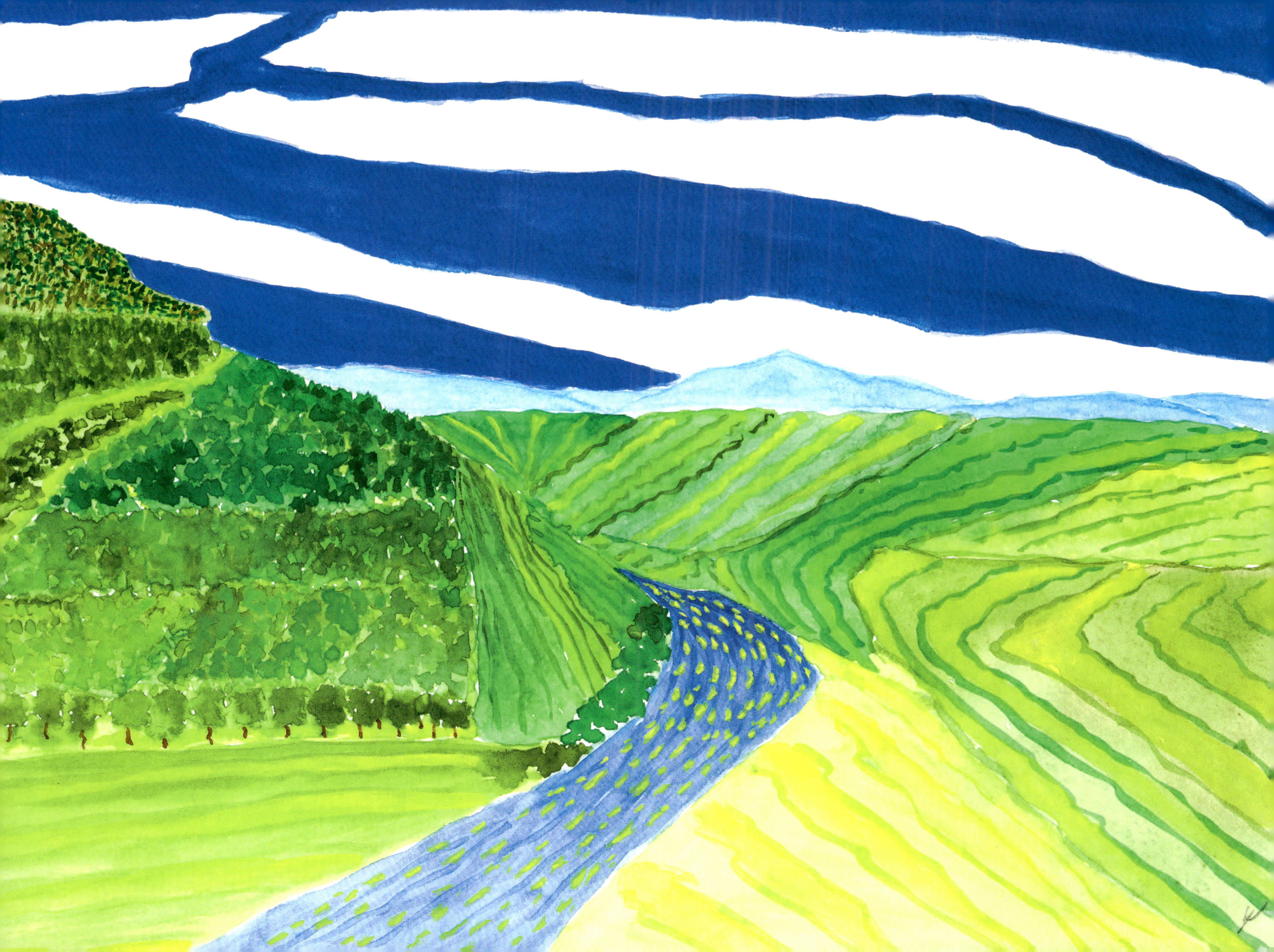

Mount Hā'upu

My old mountain
waits for me,
standing up
to rain and rainbows:
beckoning me
with its whiskered chin,
it nods
and smiles
in the early light,
as I straggle forth,
headed
for its sheltering
shadow –
there, where the road
peters out,
the mountain
shares its chants –
I listen
to the wind
and the whispering cane –
they call me
in tumbledown light,
when the clouds
have swept themselves away,
and the ancient peak
raises my eyes
to the heavens.

Rainbow Over Mount Hā'upu, Kaua'i

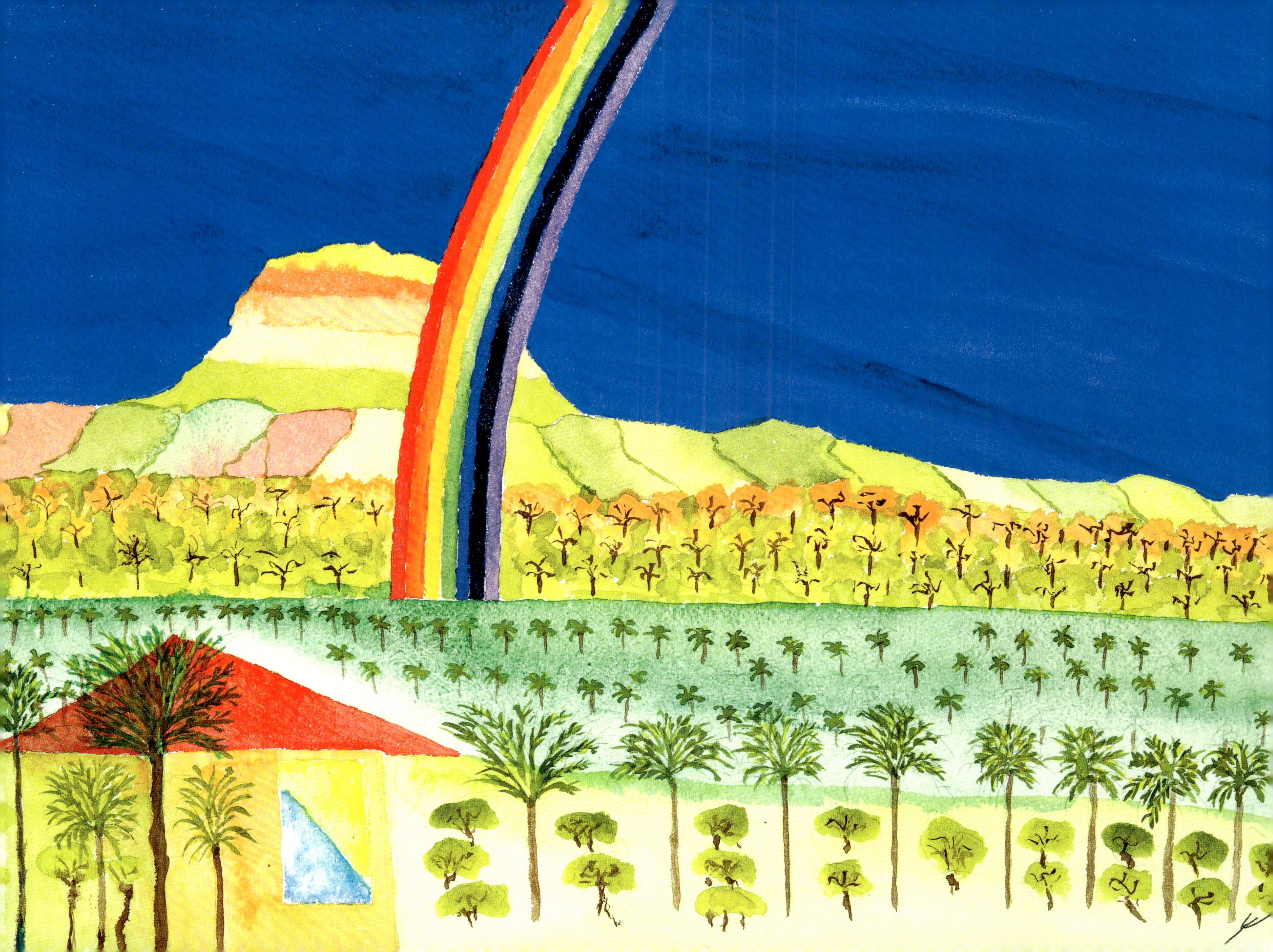

Silent Partners

A woman
with worn-out hair
sits eating barbecue,
while her baby
naps,
slumped in his stroller
in late afternoon light,
as a bird
flits into the park pavilion,
singing
and swooping,
to clean up
crumbs
that the mother
has not noticed,
while tradewinds
scatter
the fragrance of peppermint,
and the baby
shares a yawn
with his mother.

A Higher Calling

A calico cat
goes hunting
in the rain –
hiding
under a branch
that outstretches
its umbrella leaves,
she waits
for the soft patter
of raindrops
to lure a sparrow
to seek shelter,
but the bird
will hear none of it,
preferring
to shower
at the top
of a tree.

Safe Passage

Far out to sea,
the whitecaps
churn and bob –
stirring the ocean
with their ceaseless
caresses,
they pass on
the wind's greetings,
before swimming on,
happy to flirt
with the shyest
of whales.

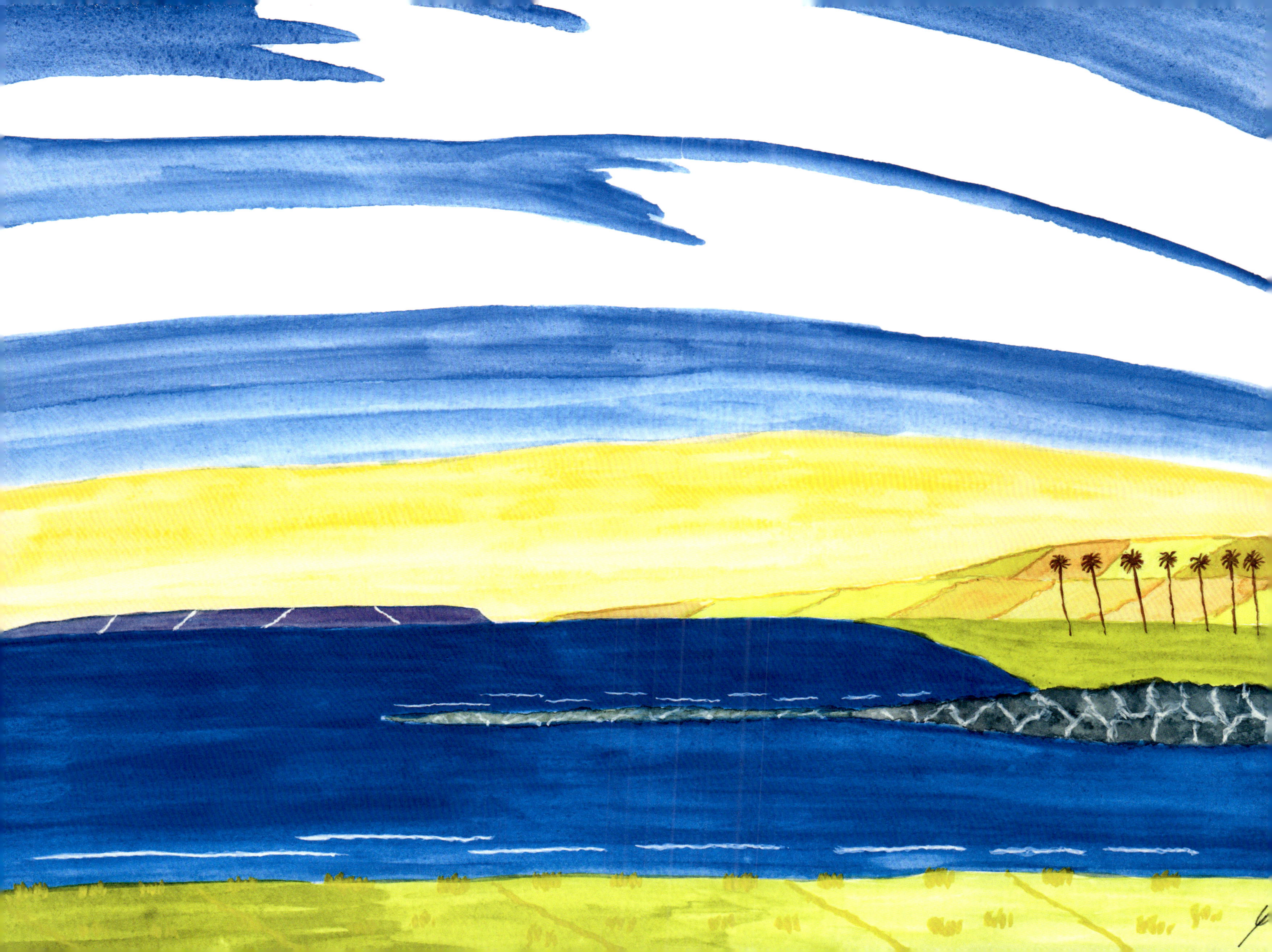

Calm Voyages

A quiet day
beside the coast
rests
in the arms
of the shore,
where waves
ride piggyback
onto the beach,
which whispers
of tranquil
journeys.

Kekaha Beach and Ni'ihau, Kaua'i

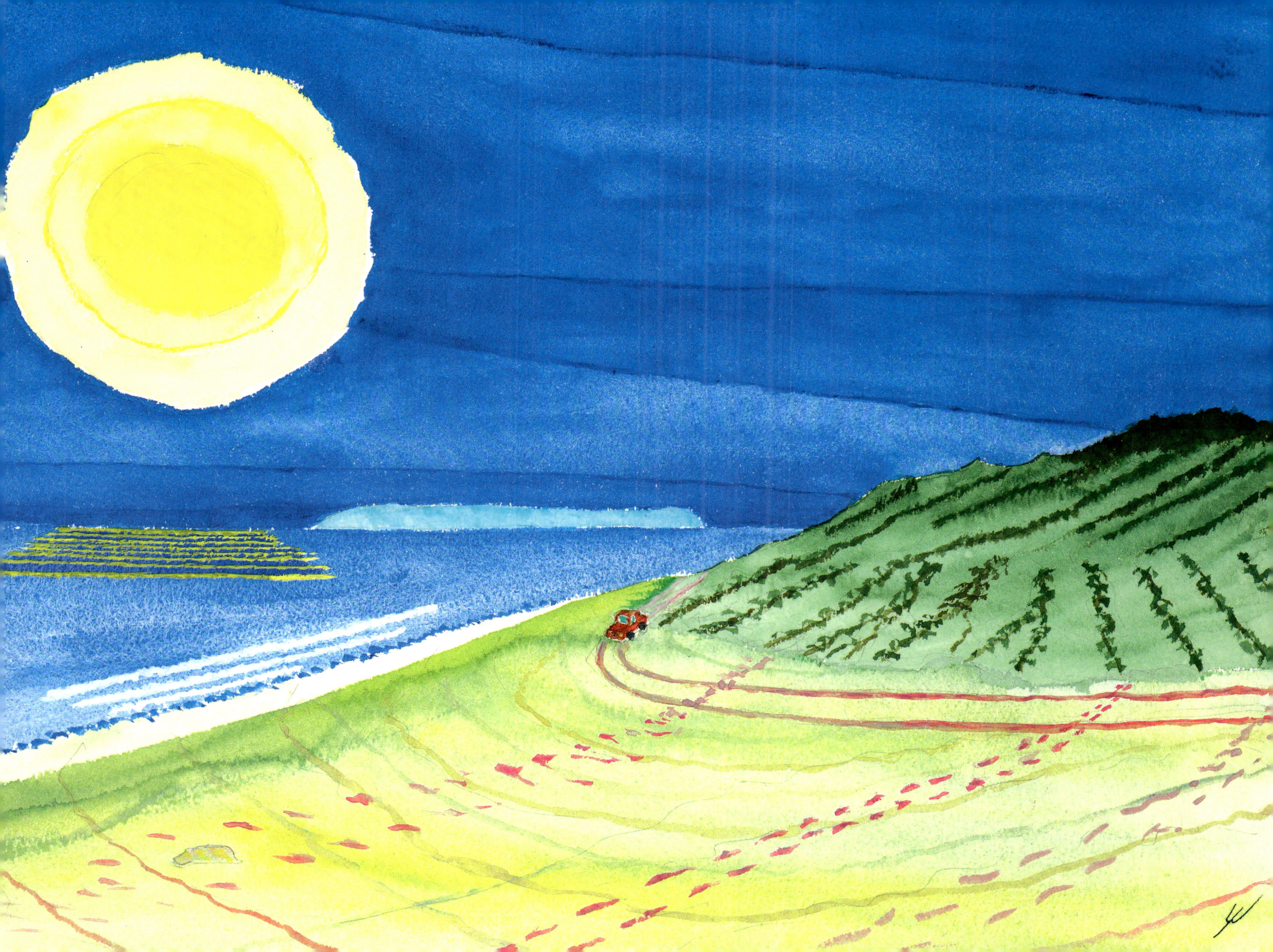

Happy Hunting

A white
cattle egret,
gazing out
from a fence post,
rises
when he sees you,
and, floating
on a breeze
that you do not
even feel,
glides
above the fields,
seeking
a slow lizard,
or a Hereford steer
with a back
that itches
to be scratched.

Cattle Egret on a Path to the Ocean, Kaua'i

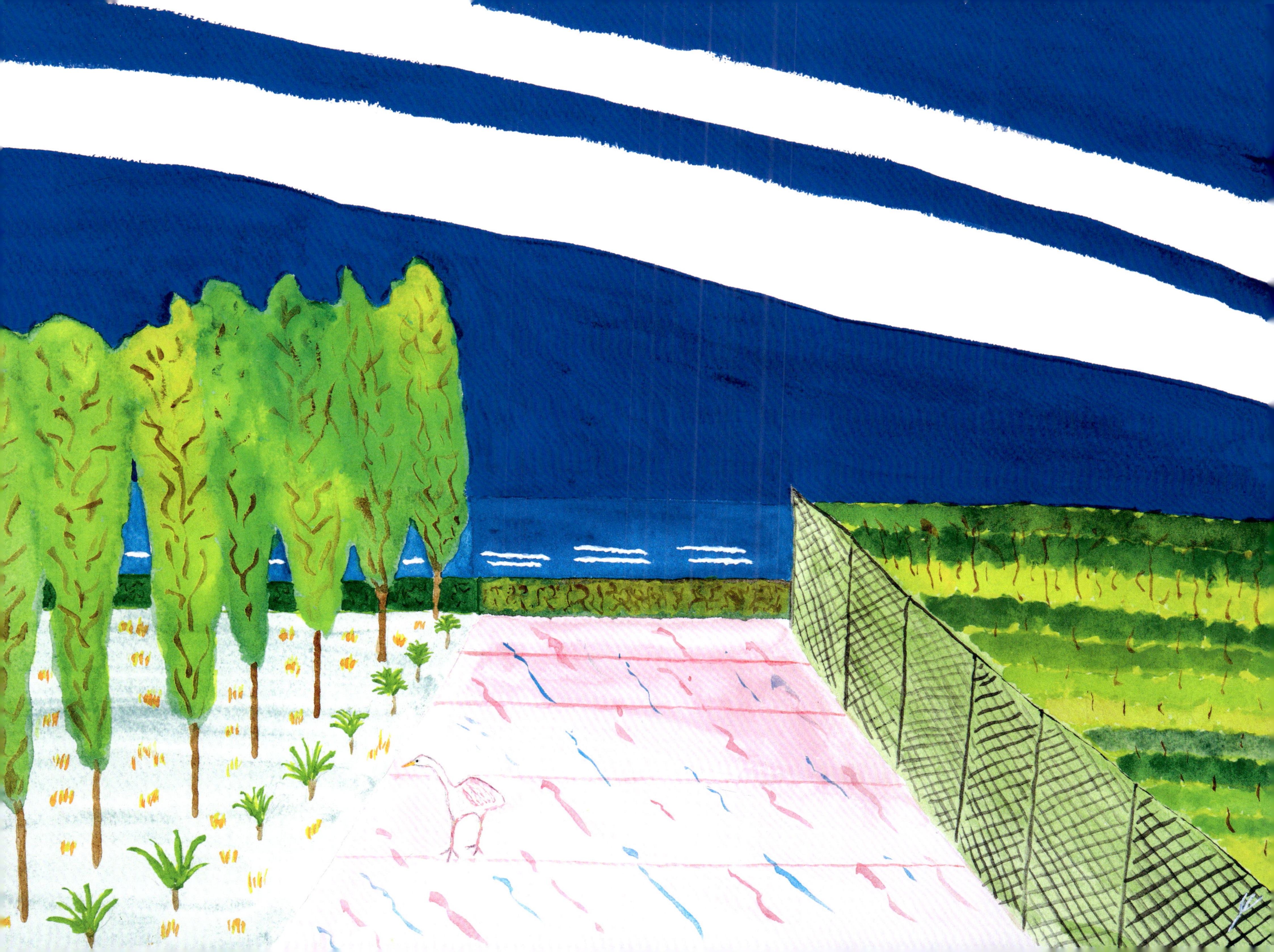

Spring Morning

The cattle egret,
a slender-winged
kite,
rises above a field,
cavorting
with a breeze,
then banks
and settles
back down,
to feast
among the straw,
which knows only
the earth's
warm embraces,
and the secret prayers
of beetles.

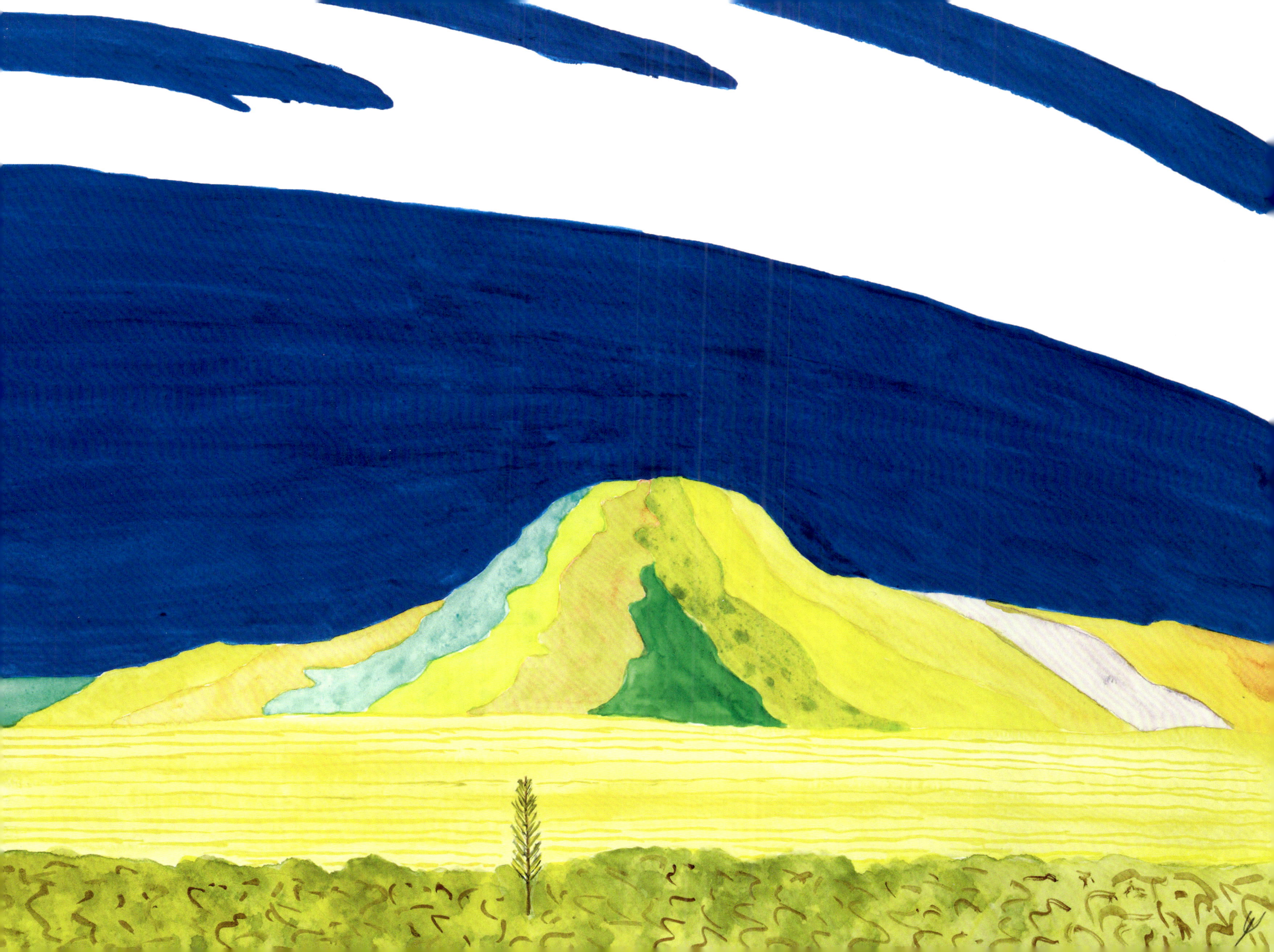

Sounding Off

Voices
echo,
then settle down –
in the canyon,
shouts
resound,
then rise
in the still air,
to welcome
strangers,
who listen
for the songs
of birds
on the wing.

Rainbow Falls, Hawai'i

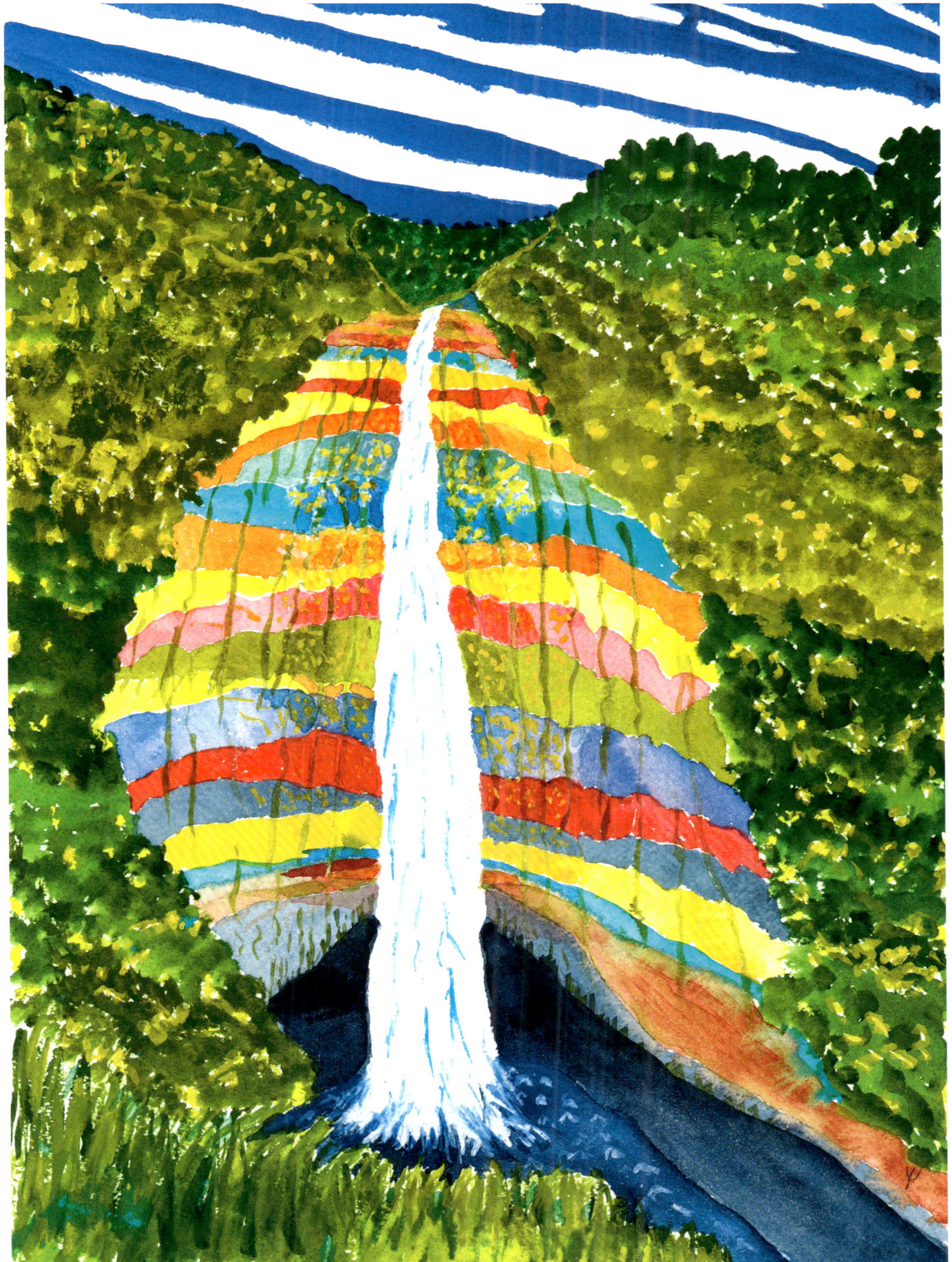

Heading Home

Brilliant light,
poured out
across the ocean,
stretches forever,
silvering the waves,
following a day
that wanders west,
certain
that islands
swim away
with golden clouds
on their backs.

Ke'e Beach in January, Kaua'i

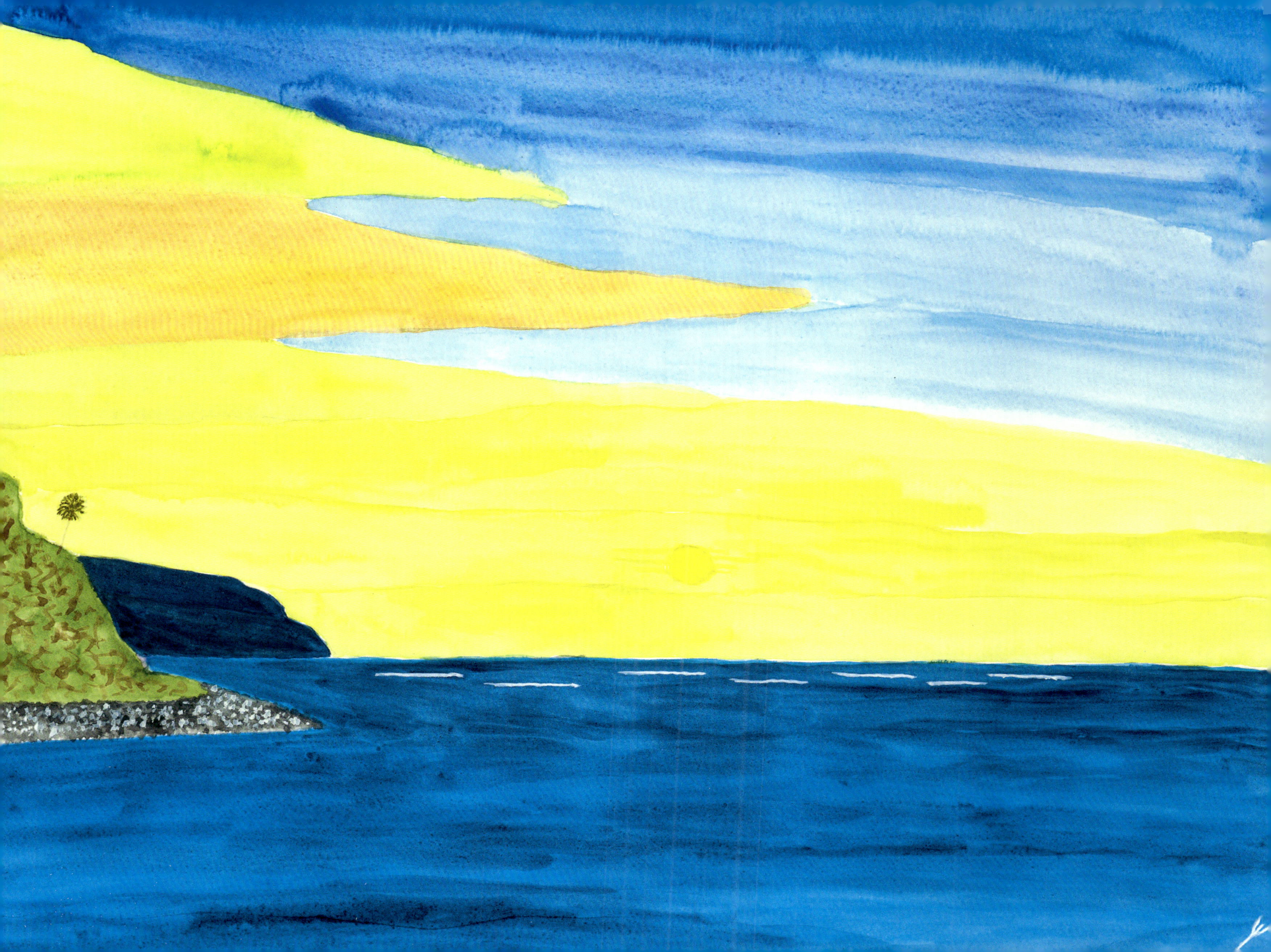

Loving the Dance

A fuzzy gray caterpillar
bustles
across the trail,
shaking
his sweatered body,
leaving
in the pink dust
a smooth path
that rumbles,
remembering
a rhythmic
passerby.

A Firebird

An old man,
working alone,
dons
a serious face –
studying a book,
he fingers
the pages,
then taps
the bright cover,
which beams
at a student,
who feels the breath
of the warm words
that fly
from the page.

A Quiet Heroine

A Hawaiian woman
in a white holokū
unfolds her body
among drooping
orchids –
with a red hibiscus
awakening
in her waves
of brown hair,
she rests
her hands
as if in a moment
of hula,
while the ferns
and the soft ground
caress
her garden
of curves,
and she lets her smile
blossom
in the fiery-eyed
shade.

Kāhili Ridge Waterfalls, Kaua'i

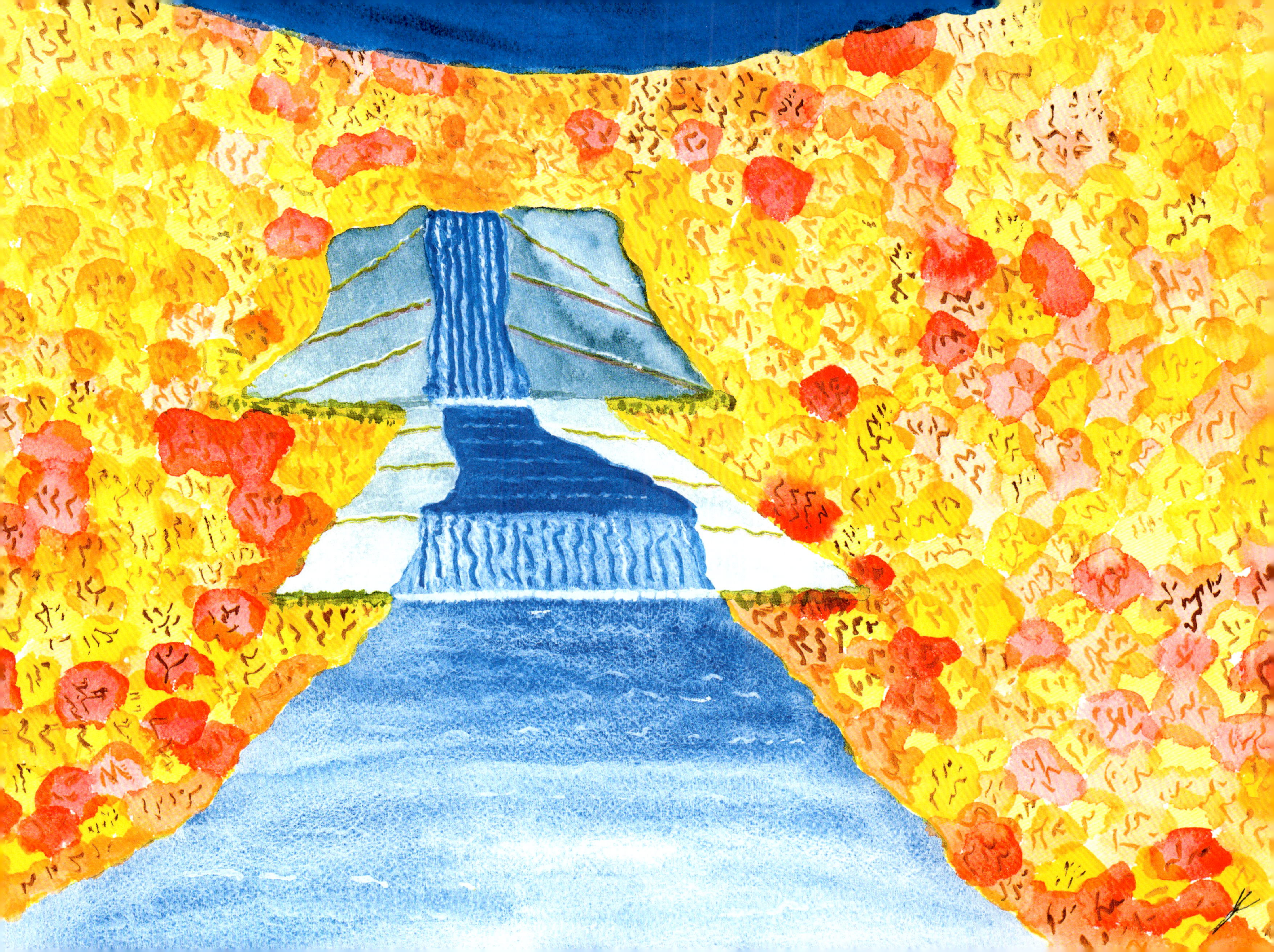

Thanksgiving

An outstretched promontory,
a slender finger
that points
beyond the horizon,
basks
in sunlight
that sails
to the west,
heading
for harbors
that open their arms,
to welcome
land-seeking
wanderers.

North Kīlauea Coast, Kaua'i

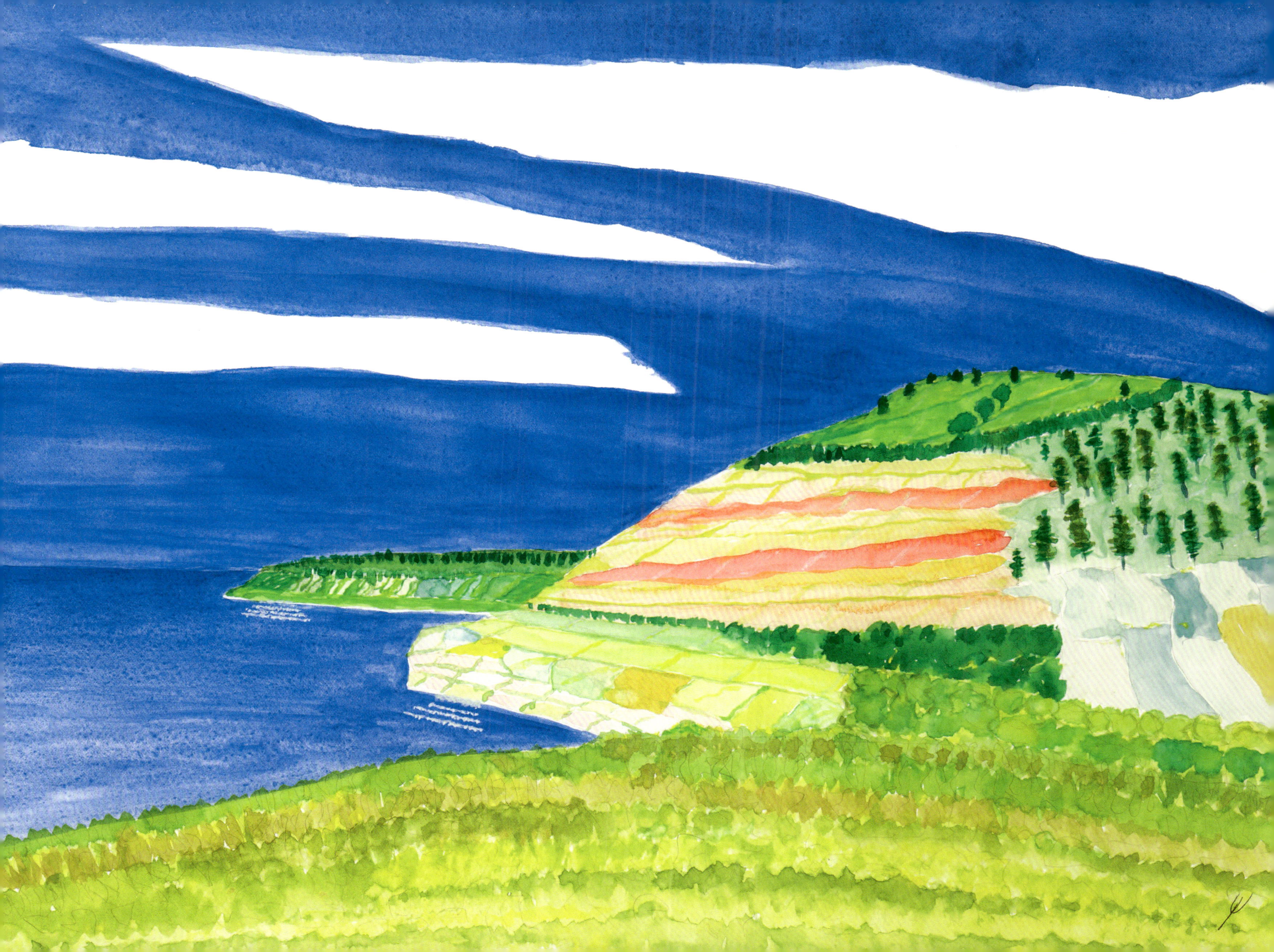

A New Day

Dawn creeps
across the horizon,
spreading
its lavender light,
as the sky
clears up,
and the land
sets out
its tablecloth,
certain
of a picnic,
on a day
when the clouds
unfurl their pink
parasols.

House on a Hill, Po'ipū, Kaua'i

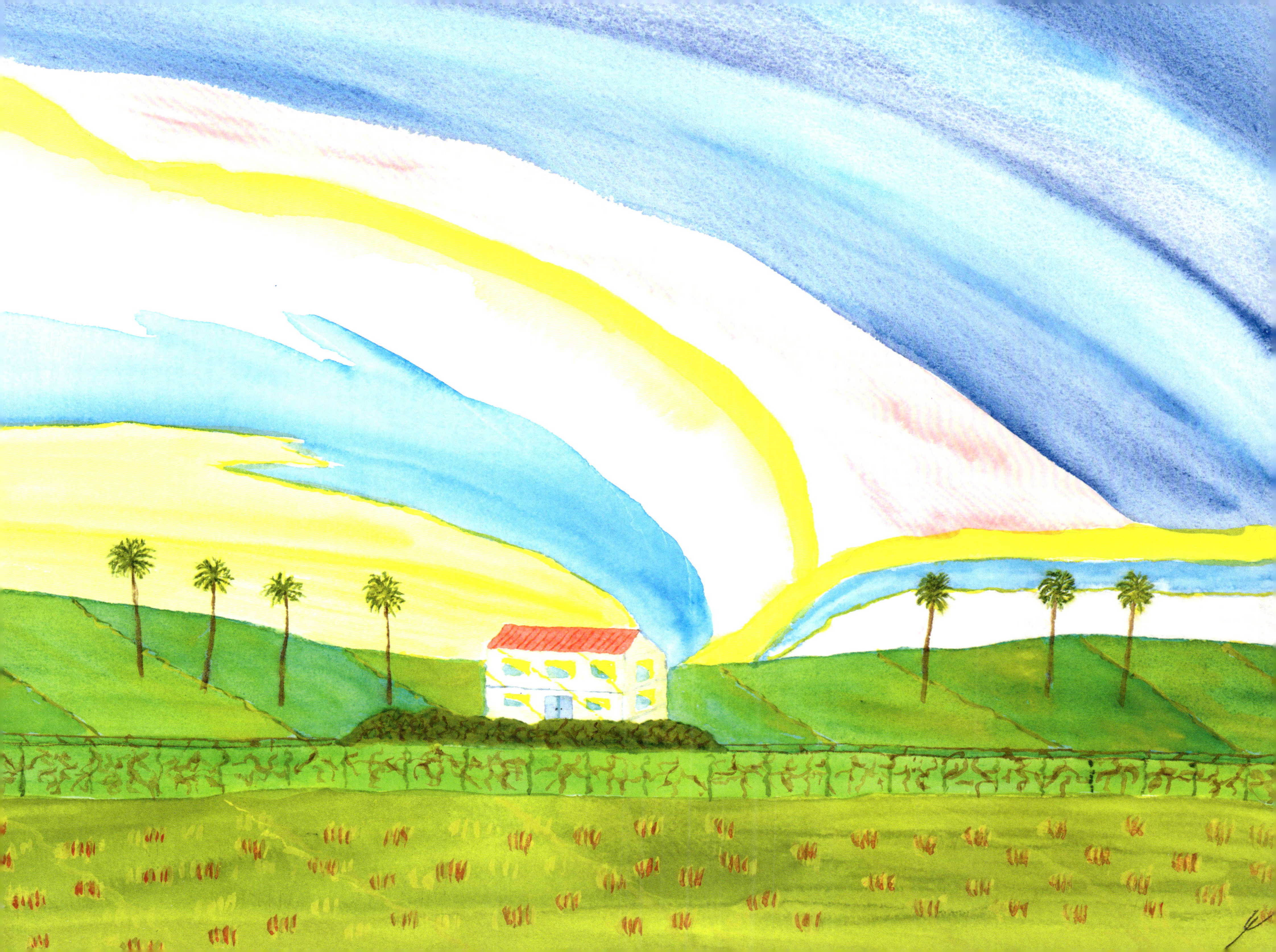

An Old Flame

A bright-eyed ocean,
gazing
at the sky,
combs out
its white locks,
while clouds
drape the waves
in silken shadows –
a sand-strewn shore,
tawny and whispering,
welcomes
the slow embrace
of breakers
that have swum
from lands
of ancient laughter.

North Shore, Kaua'i

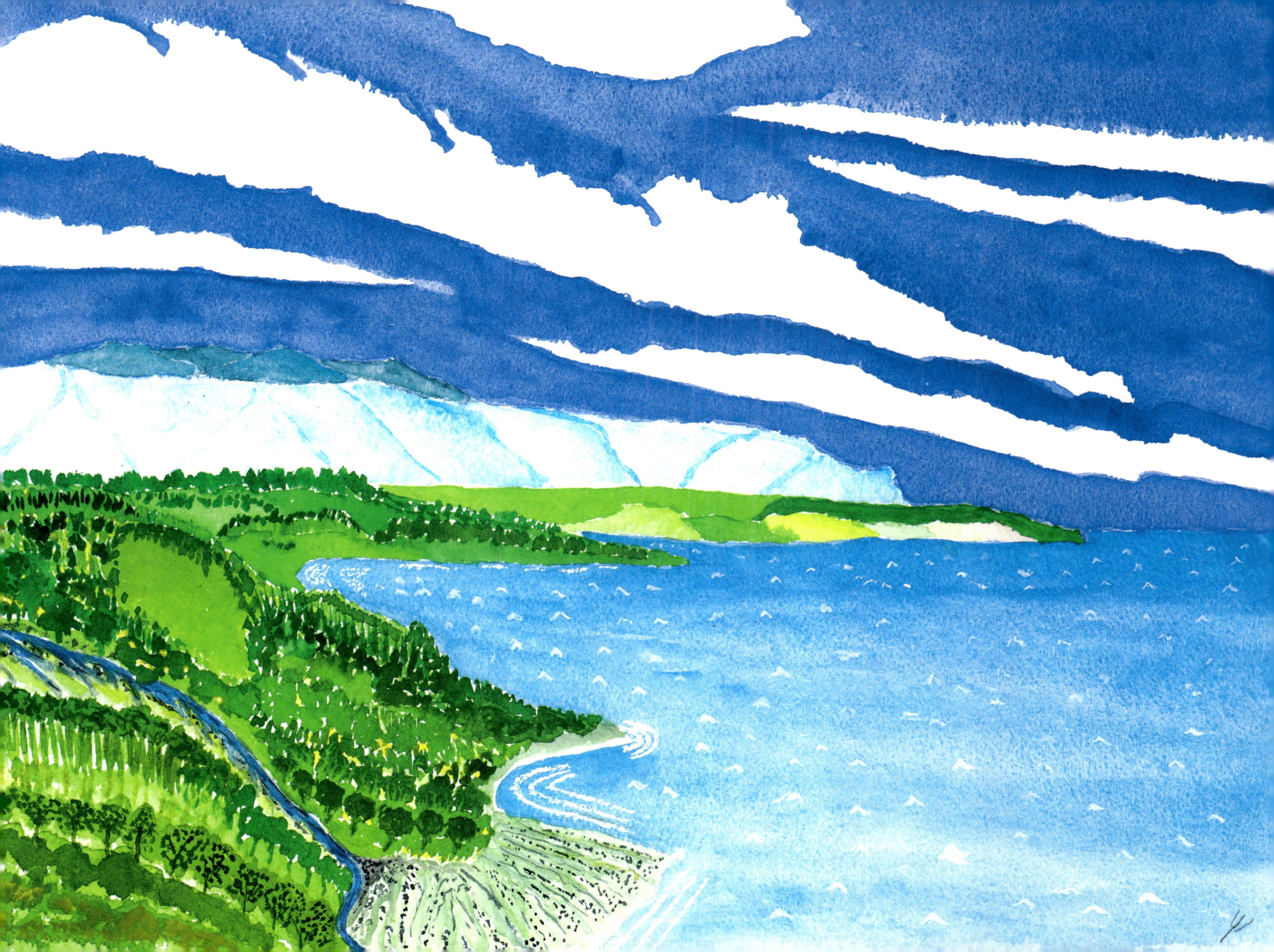

Headliner

The ocean
chuckles,
as it tumbles
over the rocks,
then does
a back flip
and raises its arms high,
to accept
its own
thunderous
applause.

Ninini Lighthouse, Kaua'i, Hawai'i

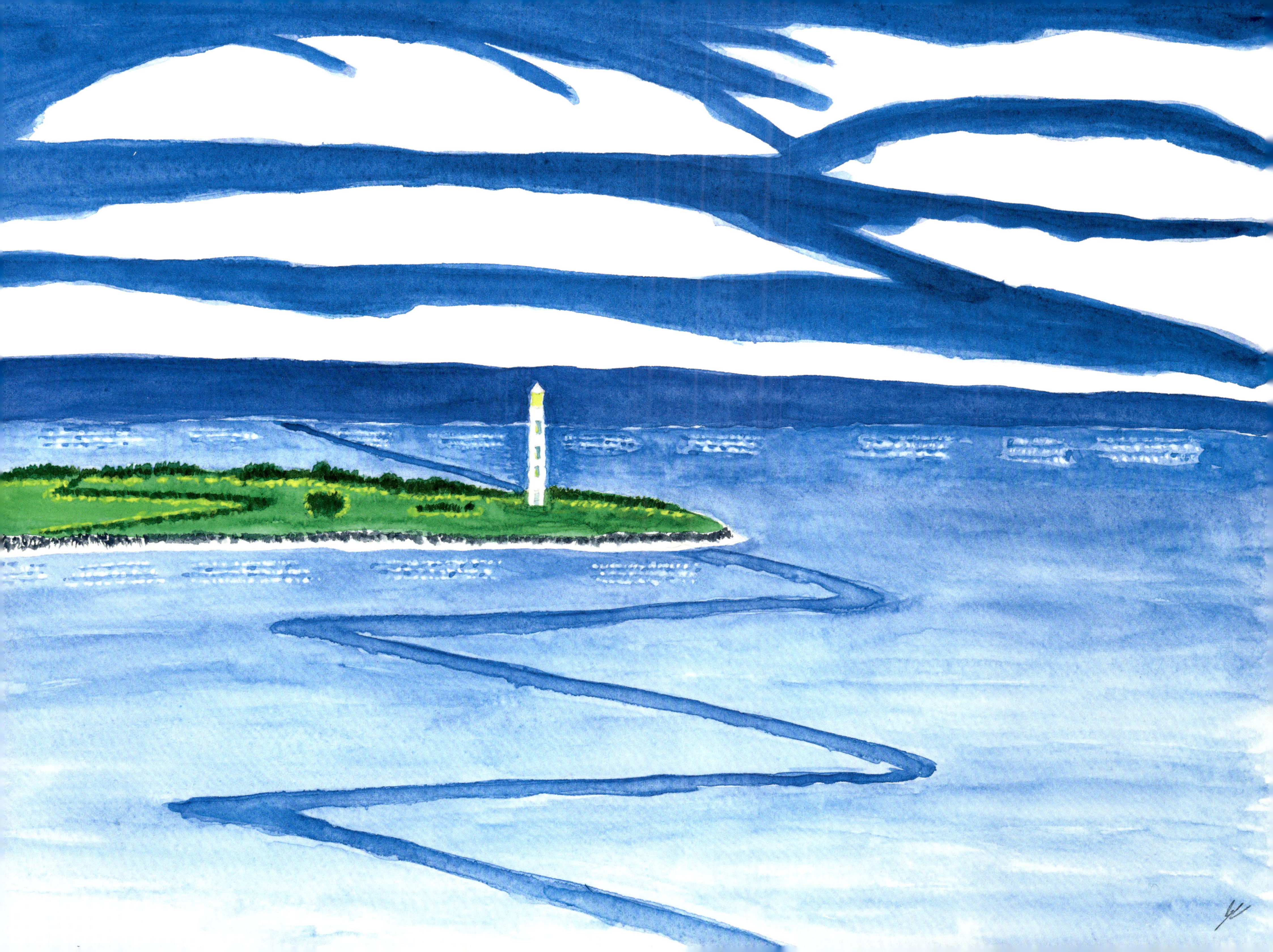

Celebrating Hawai'i

The womp-womp lady,
bedecked with red and yellow and lavender and white leis,
steers her bashful husband,
wearing khaki shorts
and a gray canvas hat,
as they walk off the cruise ship
into a flood
of sunlight,
at which he blinks,
while she raises high
her hands,
to form a V
that signals
the sky
to make room
for a palm tree
that knows
how to shimmy.

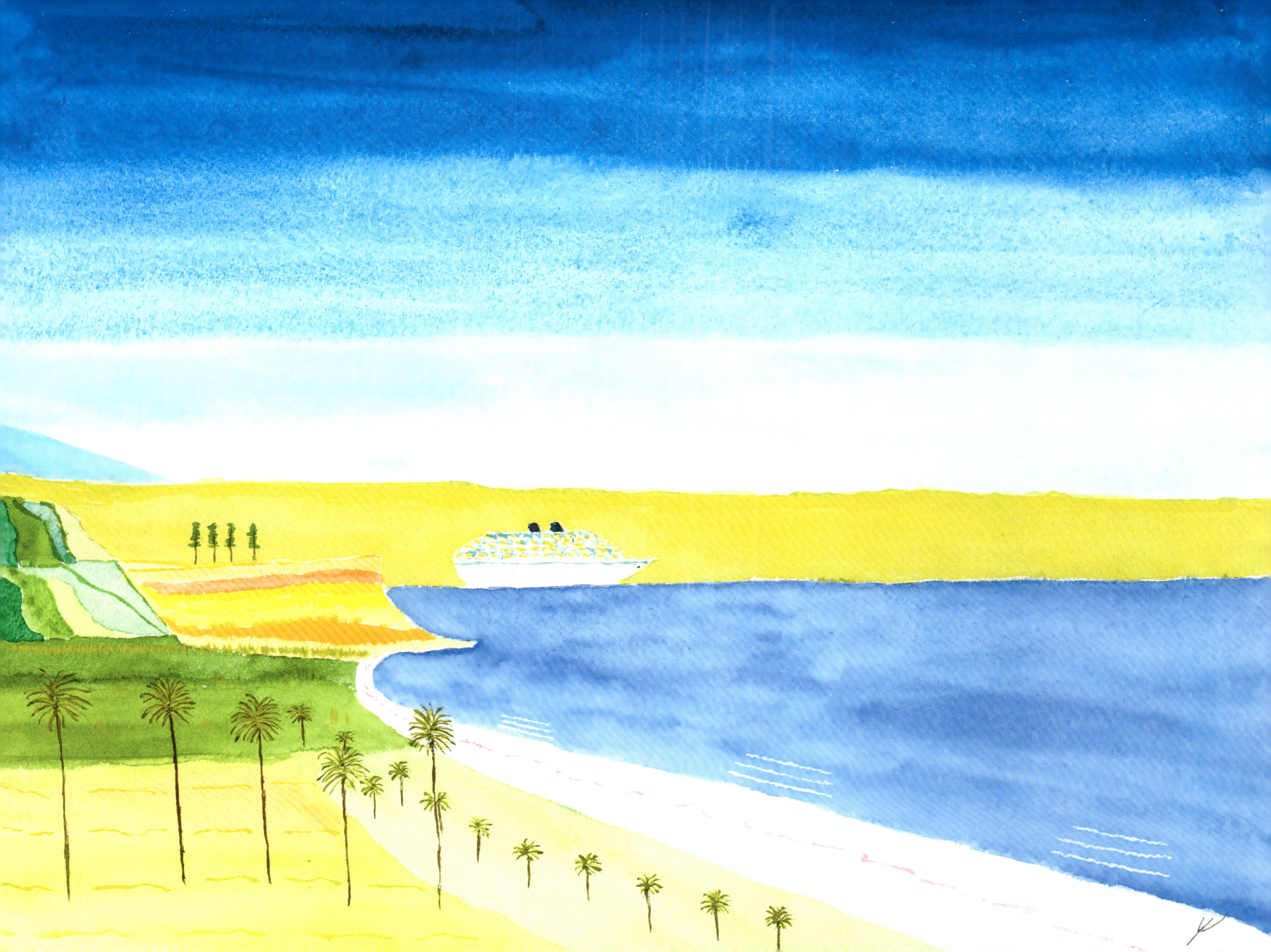

Early Courtships

A bird
sings out
at dawn,
complimenting
the sunrise,
while in a high tree,
a breeze
stirs a bough,
tempting a leaf
to dance
till it drops.

In Charge

An infant girl,
reaching out
to her mother's long hair,
giggles
as she snatches
a few blond strands,
until her mother
snaps, "No!"
and the little girl,
looking up,
surprises her mother
with a piercing cry
and two arms
outstretched
to her dad.

Shipwreck Beach got its name, which really is its nickname, because of a wooden ship that beached there decades ago. Its wreckage remained there for years but has long since been removed. The beach's real name is Keoneloa, meaning "long beach" in Hawaiian. The nearby high cliff, overlooking the beach at Makawehi Point, is well-known, because teenagers, as well as intrepid celebrities, enjoy jumping from it into the ocean. Avoiding this peril is a wise decision. I love painting this beach and its environs. The diverse bands of color on the cliff, and the lush greenery that surrounds it, stand in sharp contrast to the rugged mountainscape to its northwest, and the sapphire tranquility of the bay that cuddles with the beach.

Shipwreck Beach at Dawn, Kaua'i

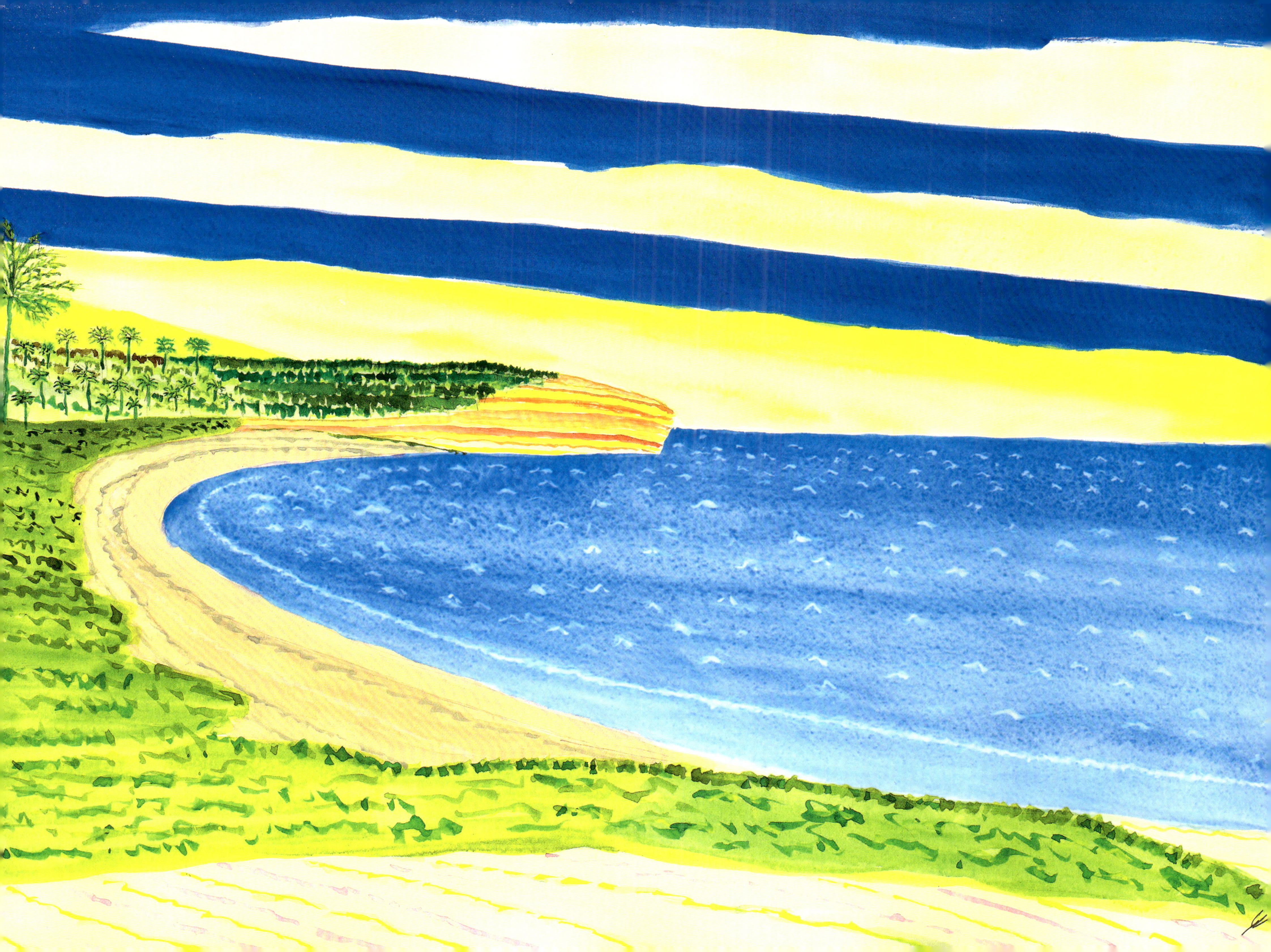

Tender Mercies

God
watered my tree
last night,
just when the hose and I
were too tired and tangled
to do it
one more time –
the wind and rain
crashed down
all around my sapling,
quenching its thirst
for at least a day,
while I,
standing inside,
keeping the teary-eyed window
company,
thanked the Lord
for the drink that he saved for me,
from a tumbledown storm
that pitched its tent
over
my would-be
forest.

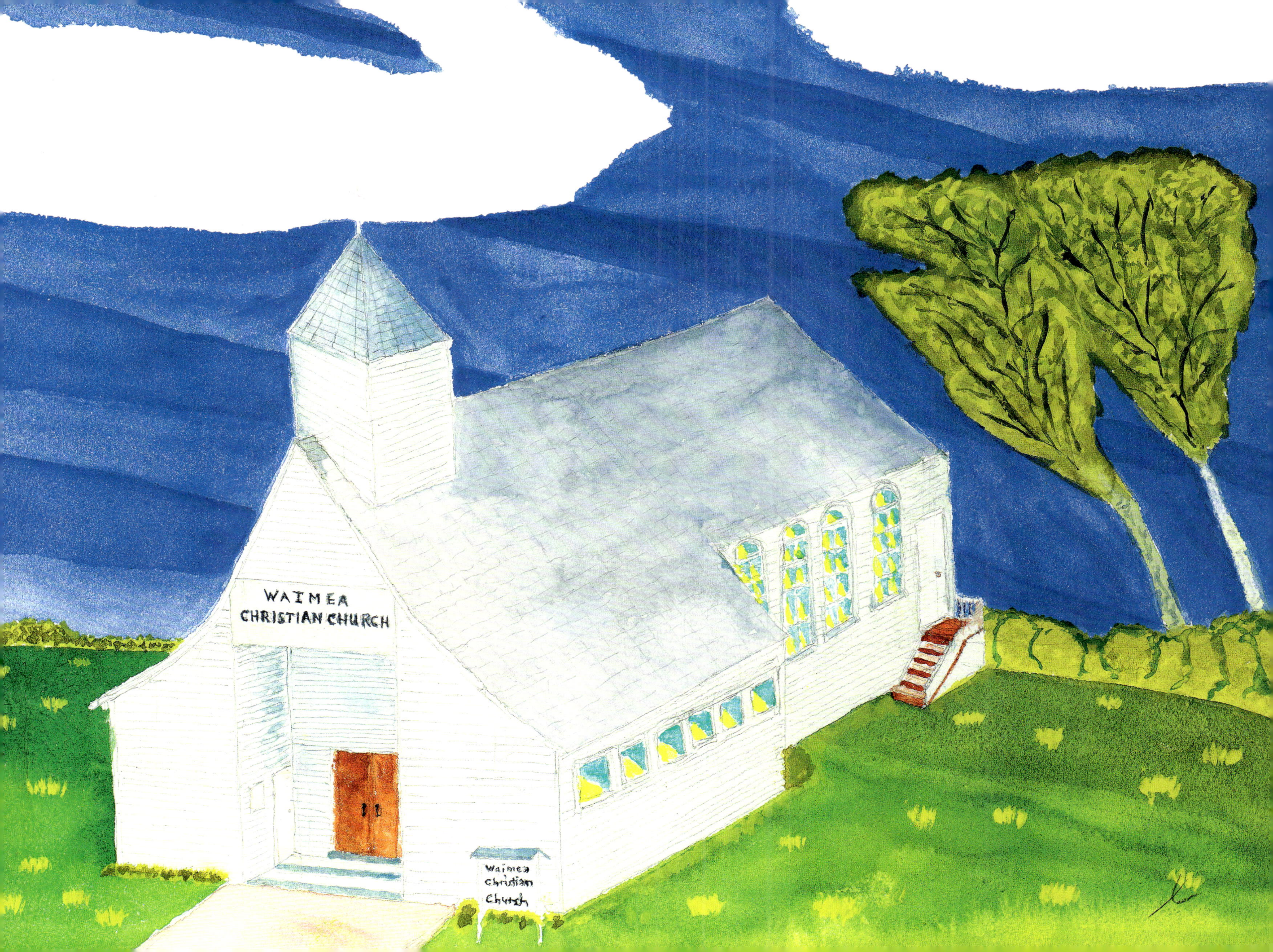
WAIMEA
CHRISTIAN CHURCH
Waimea
Christian
Church

Trapeze Artists

Clouds at dawn,
tanned
and restless,
somersault
over each other,
and, riding piggyback
on breezes,
tumble
above the land,
to catapult their shadows
onto the the shoulders
of mountains –
TA-DAH!

Menehune Fishpond, Kaua'i

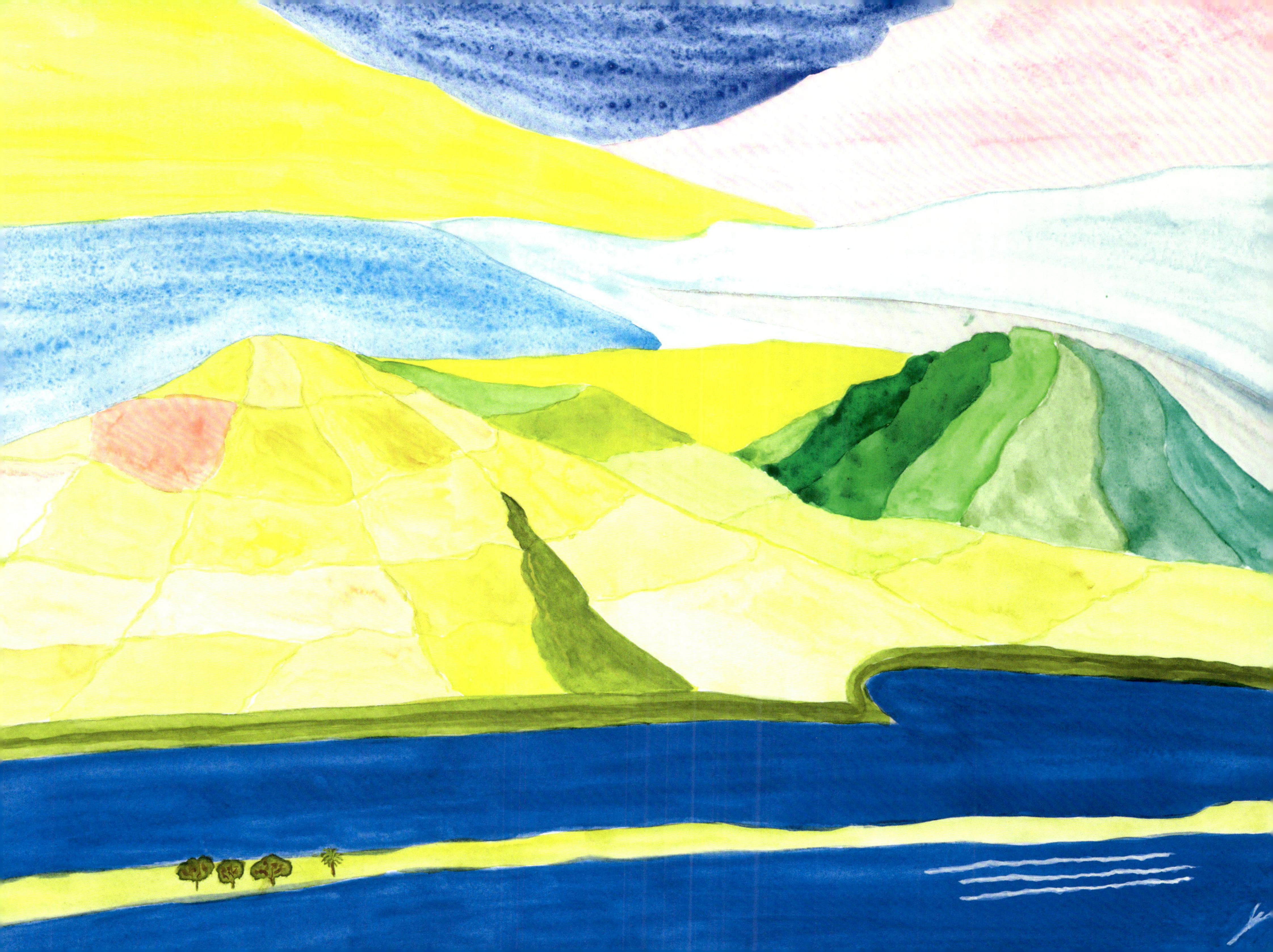

A Sharp Lookout

A bamboo cottage,
perched on a hilltop,
beams its sunlit smile,
as it overlooks
the ocean,
the palm trees,
the barefoot path,
while beyond it,
the sky clears,
and the waves
paddle away,
and the cottage sighs
as it dozes,
longing
to fling open
its bright-eyed door,
welcoming every
seafaring breeze.

Bamboo Cottage, O'ahu

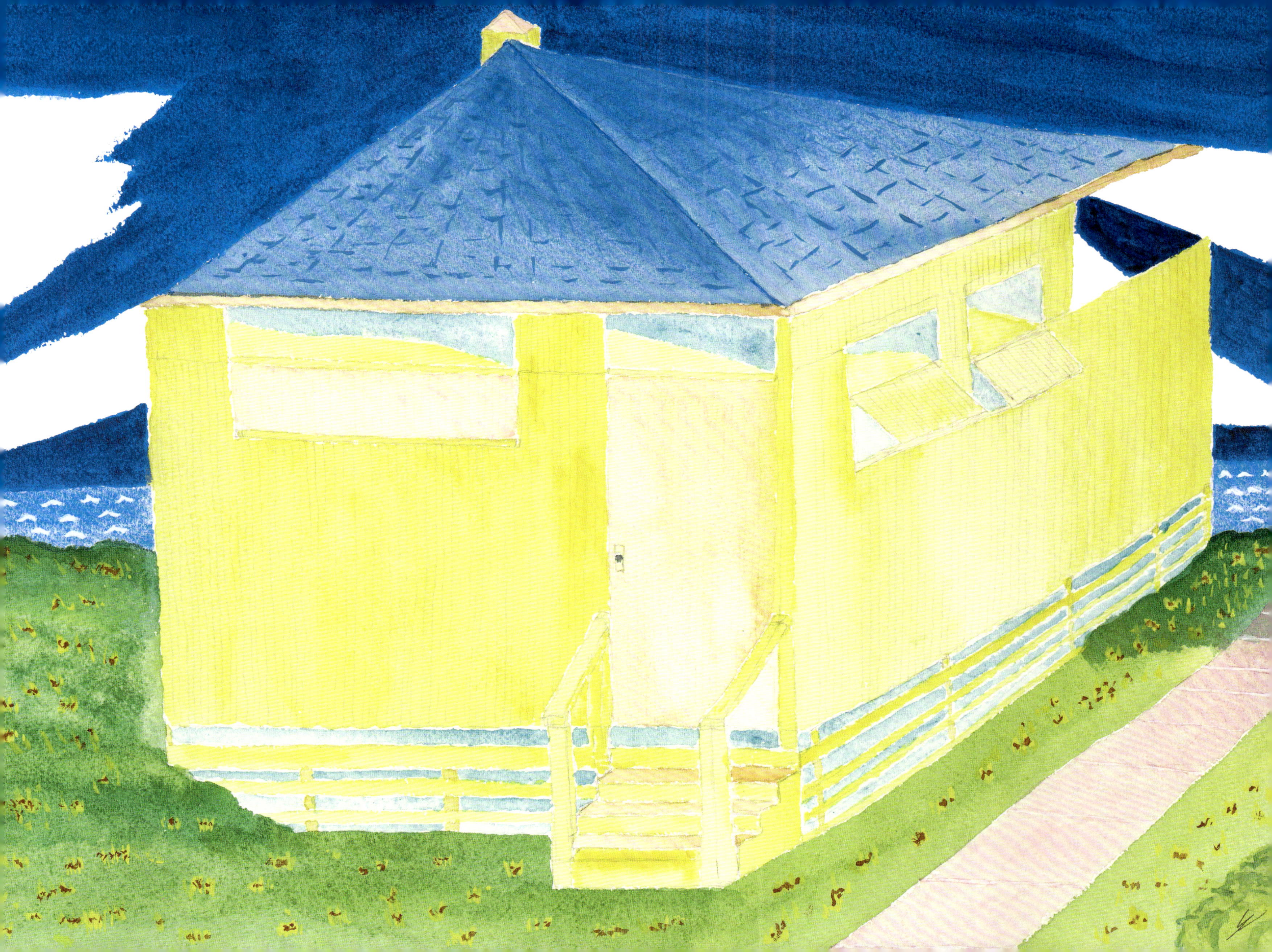

Turning the Tables

Every day
a young man
sits on a park bench,
gazing
with downcast eyes,
and when,
as last,
you ask him
if he is all right,
he glances up,
startled,
and tells you
that he was praying
and wants to know,
Are you all right?

You smile
and reply
that you are,
but his dark eyes
do not turn away from you,
while yours ask him
to remember you
tomorrow.

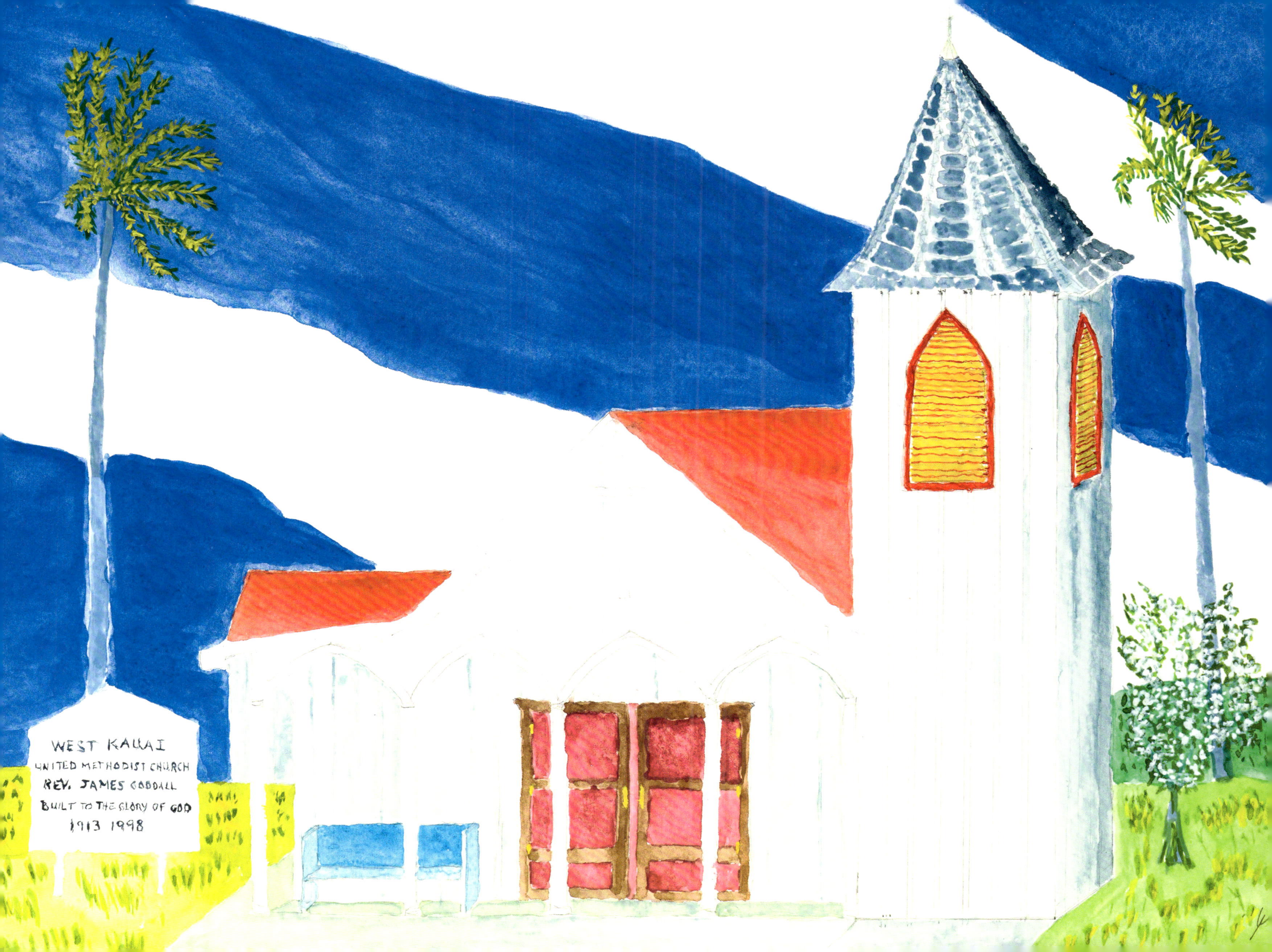
WEST KAUAI
UNITED METHODIST CHURCH
REV. JAMES GOODALL
BUILT TO THE GLORY OF GOD
1913 1998

White Caps

A calm-eyed sky,
inviting clouds
to settle down,
stretches out
beyond the horizon,
while mountains
retreat –
they will have their day
in the sunlight
and the shadows,
and as for the ocean,
it is the firmament's
disobedient
mirror.

Kuahonu Point, Kaua'i

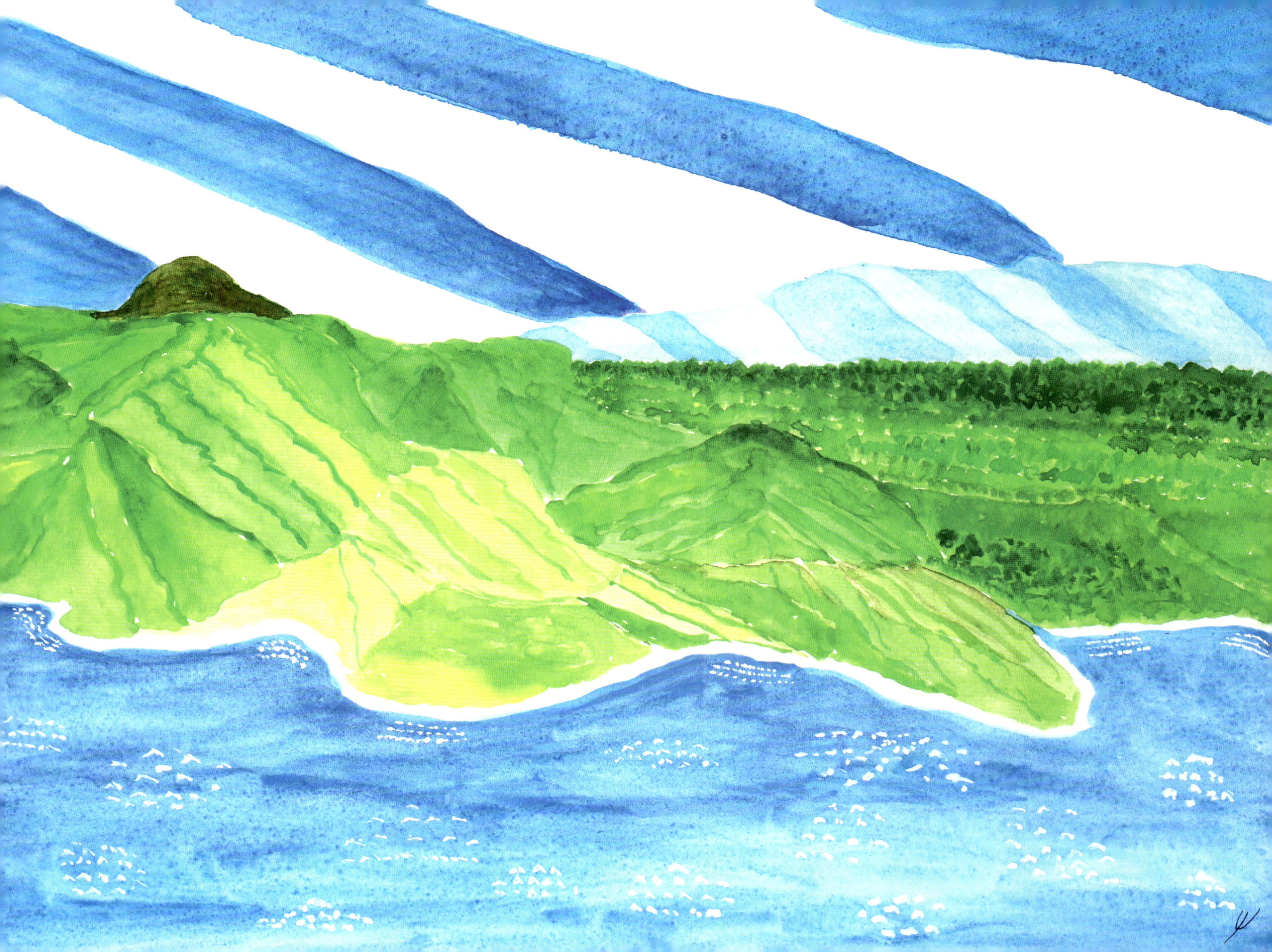

Together

Rough
is a large
black and white
dog,
who barks at me
when I
run past him
in my dreams.

Ruff
is probably
his real name,
but I call him
Rough,
because he is,
with his curly spaniel hair
and his chubby body,
which shimmies
as he runs.

Today
I got caught
running
inside his low rock wall,
which made him
growl,
until his owner
bade him stop,
and I petted
his matted fur.

Rough
looks
more like a fat sheep
than a dog,
and lopes
like a fat sheep,
too,
but he and I
are steadfast
friends,
even now,
on the night before Christmas,
when all of the ghosts
of the past
and the nightmares of the future
come out
to jeer.

So there I stand,
petting Rough's
grizzled fur,
and we are
happy
enough,
just standing there,
inside a tumbledown
rock wall,
with no need
to race or chase,
or explore
a new path up the hill.

Standing Out

Brides
brides
brides
brides
brides,
dazzling in white
as they float
down the aisle,
and behind
them,
the bridegrooms,
asterisks
in black,
with
rosebuds
stuck
in their
lapels,
as afterthoughts
of timid
adornment.

Going the Distance

The Pacific,
boundless and yearning,
outstretches its arms
to breezes and sunlight –
making room
for islands and clouds,
it swims on its back,
into the embrace
of the wandering
horizon.

Hanalei Bay from Alaka'i Swamp, Kaua'i

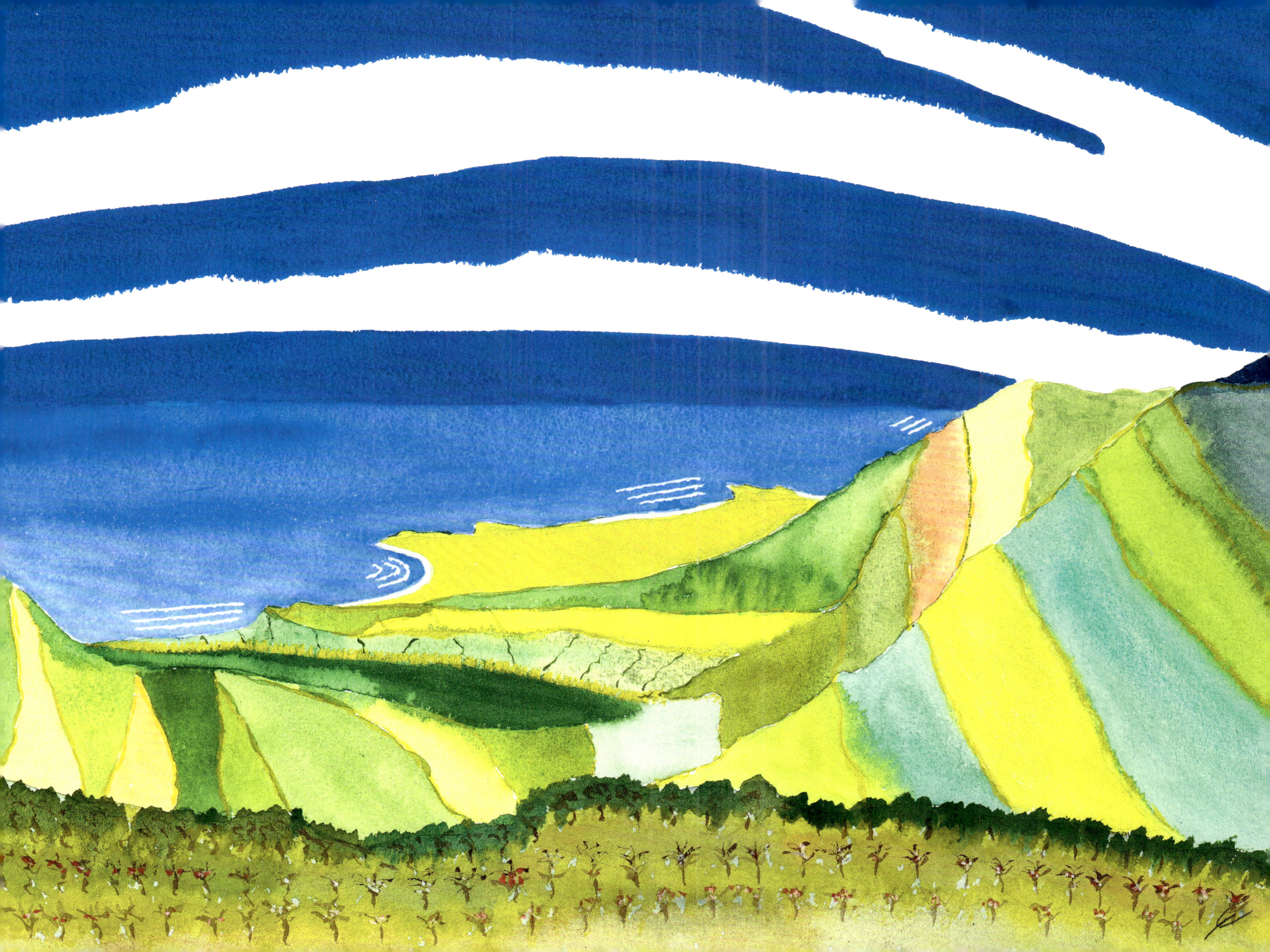

Pacific Navigation

Far
out to sea,
the waves
paddle home,
to lands
that float
in an ocean
that never
loses
its bearings.

Hanalei Bay, Kaua'i

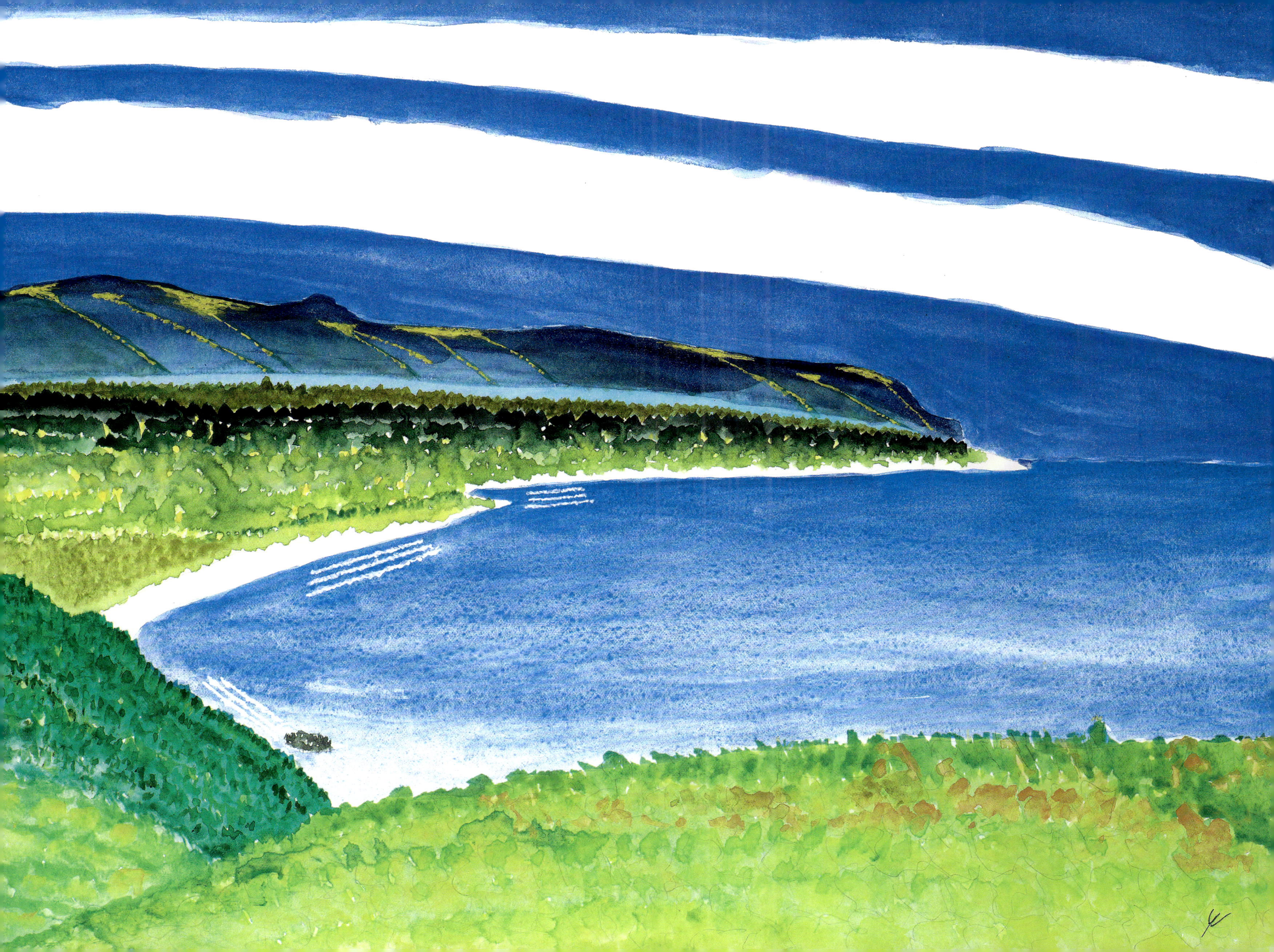

Hawai'i Nei

An old Hawaiian man
talks story,
reeling out
a tale
that murmurs
all afternoon –
unfurling
his wrinkled face,
he tells
of forgotten heroes,
high-spirited
islanders
who rode
horses
over mountain trails
that laughed at the wind,
and who sang love songs
to waves
that had swum all night,
to bring news
of slender-hipped
canoes.

Sugar Plantation Cottage, Waimea, Kaua'i

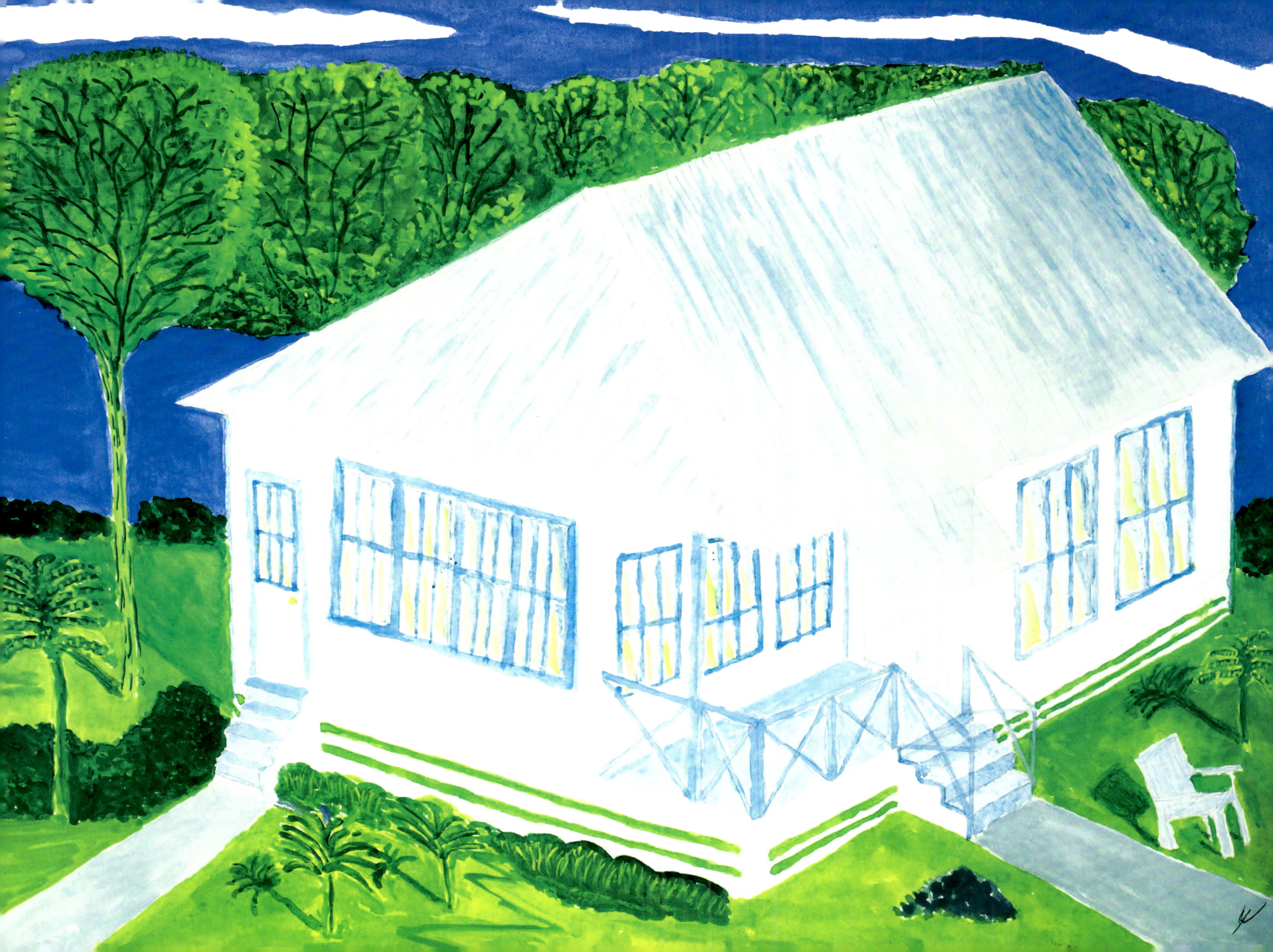

Never Saying Goodbye

Returning home
after a lackluster
day,
you watch the mountains
climb down
to the coast –
the blue sky
brightens,
and the ocean
blinks,
and in the distance,
an island
promises
to wait
for your arrival.

In the morning,
you will awaken
to kindly sunlight
on your pillow,
without looking back
at a busy world
that you thank
for forgetting
the way
to your house.

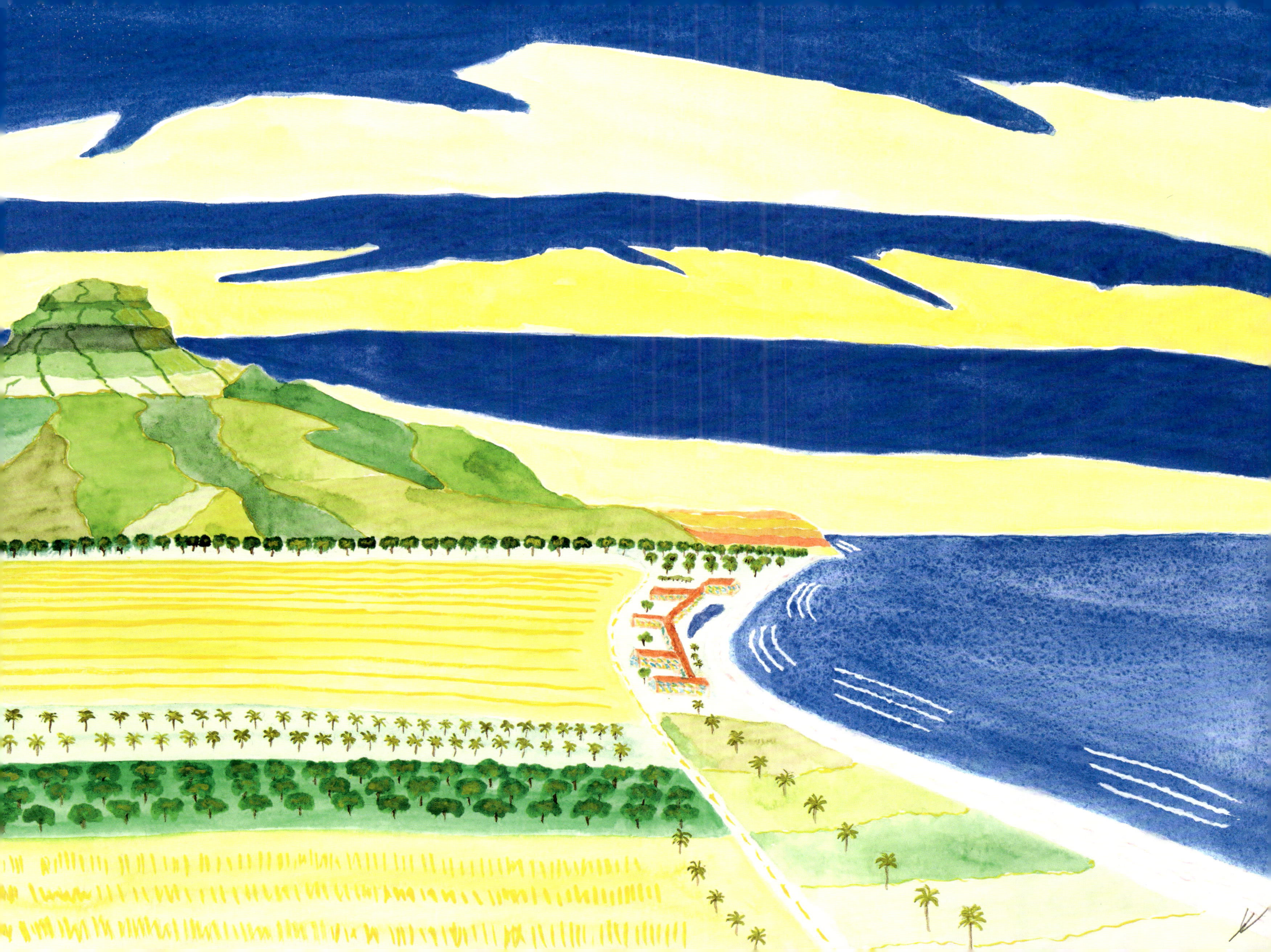

Stranded Voices

Palm fronds,
tittering
all afternoon,
tell tales
of distant islands,
sheltered
by an ocean
that daily
brings news
of shores
that repeat
the same old stories
in whispers.

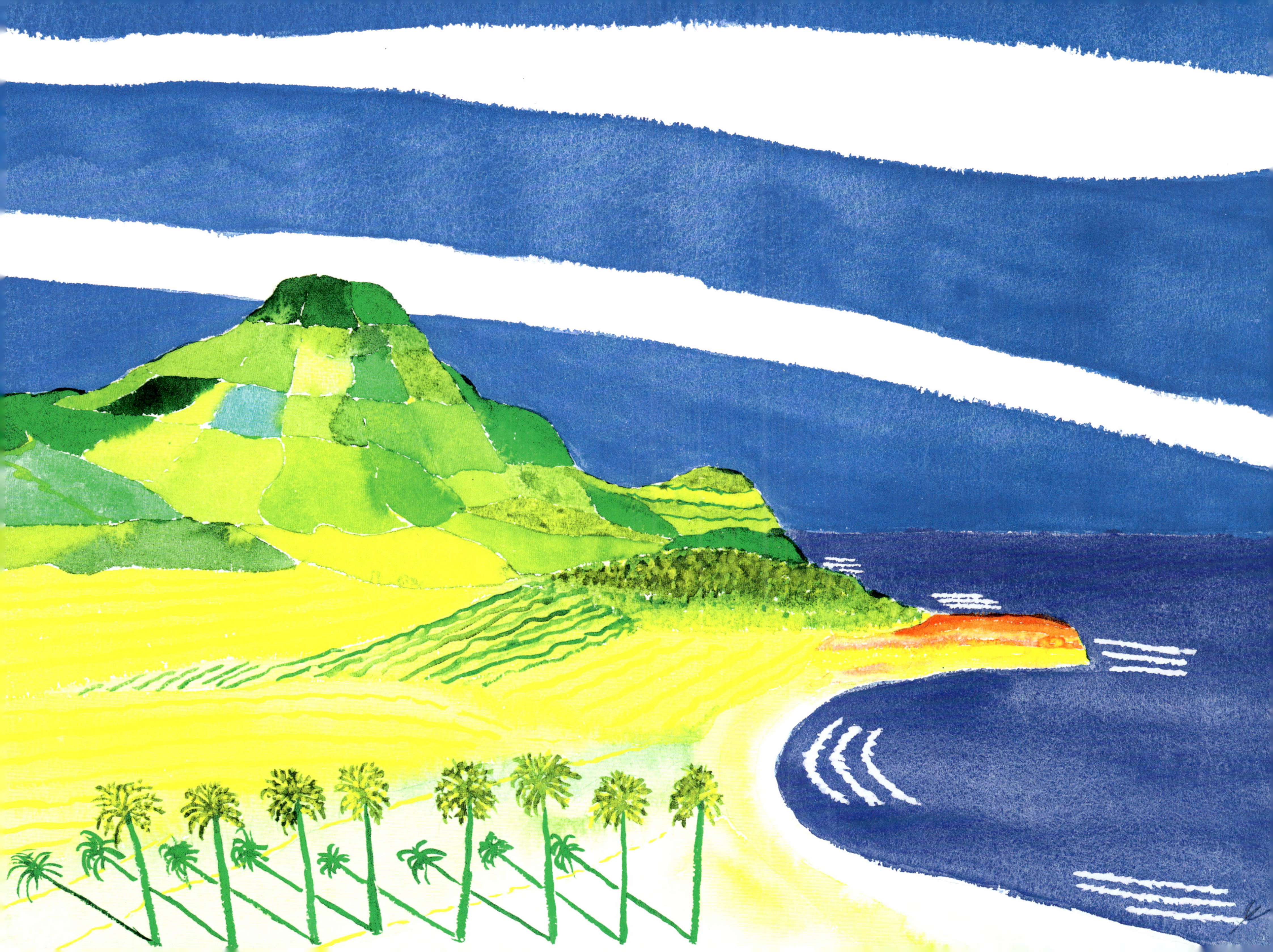

Private Libraries

Two women
in a waiting room
sit reading their books,
one with a wrinkled smile,
the other
with a guiding finger –
one, dressed in red,
devours the chocolate words,
while the other,
all in white,
caresses the pages,
turning each over
as she welcomes
its best friend.

A torrid
love story
and a mystery-ensnared
novel
hold hands
with the two women,
who glance up
at a clock
that never
tells the same story
to two readers
twice.

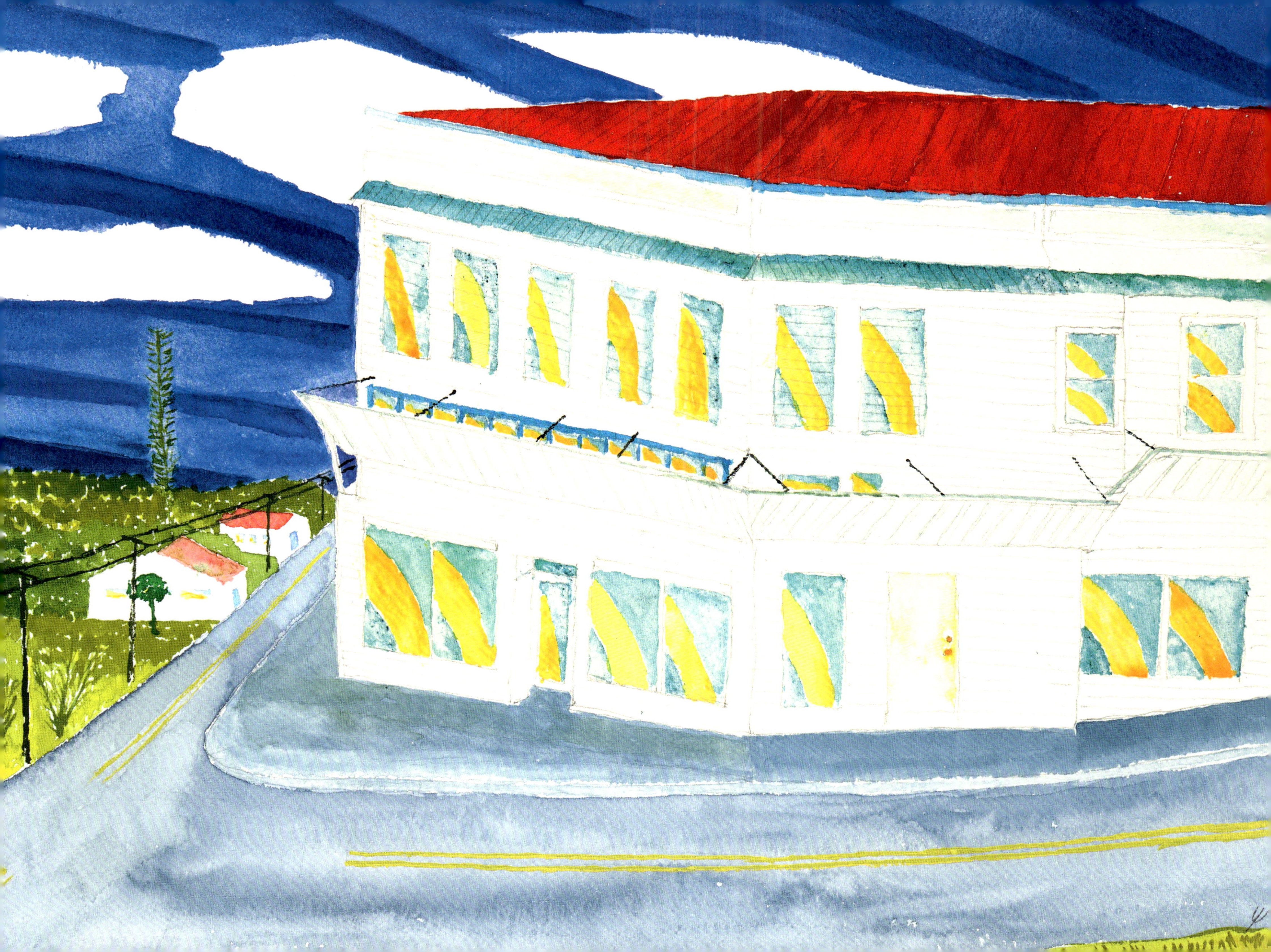

High and Low

Rain
blesses
the roof,
while chatting
with the eaves,
and on the wet pavement,
the moon
swims
in a puddle
of silver.

A Weekday Vigil

An old man,
gray-haired
and red-shirted,
sits on your
back porch,
enjoying the calm breeze
and the boisterous sunlight,
and the absence
of rain,
which the weatherman
had forecast –
you ask him
if there is anything
that you can get him,
and he smiles
and says no,
while he lets
his cane
rest
on a broad-backed
lawn chair.

He asks you
your age,
and you tell him,
as he laughs –
the very same age,
he declares
with a grin.

And the breeze
and the sunlight
are suddenly
enough,
and the fact
that the weatherman,
after all these years,
is sometimes blessed
for his kindly
errors.

Overhearing the Melody

Honolulu –
even the name beckons,
as green slopes
guard its harbor,
and palm trees
sigh together –
the waves
comb out
their white curls,
while distant clouds
glow
on the shoulders
of the horizon,
and breezes
share their secrets,
and laughter brims up
in words,
welcoming you home
when you least expect it,
until the night
embraces the island,
and they bed down together,
while you sing
in your dreams.

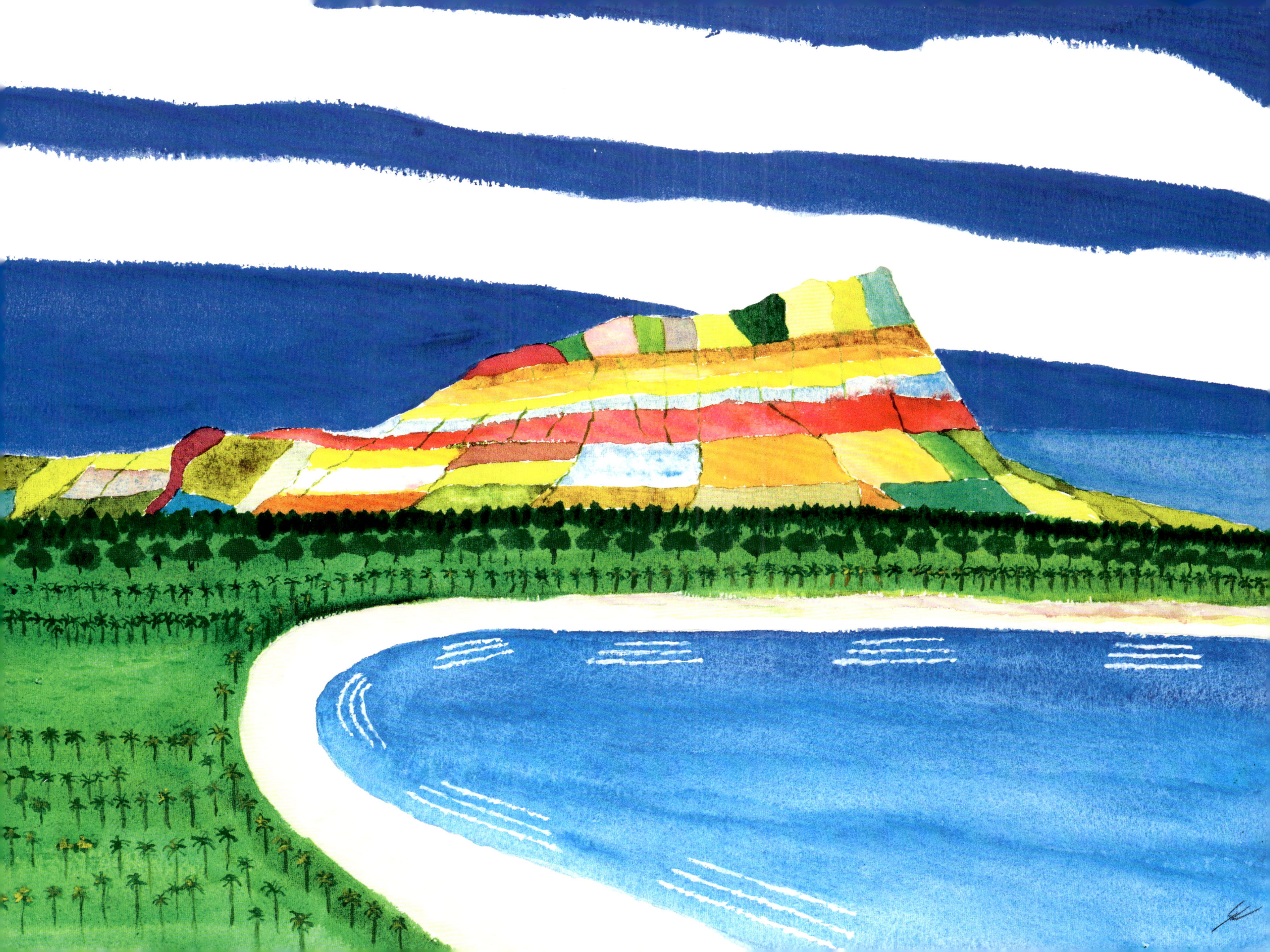

Ford Island, in the middle of Pearl Harbor on O'ahu, was once owned by Dr. Seth Porter Ford. By 1939, it had become the center of the U.S. Navy's maintenance facilities for the Pacific Fleet. As a result, it was the focus of the attack on Pearl Harbor on December 7, 1941. Today, Ford Island is a peaceful refuge near the shores of Pearl Harbor. It is the home of the Pearl Harbor Aviation Museum and the battleship USS *Missouri,* both of which are fascinating. The present tranquility of the island makes it hard to imagine the chaos and destruction that it witnessed over eighty years ago. The air control tower was under construction in 1941. It was strafed but not destroyed and was completed in 1942. It got its bright stripes in the 1960's. The structure contains a water tank and meteorological tower, which was used until 1999.

This colorful monument to the military operations that were centered on Ford Island, and that still surround it in Pearl Harbor, stands like a flag that salutes the surrounding harbor and the high hills that rise behind it.

Air Traffic Control Tower, Ford Island, Honolulu

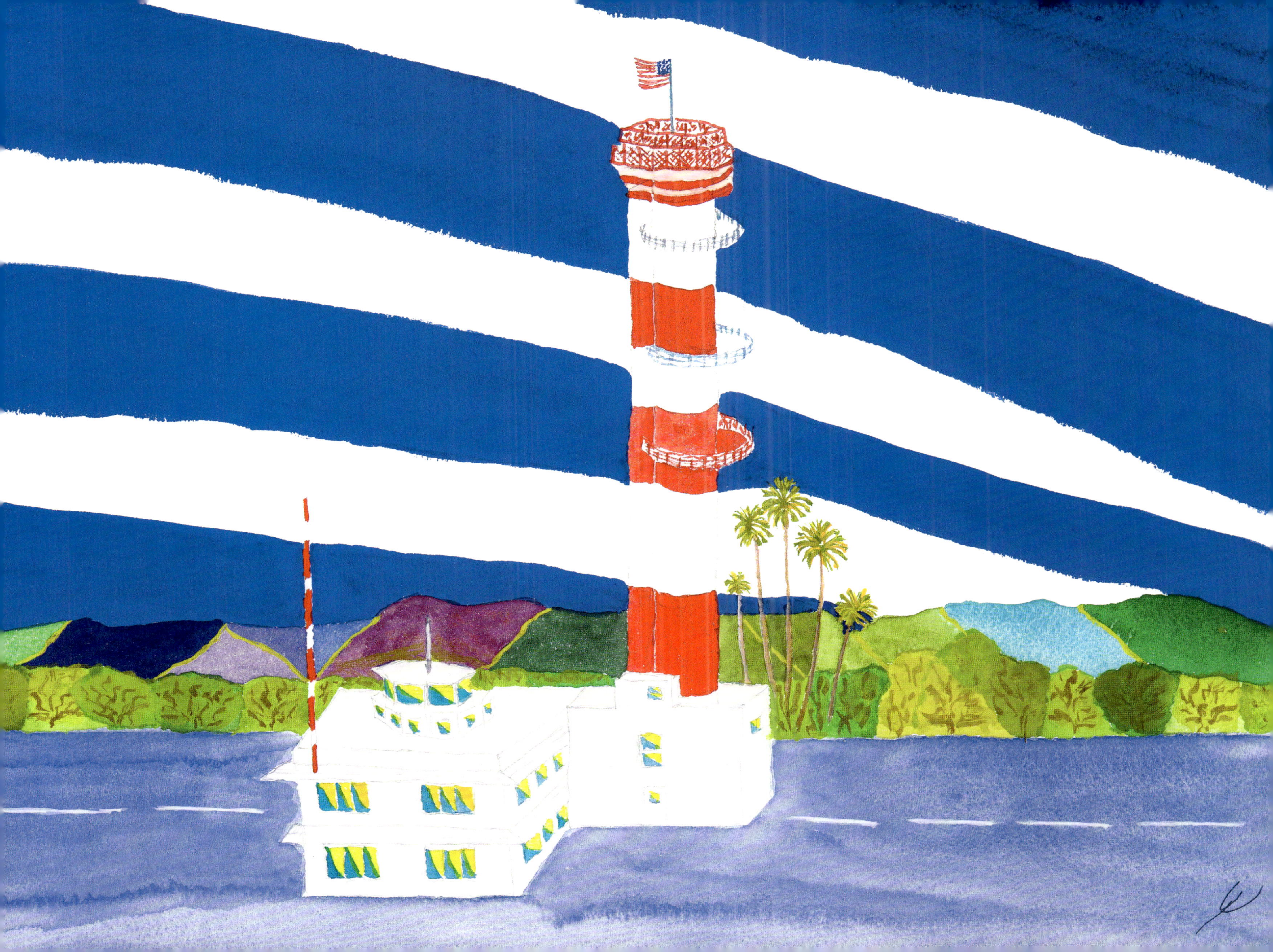

Kind Tears

A lagoon
beside the ocean
glitters
in winter
sunlight –
watching it
shimmer,
you touch
the soft-tongued waves,
warm
to the hand,
as a shower
passes its cool fingers
over the brow
of a warmhearted
mountain.

Lake and Mountains, Kāneʻohe, Oʻahu

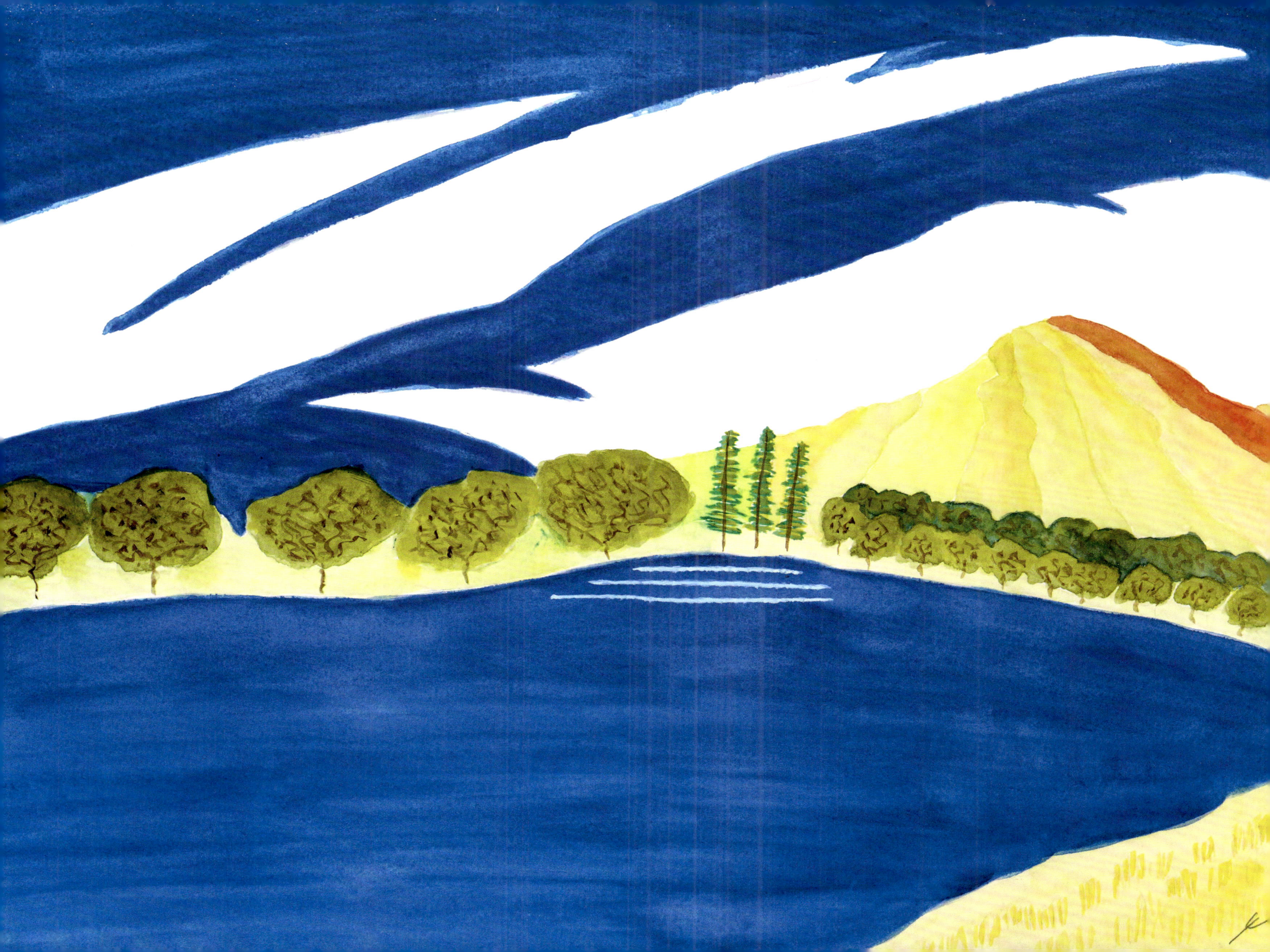

Paddling Home

Nothing
except islands
and the shadows
of clouds
stretches out
across the Pacific –
following the sunlight,
they gleam,
unfurling
their quilt
for tireless
voyagers.

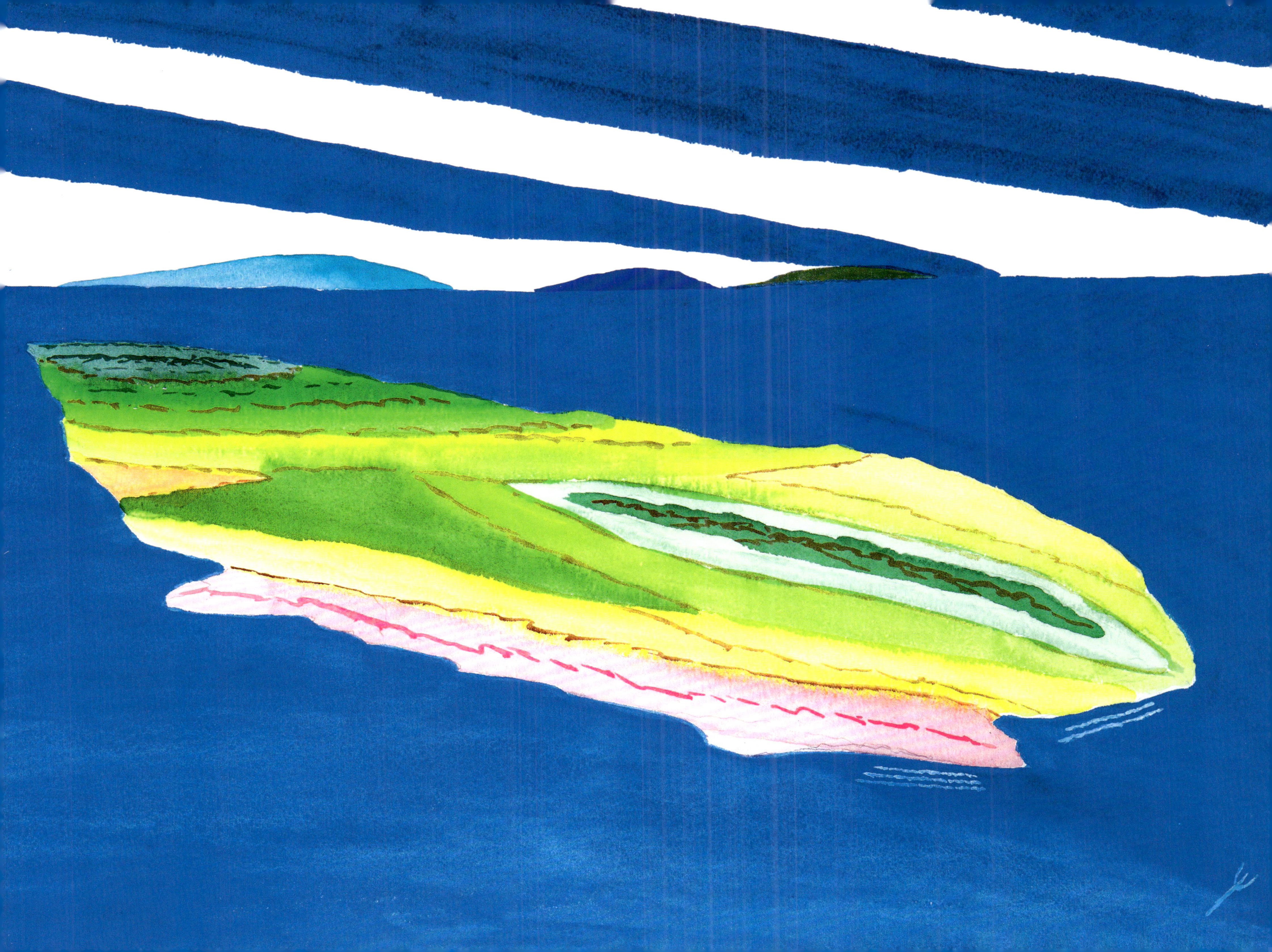

High Rollers

Waves roll in,
riding
their white surfboards –
letting the wind
comb back
their long hair,
they somersault
toward the beach,
inviting the sunlight
to smile at their antics,
while beaches admire
their homecomings
on tightropes.

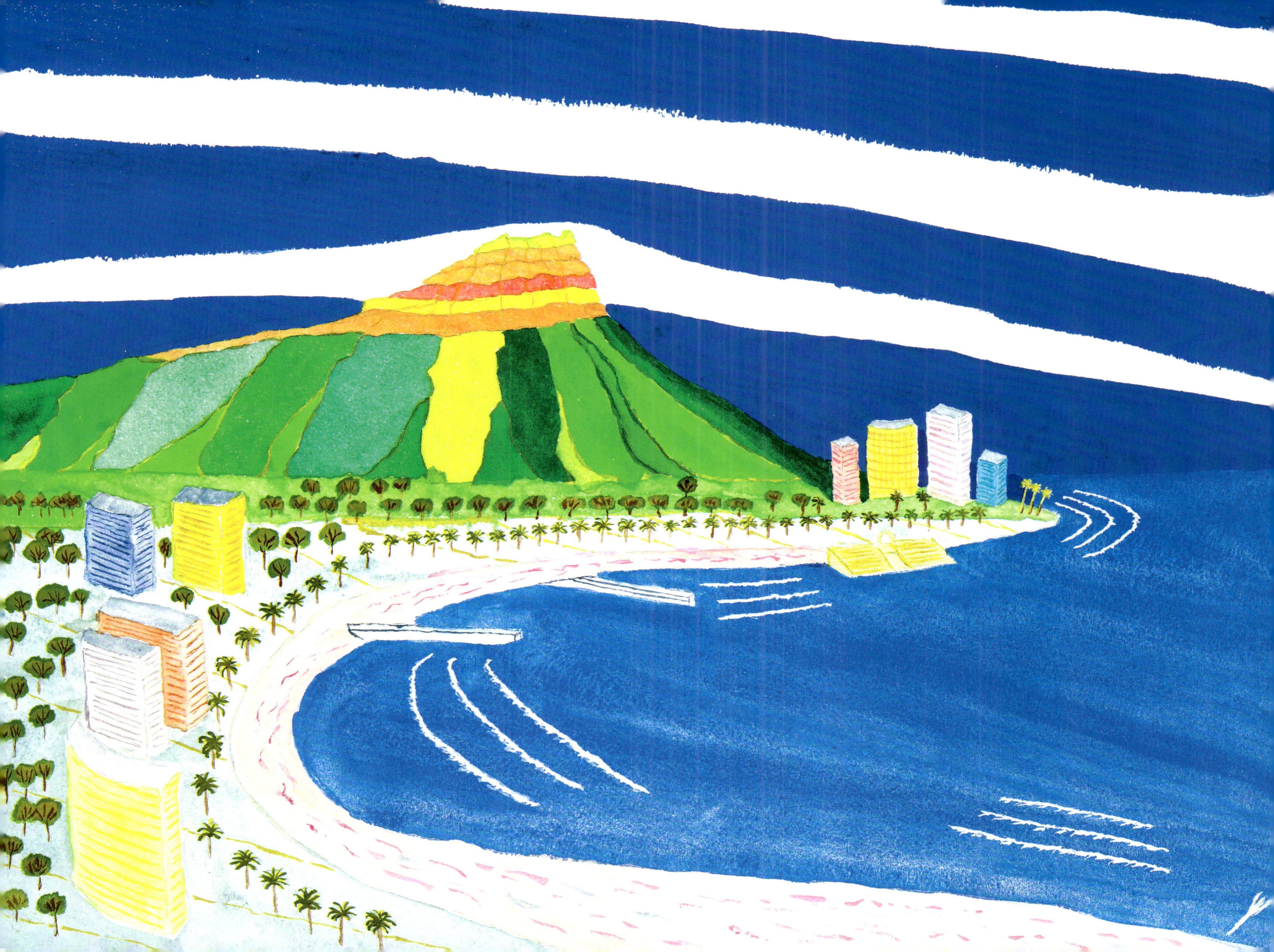

Living It Up

The vast Pacific,
all ocean
and clouds,
swims
for Hawai'i,
with laughter
in the mouths
of its waves –
why should it not long
for green shores
and yellow-vested
songbirds,
when the ocean
must go so far
to find a family
of sisters
who welcome
a voyager's
soft embraces?

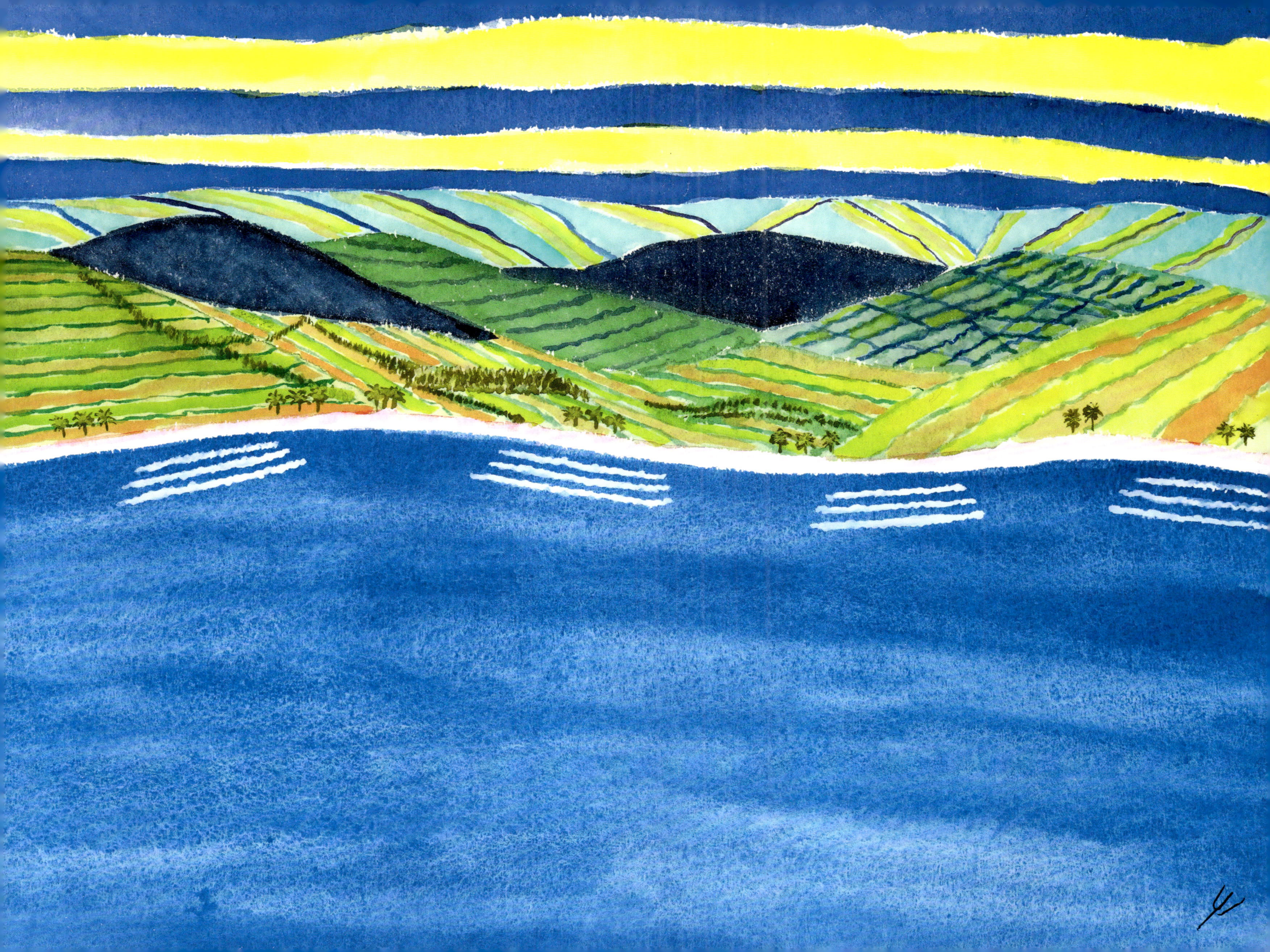

Ala Wai

The fiery-eyed canal,
where gaudy streetlights'
reflections
leer
at law-abiding
traffic signals,
flows
to the ocean,
with a calm
unknown
to rivers:
between its concrete banks,
it unfurls
its rainbow-clad
ribbon.

Friends in the Circus

A little boy
stands facing
the ocean,
staring
at the breakers,
with their clowns' ruffled collars –
watching them
turn cartwheels
and tumble
and balance
on each other's shoulders,
he claps
his hands
together,
until the waves
somersault
to his feet.

Honolulu

The gleaming city,
climbing a hill,
dozes
by the ocean,
which comes calling
all afternoon –
mountains tumble down,
with leis of gardenia clouds
around their necks,
as a rainbow
hoists its banner,
and the sunlight
goes westering.

The city,
a host of fireflies,
glimmers
in the dusk,
and, gazing out
at the flat horizon,
watches
a ship
light its lamps.

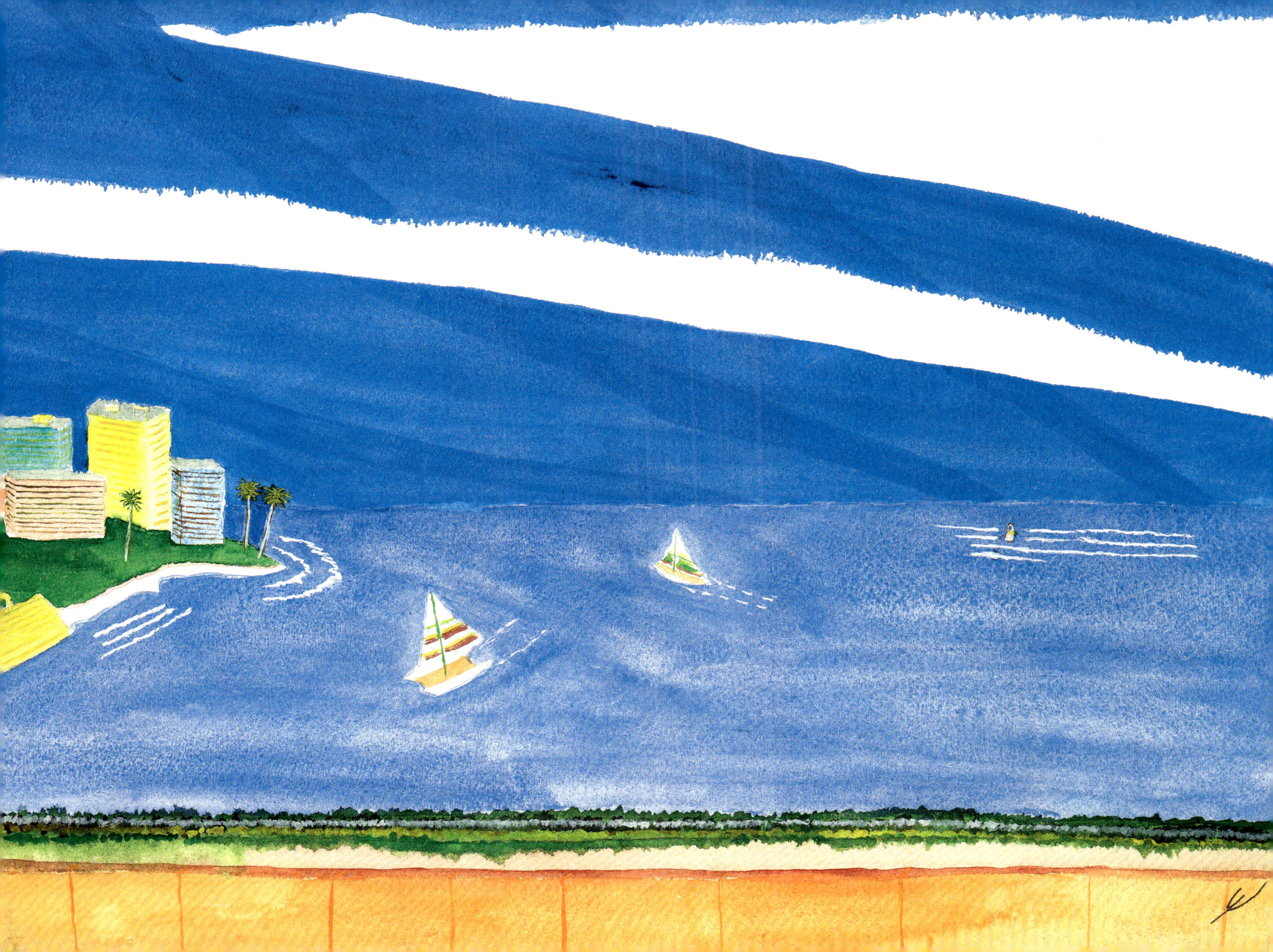

On a Mission

A ragged mountain,
a herd
of red-headed cattle,
a meandering fence
greet
the hydrangea clouds,
the whispering beaches,
the palm trees
that titter all day,
while a gravel road
meanders
across the hills,
and the ocean,
always waiting,
voyages,
with the horizon
on its back,
an easy burden,
a gentle passenger,
on a journey
that an island takes
every day,
as it swims
among pools
of light.

North Kohala Coast, Hawai'i

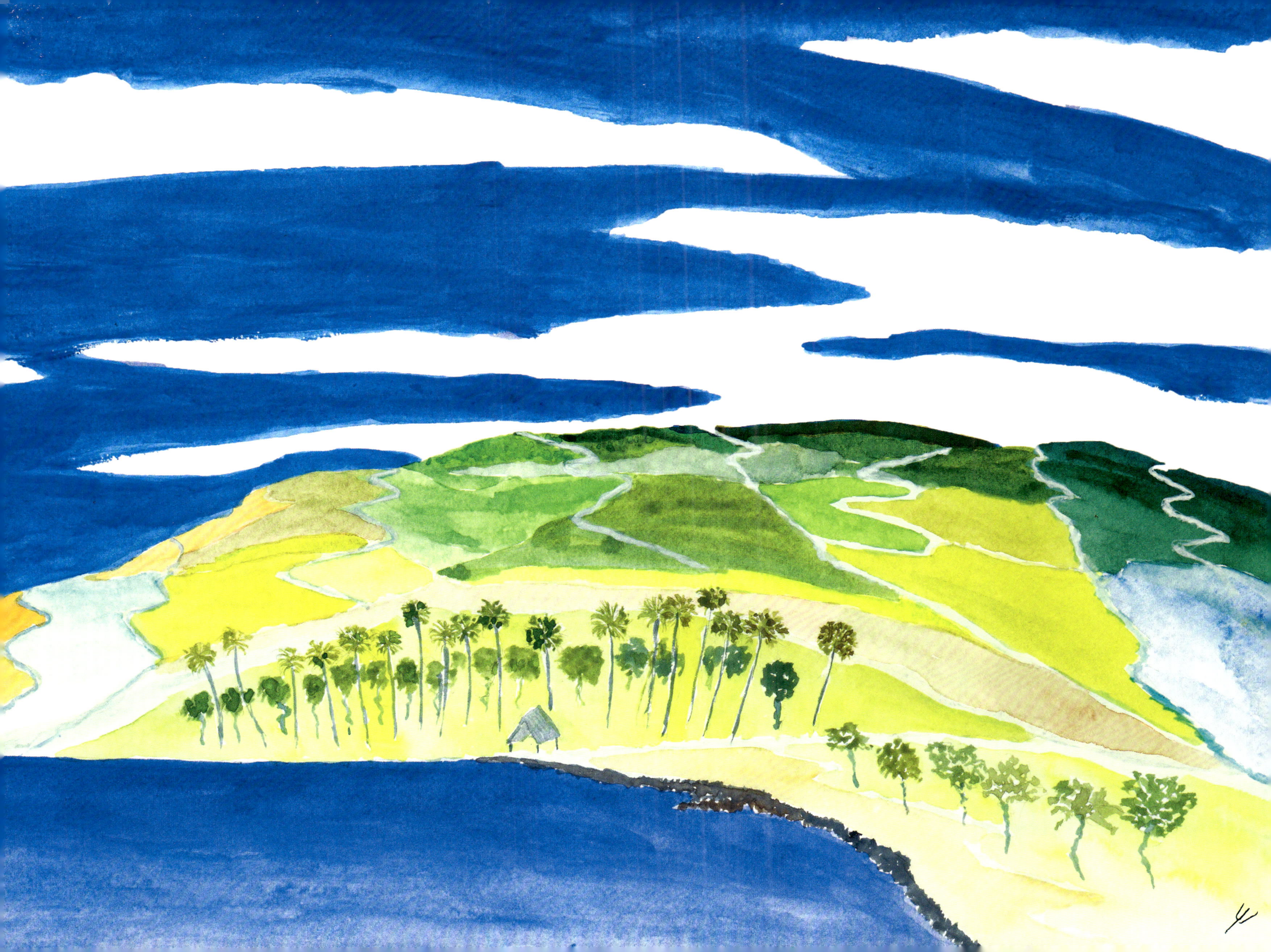

A Tropical Duet

A young man
with a scruffy
blond beard
sits strumming his ukulele,
watching the breeze
toy with the grass,
while the palm fronds
ask their shadows
to dance –
picking out
a tune,
he smiles
at the far-flung ocean,
which sings
its own song
in the morning light,
while the young man
tickles the whiskers
of his melodies'
traveling companion.

Diamond Head Seen from Kāhala, O'ahu

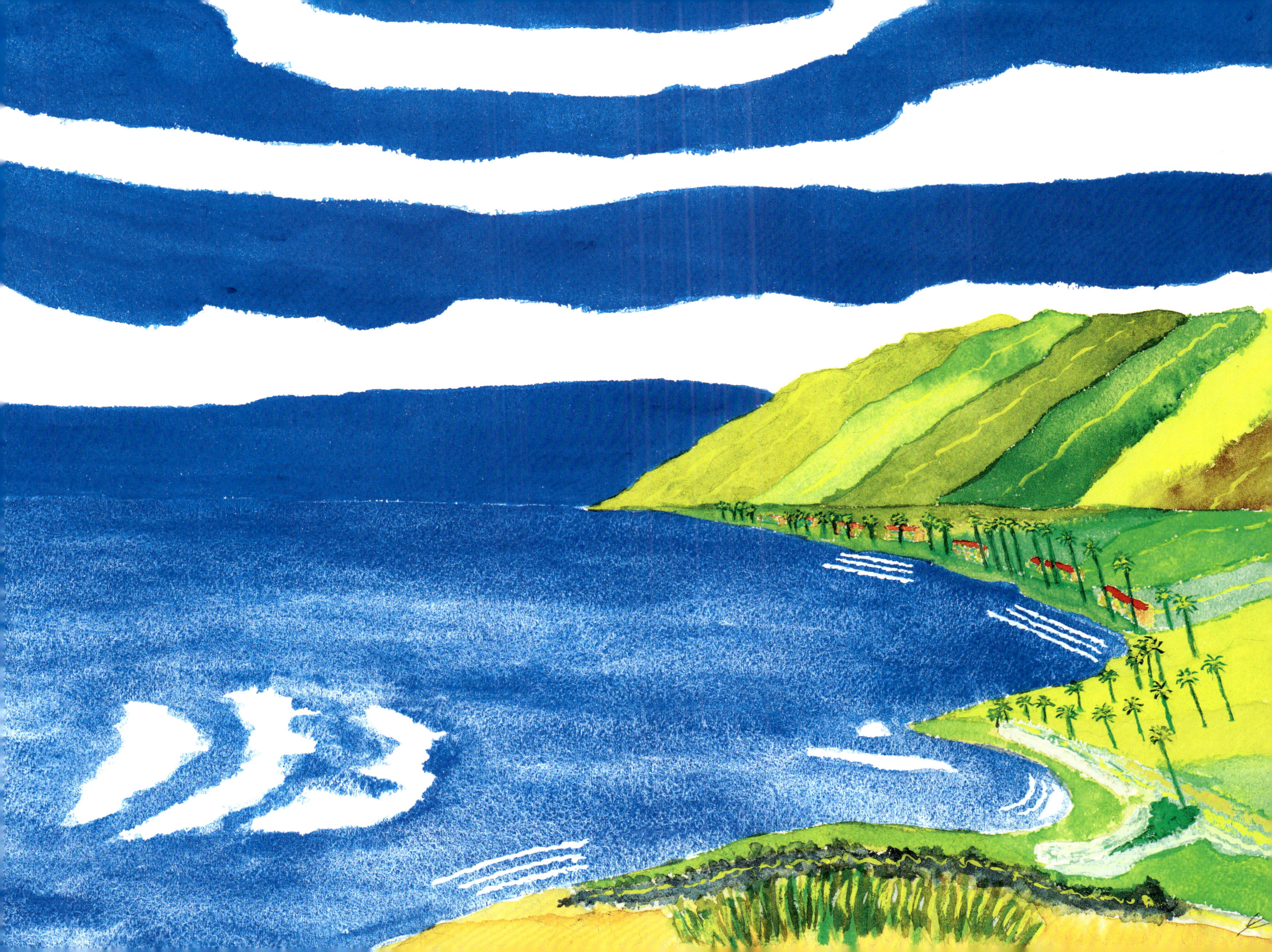

A Last Gasp

The wind
huffs and puff
all night long,
bellowing
from east to west –
wearing itself out,
it settles
down
to sigh,
still snatching
at tree branches,
to coax from them
applause.

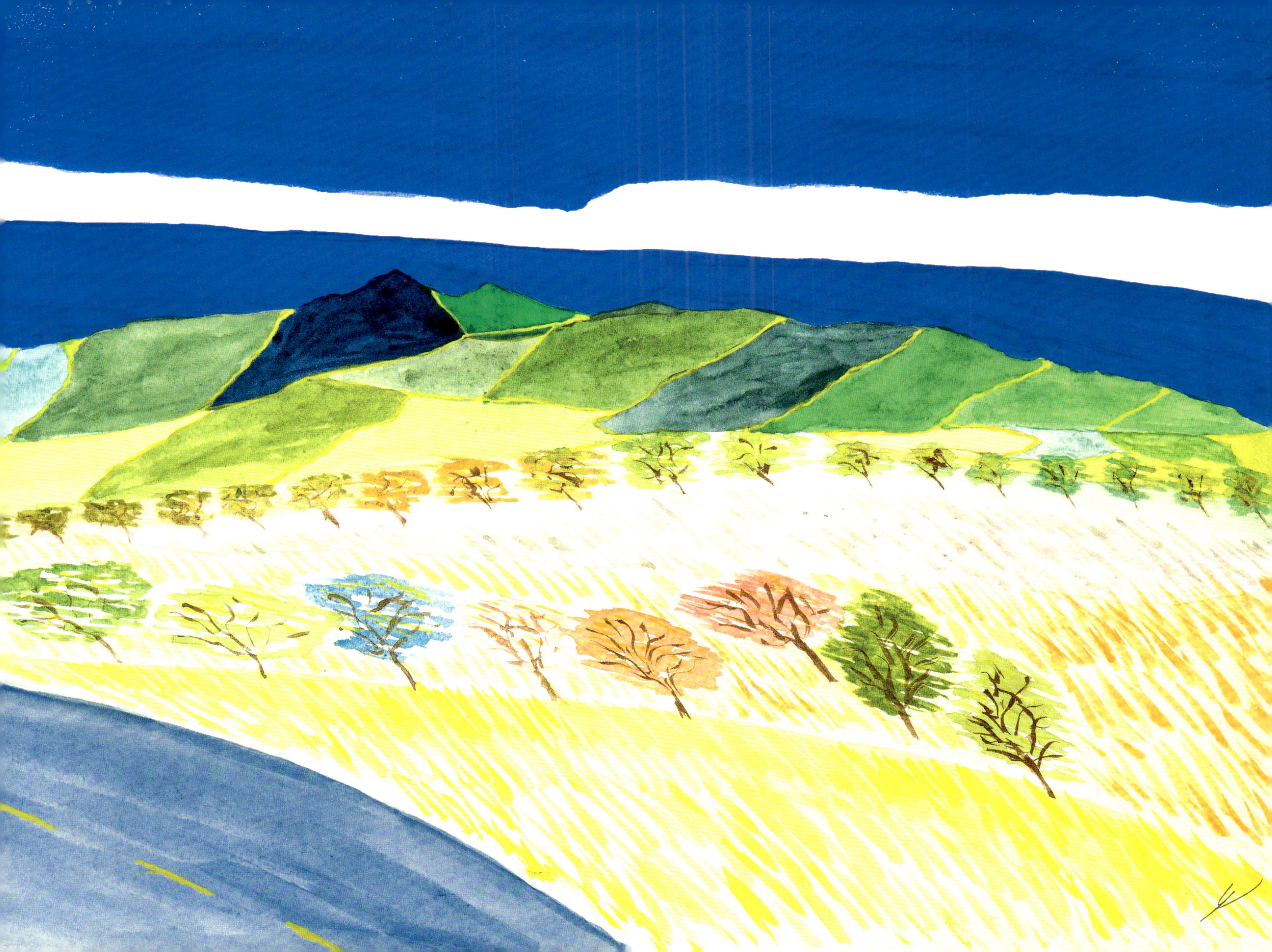

The 3rd of July

On a calm day
by the ocean,
a family
wades
into the waves,
while behind them,
a palm tree
titters,
and a beach umbrella
outspreads
dusk
on a sunny day.

The shadows lengthen,
and the ocean
settles down,
whispering
to young
and old
swimmers
that the tide
has escaped
for the night.

A Calm Day at Hanauma Bay, O'ahu

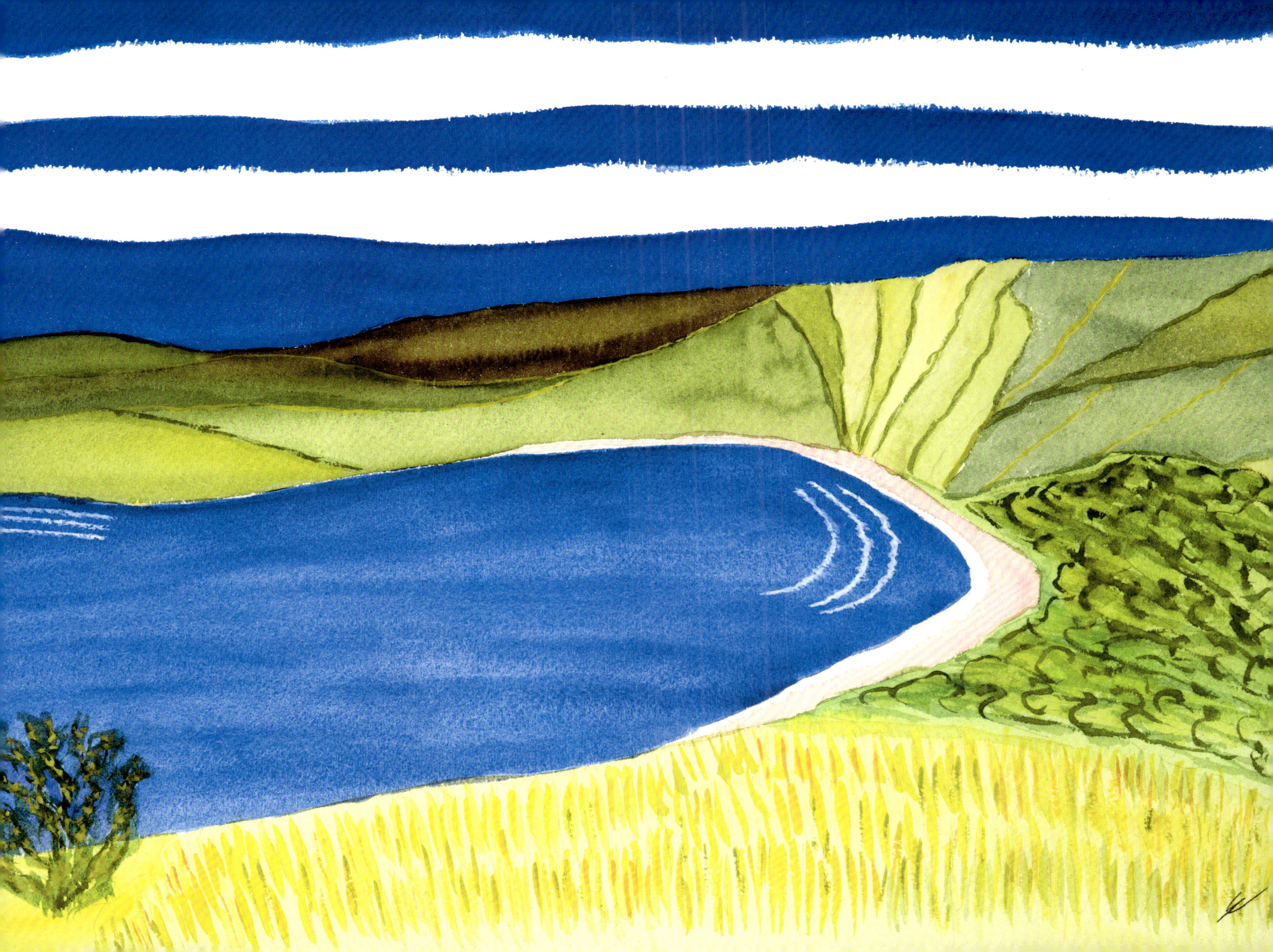

Hawai'i

One island
reaches out
to another,
pointing
at its green-vested
brother –
sharing
the same sky umbrella,
they paddle
in a school,
crossing the Pacific
in the company
of a laughing
family.

Diamond Head Beach, O'ahu

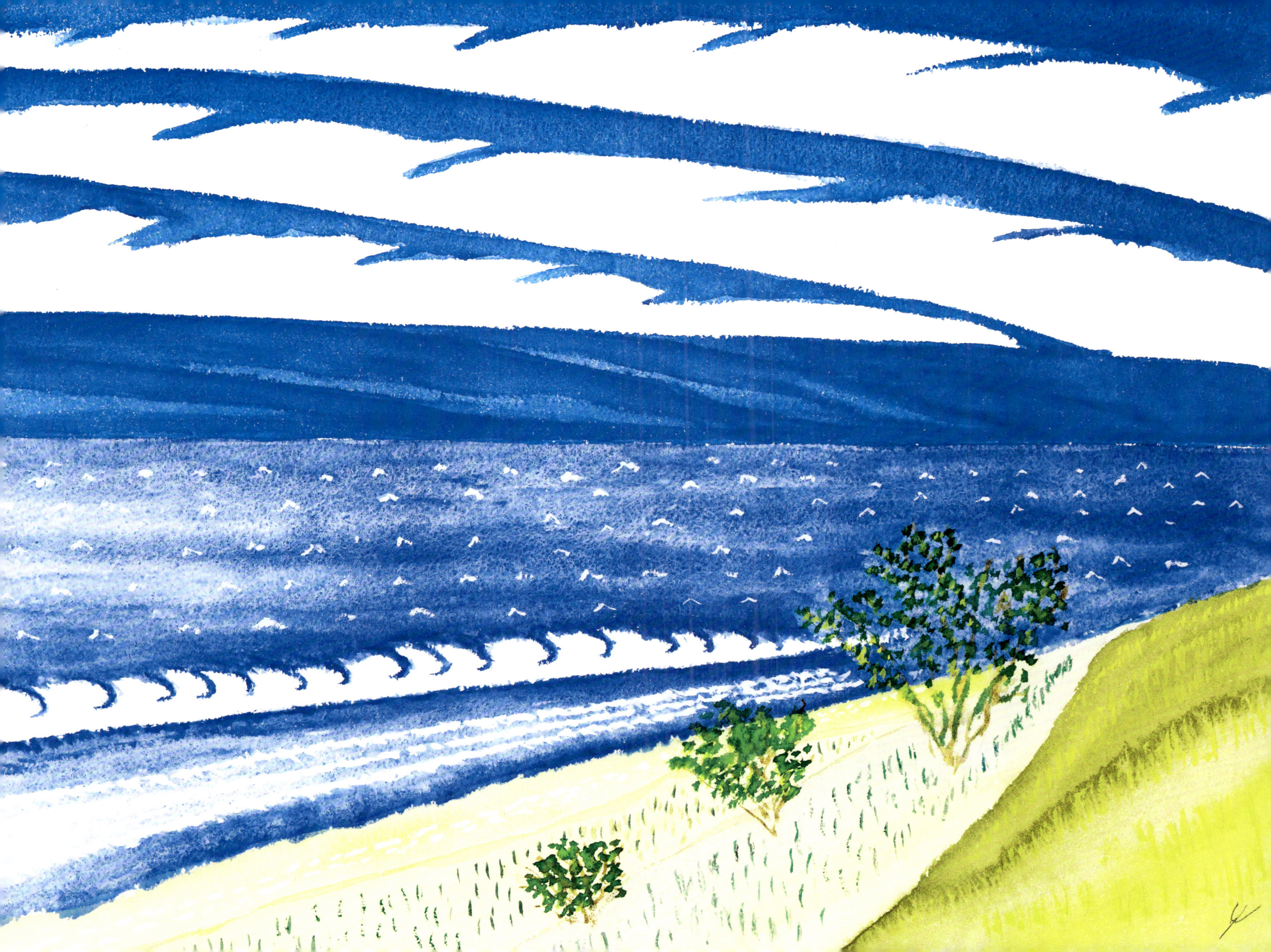

Old Enough

The gray mountain
dons
its jaunty
cap of fog,
letting a stiff breeze
whistle
about its ears –
with nothing
to hide,
it coaxes out
the sunlight,
then waits
for a cloud
to cry
on its shoulder.

An Ancient Romance

Clouds
drape themselves
around the shoulders
of mountains,
caressing
the purple slopes,
the shadow-clad
valleys,
and when the clouds
have tired
of their perches,
they amble
out to sea,
where whitecaps
claim
to be their
forgotten
lovers.

Truth Angels

The orange and gold and lavender
mountain,
gleaming
under a bright-winged cloud,
smiles
at the plain,
with its long-limbed fields,
lined by four palm trees
that have traveled from afar
to gape
at a mountain,
while whispering
sweet nothings
to corn
that has made a feast
out of sunshine.

Summer Cloud Over Mount Hā'upu, Kaua'i

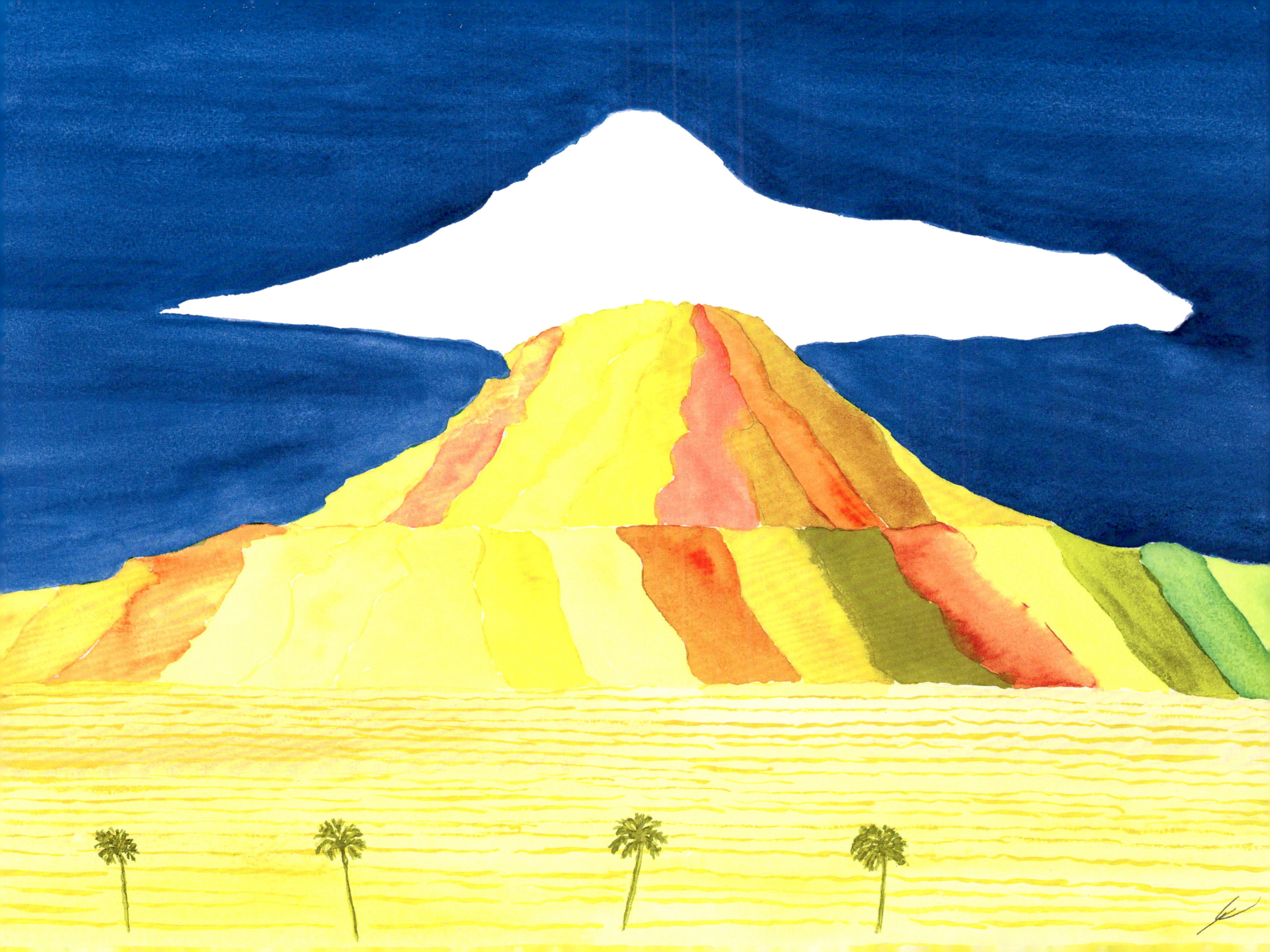

Old Roots

The monkeypod trees
have had their way,
uprooting the sidewalk
as they grow
beneath the ground,
while holding hands
with the soil,
and, now and again,
entwining their fingers
around a drainage pipe,
to plead
for a secret drink
in the privacy
of a friendly
basement.

Old Hawaiian Tree and House, O'ahu

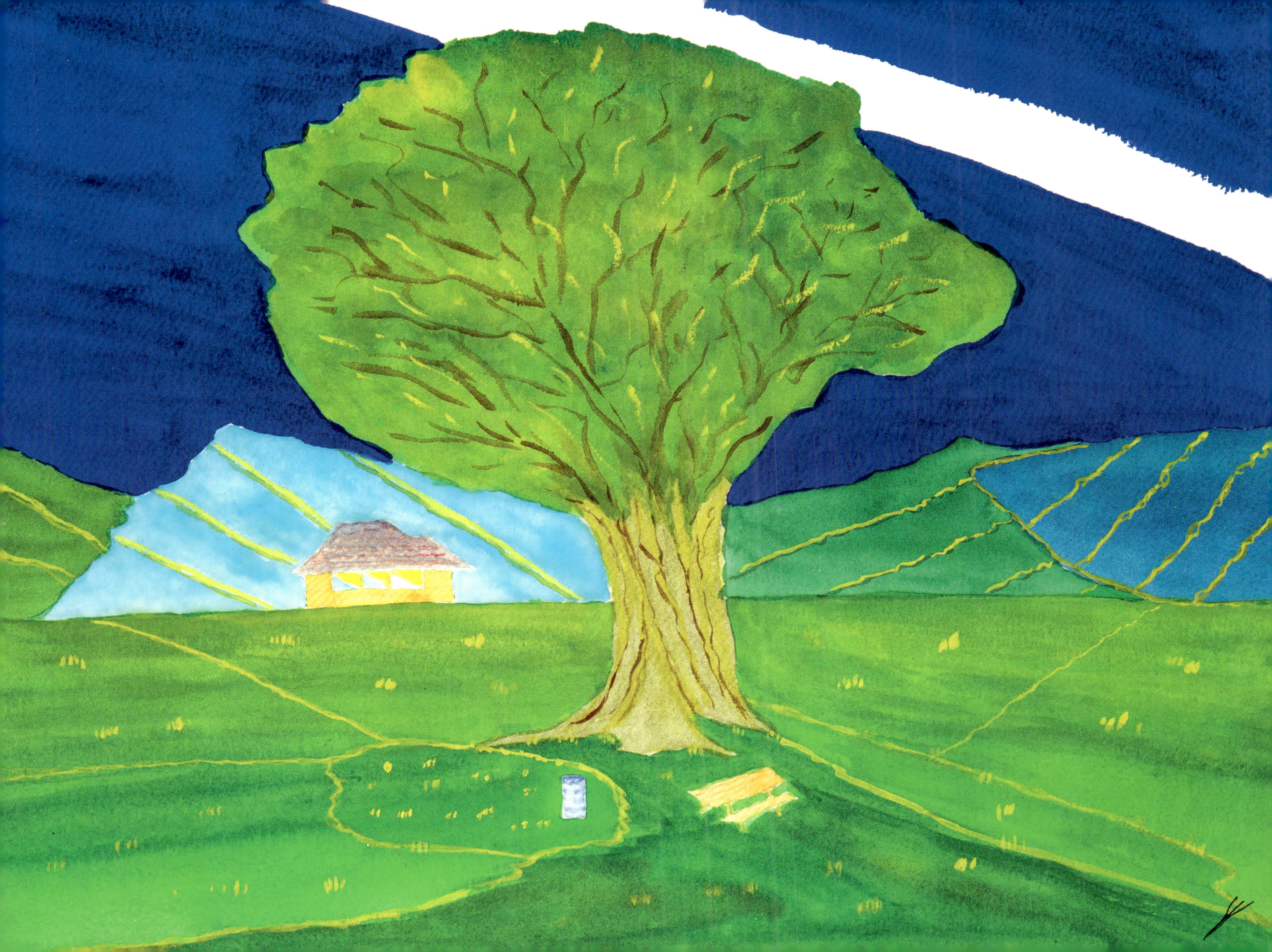

House on Mount Tantalus

Night after night,
they sat
by the window,
watching the light
tremble
on the horizon,
while the hills
tumbled down to the ocean,
and the city's lights
raised their lamps.

They must have known
that nothing could change,
so long as the ships
pulled in
and pulled out,
and the harbor sparkled
every dawn.

Now their table
sits alone,
and the shadows
of ohia trees
cradle their home,
and they,
who no longer
perch here,
have left behind
their walls
and their windows,
open to breezes
that teach dust
how to fly.

Sunset Off Waikīkī, Hawai'i

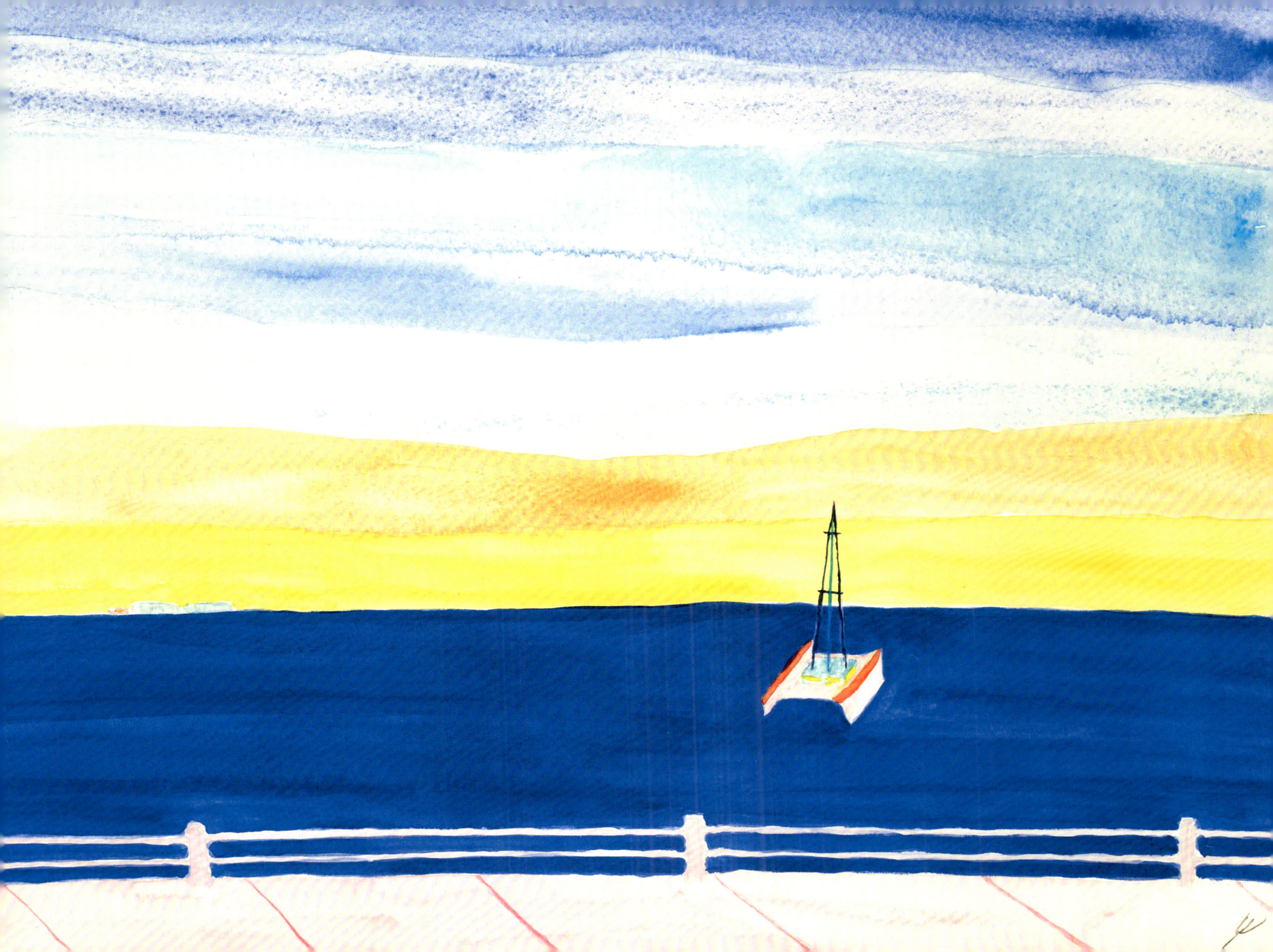

Trysts

Mountains and clouds,
faithful companions,
raise the horizon
to light-flooded
heights,
while the sky
sails away,
a witness
to lovers,
as the ocean,
curling its toes,
floats
in the embrace
of a beach
that whispers
its farewell
to will-o'-the-wisp
sailboats.

Diamond Head and Sailboat

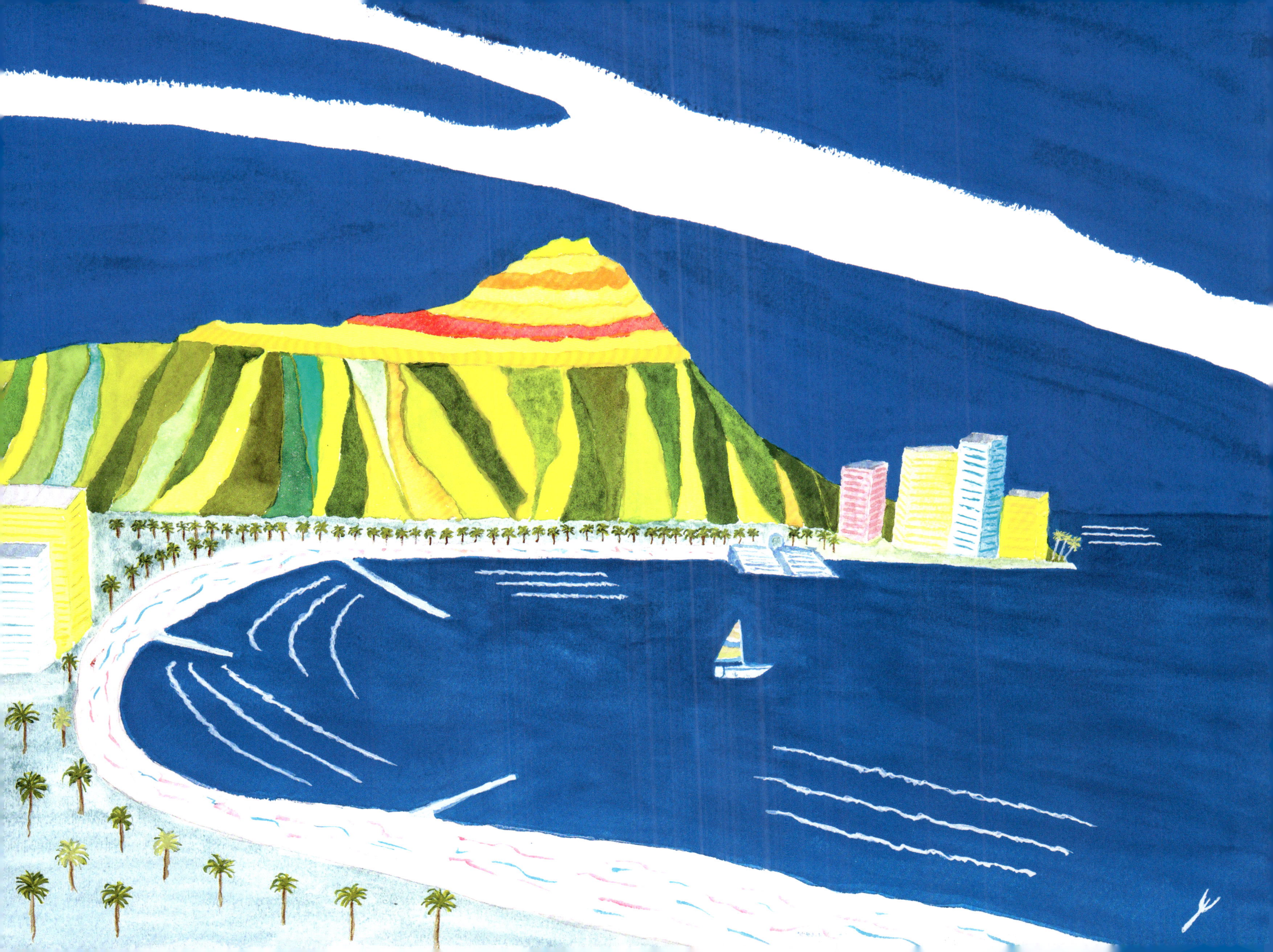

Hawaiian Mele

The notes
of the song
echo
and fade away,
while an old man
rests his eyes,
and a young couple
hold hands
beneath a table
that has grown tipsy,
on the reflections of singers
and the sweat
of Mai Tai glasses
that welcome
the soft tittering
of ice cubes.

Sunset at Turtle Bay, O'ahu

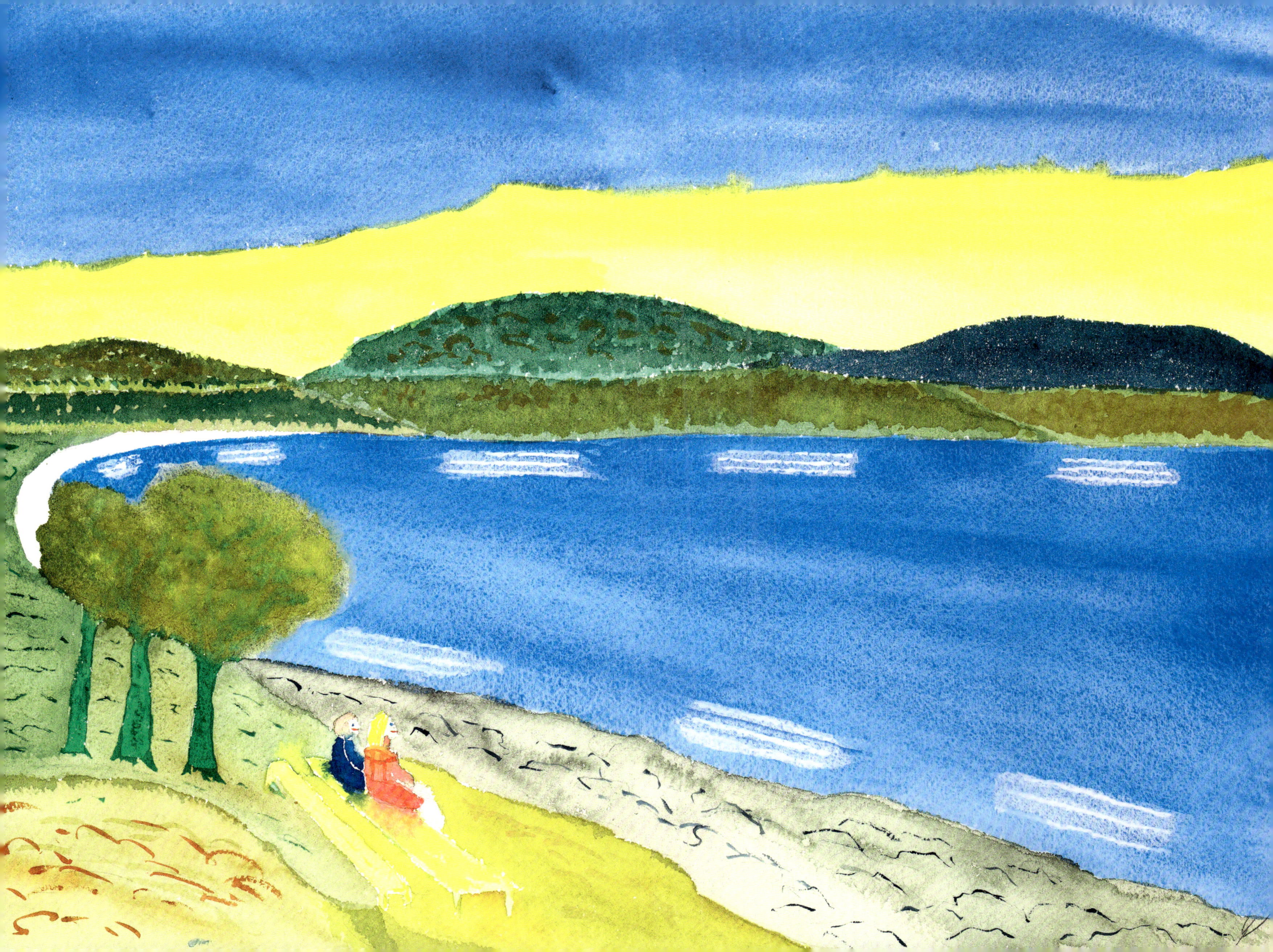

Peace in the Storm

A palm frond
plummets to earth,
torn from its companions
by a long-winded winter gale,
which trumpets
its martial hymn,
until the palm tree
brushes aside the clouds,
and, discarding
all caution,
drinks deeply
of the rain
that the storm
has squandered
on the soft-lipped
earth.

Spring Sunset, O'ahu

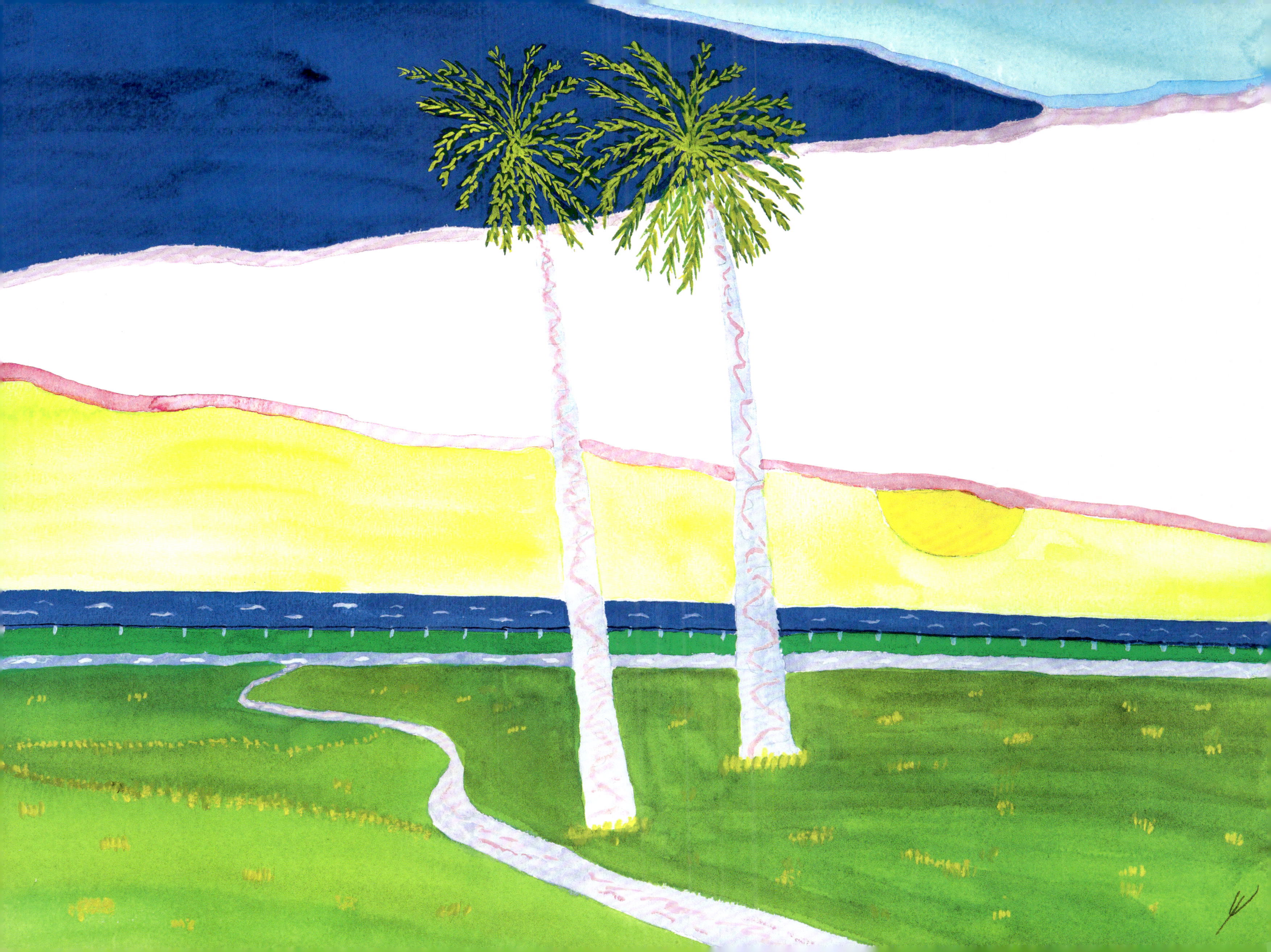

Catching a Ride

The white
cattle egret,
perched
on a pickup truck
laden with palm fronds,
hitches a ride
down the cane roads,
to a mountain
of cut foliage,
where he must work
for a living,
seeking out
insects
who never thought
that anyone
would chop down
their summer palace.

Resting, the egret
enjoys
the rough ride,
content to save his wings
to hoist high
a full belly.

Ohana

An old
Hawaiian woman
speaks in poetry,
as her wrinkles
and her graying hair
meet in peace –
gazing up,
she smiles
at clouds that part,
then straightens out
her long cotton skirt,
a garden
that she has tended
since the sun
was a reckless
teenager.

A Calm Farewell

An old
paniolo,
a Hawaiian cowboy,
yodels
at the edge
of a pasture –
standing
by his truck,
he glances
at his herd of cattle,
raising their heads
to listen,
then grazing
again,
as a breeze
tugs at the grass,
and a canyon
corrals
the last
of his echoes.

Pickup Truck and Sunset, Po'ipū, Kaua'i

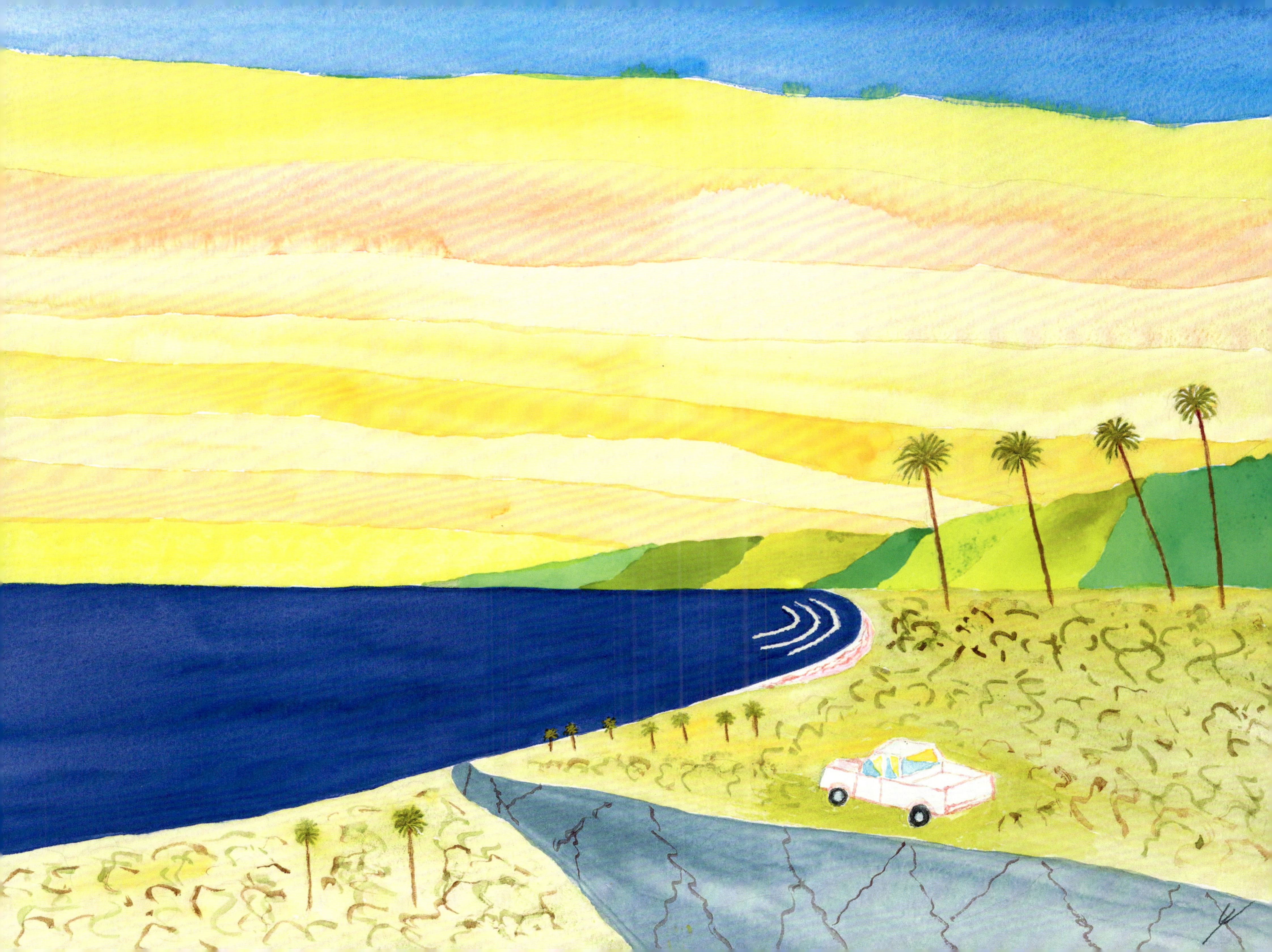

Hawaiian Laughter

Green islands
outstretch their long fingertips,
which dangle
in the surf,
as palm trees
send their shadows
swimming,
and beaches line up,
to welcome
the last
of the sunlight,
which warms them
with its gaze,
while the rainbow-clad cliffs,
unfazed,
stare
at the ocean,
their ancient
companion,
their far-wandering
neighbor.

Turtle Cove, Kaua'i

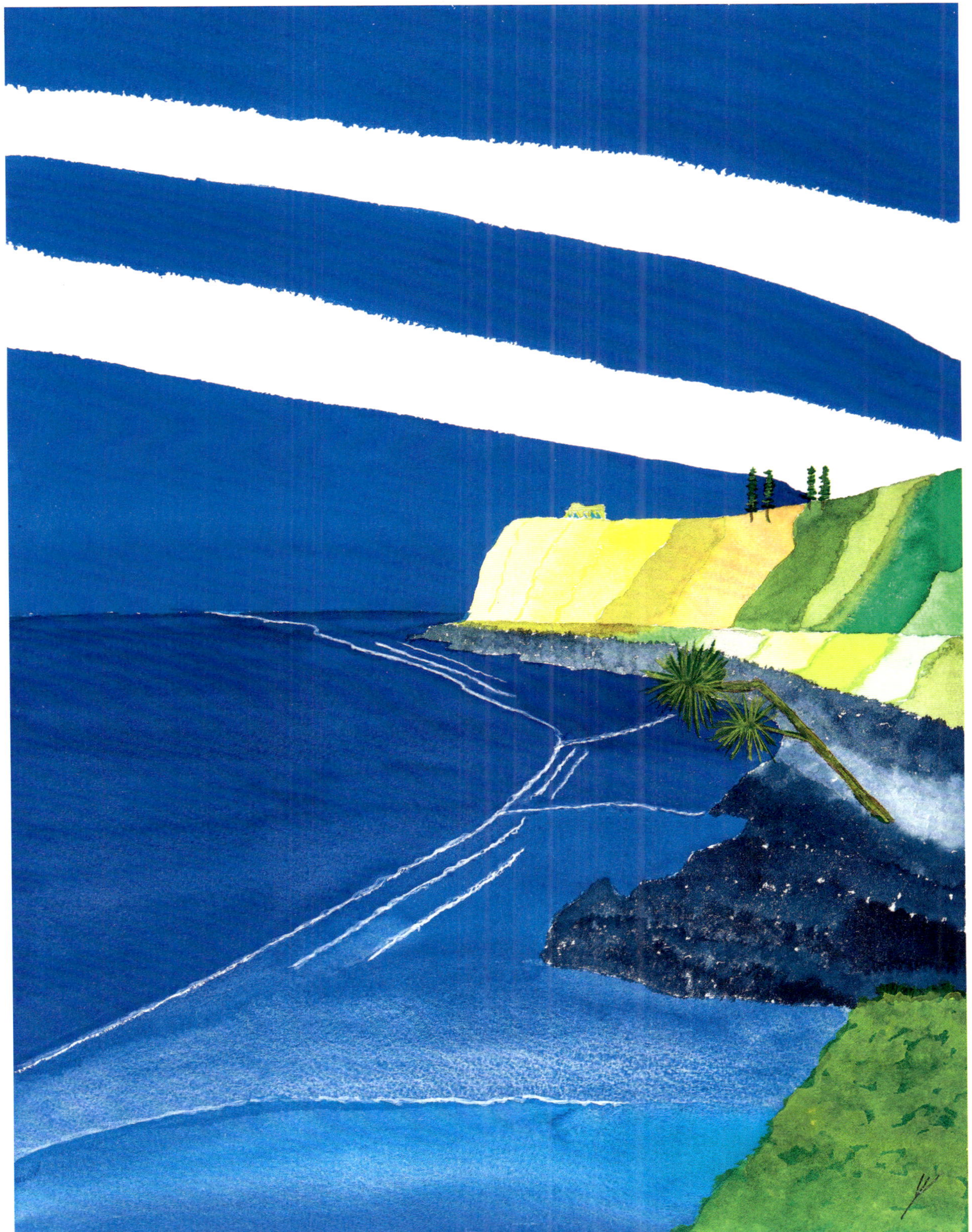

An Autumn Visitor

The ocean,
so calm
and golden-faced,
rests
on a dreamy afternoon,
when islands float
on their backs,
watching
the clouds
drift
into uncharted
heavens.

Afternoon Light at the Beach, Po'ipū, Kaua'i

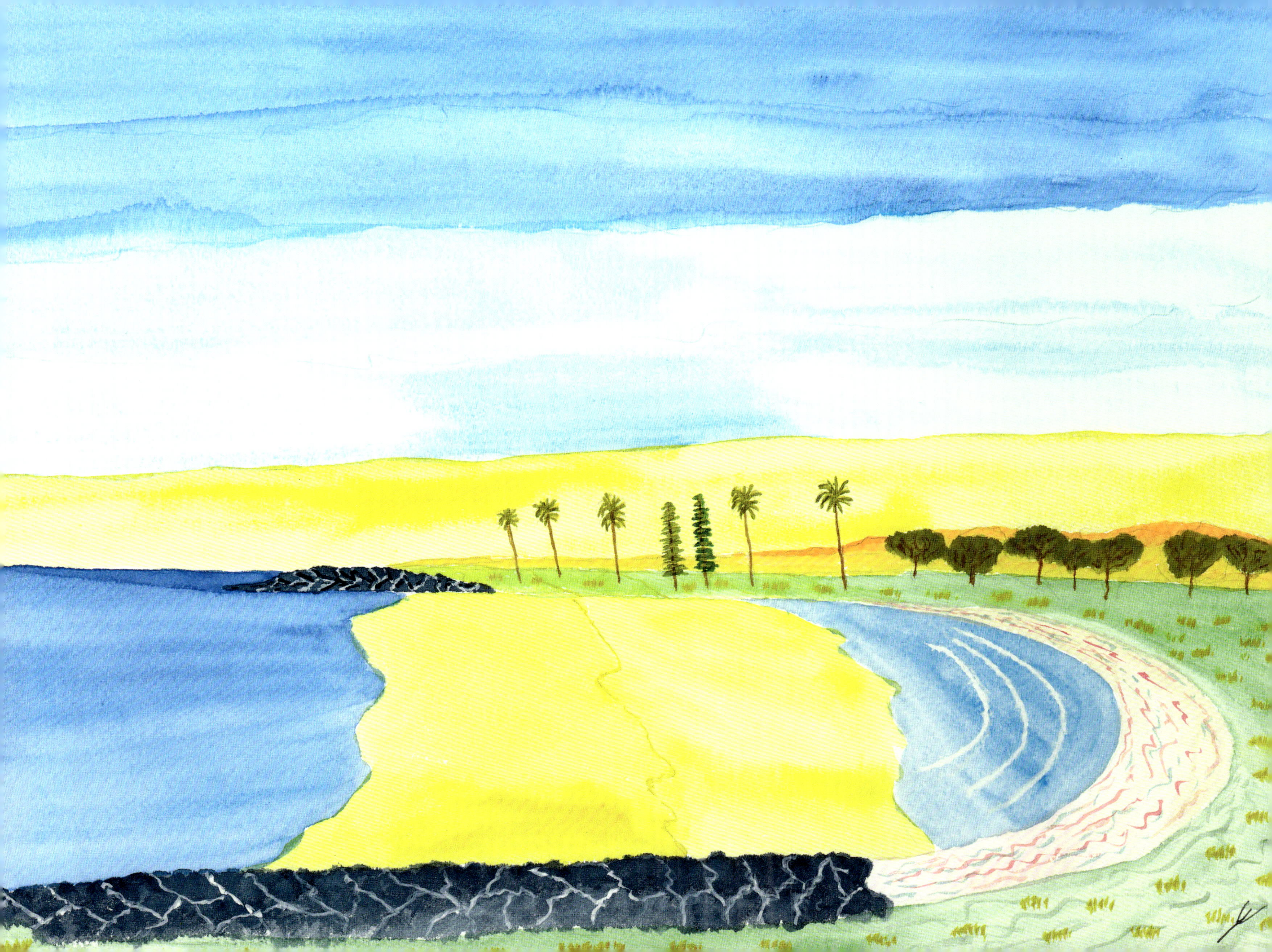

The Nā Pali (the cliffs) Coast, on the western side of Kaua'i, is spectacular from the ocean or from outlooks at its summit. No road has been cut around these rugged cliffs, which rise from sea level to about 4000 feet. One theory of how the cliffs were formed postulates that a gigantic landslide, or series of landslides, including submarine landslides, created this dramatic feature of Kaua'i's topography. While this scenario is possible, scientists now theorize that wave erosion and gradual subsidence of the shield volcano that is Kaua'i, along with changing sea levels, were probably the most important factors in the sculpting of this shoreline.

Regardless of their origin, the cliffs inspire awe and reverence. The valleys that lie nestled among Nā Pali canyons once were home to thousands of Native Hawaiians. These valleys still retain an aura of spirituality that Hawaiians have revered for centuries.

One of the most appealing characteristics of Hawai'i, including the Nā Pali Coast, is the relationship between place names and stories. Many of the names of Hawaiian places refer to stories of mythical or historical adventures by human beings and gods. Thus, the name of a place confers upon it a history and a mythology, and therefore a spiritual presence that resides not only in the place but also in the thoughts of all who speak or hear its name.

Nā Pali Coastline, Kaua'i

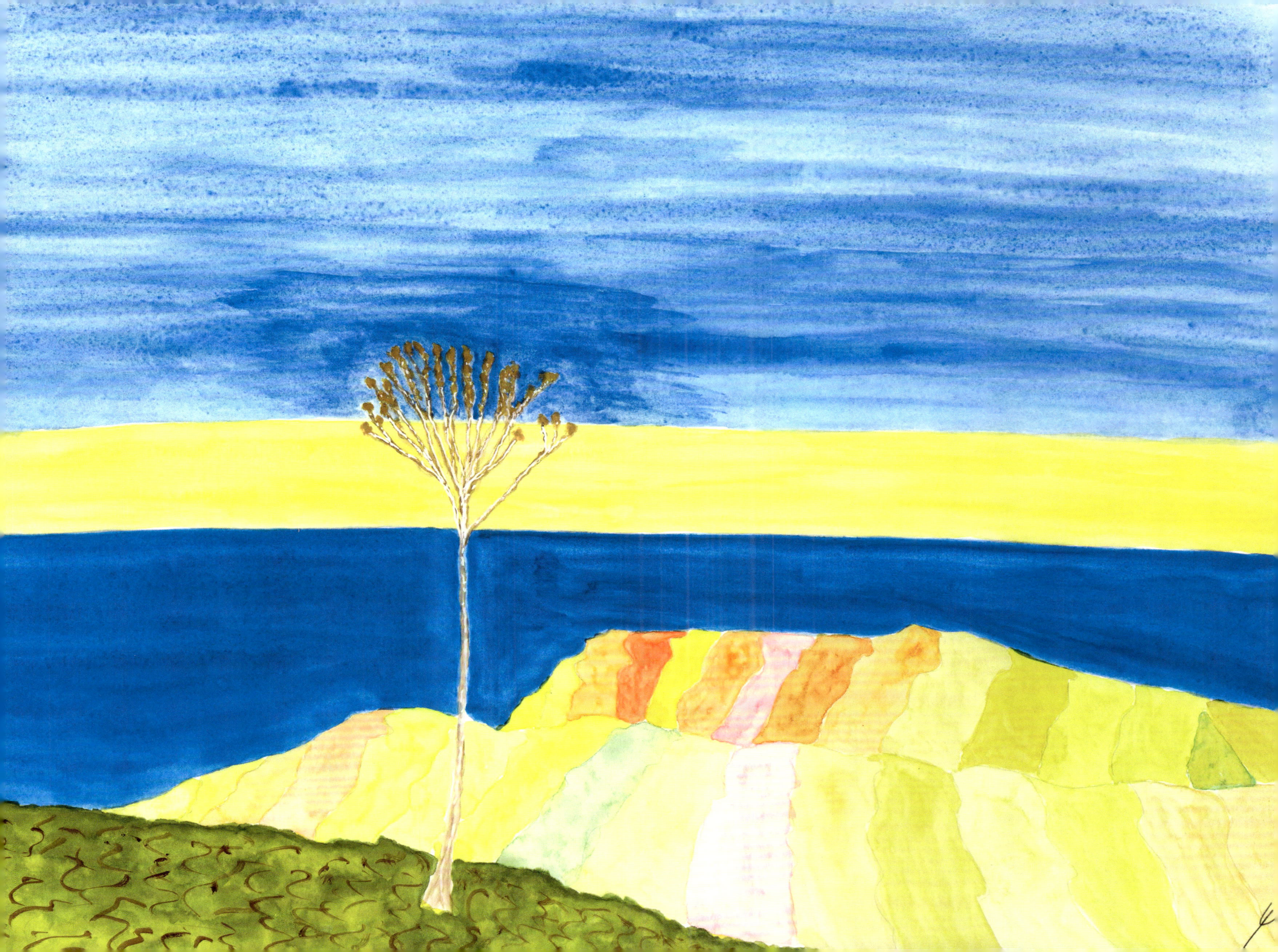

A Surprise Ascent

A mountain of a man,
wearing
a flowering
aloha shirt,
sits waiting
in a wheelchair
in an airport,
watching passengers disembark,
and when his flight
is announced,
he rises,
in his mind of minds,
to let
his garden
of red hibiscus
and white plumeria
and bird of paradise
and fragrant gardenia
and orchids with purple eyeshade
dance
with breezes
that are as light on their wings
as hummingbirds.

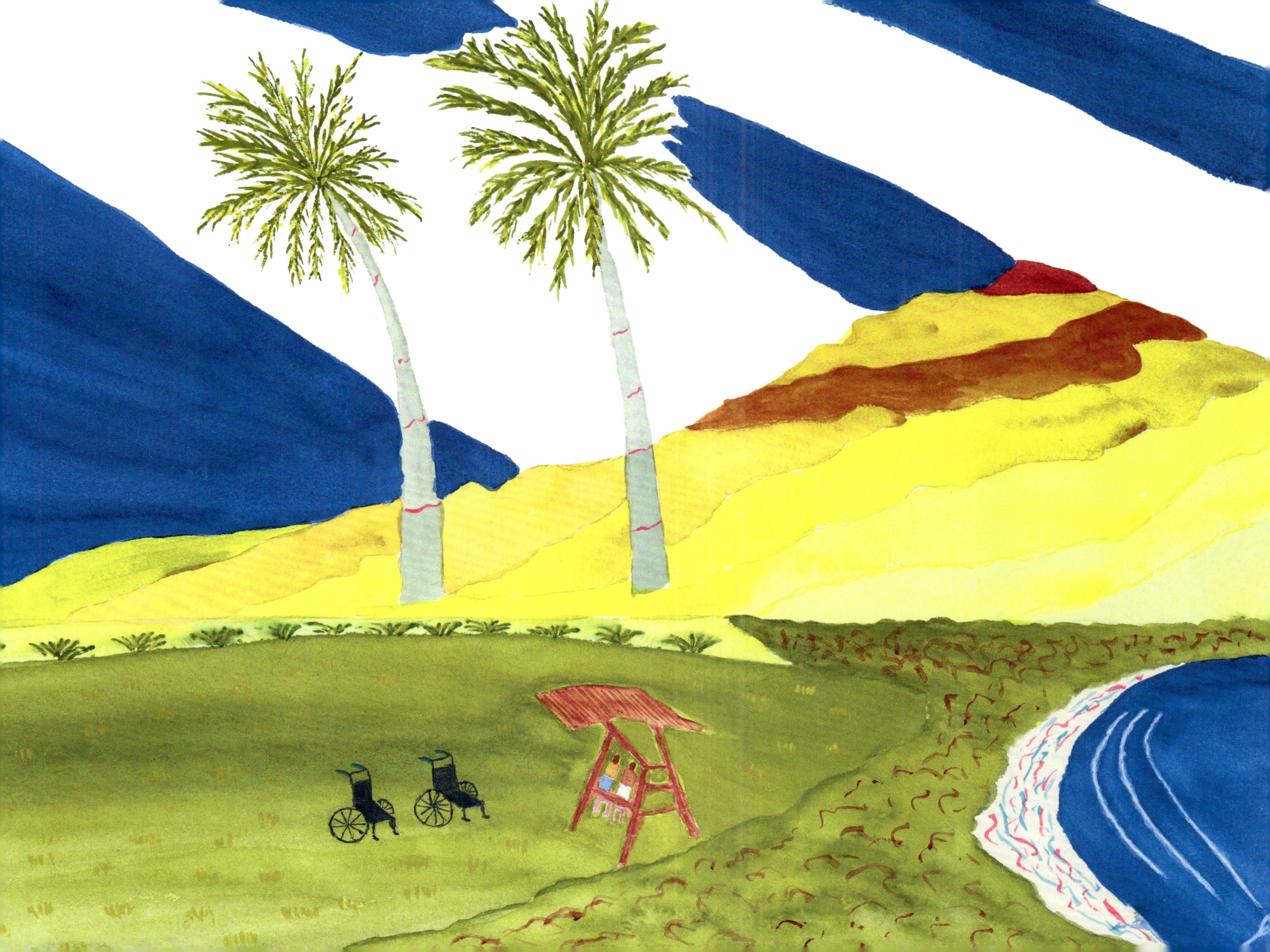

The Faithful

Small boats,
circling
each other,
nod
to one another,
bobbing
on a sparkling ocean,
where the fish
share no news
of their congregation's
prayer meeting.

Small Boat Harbor in Spring, Kaua'i

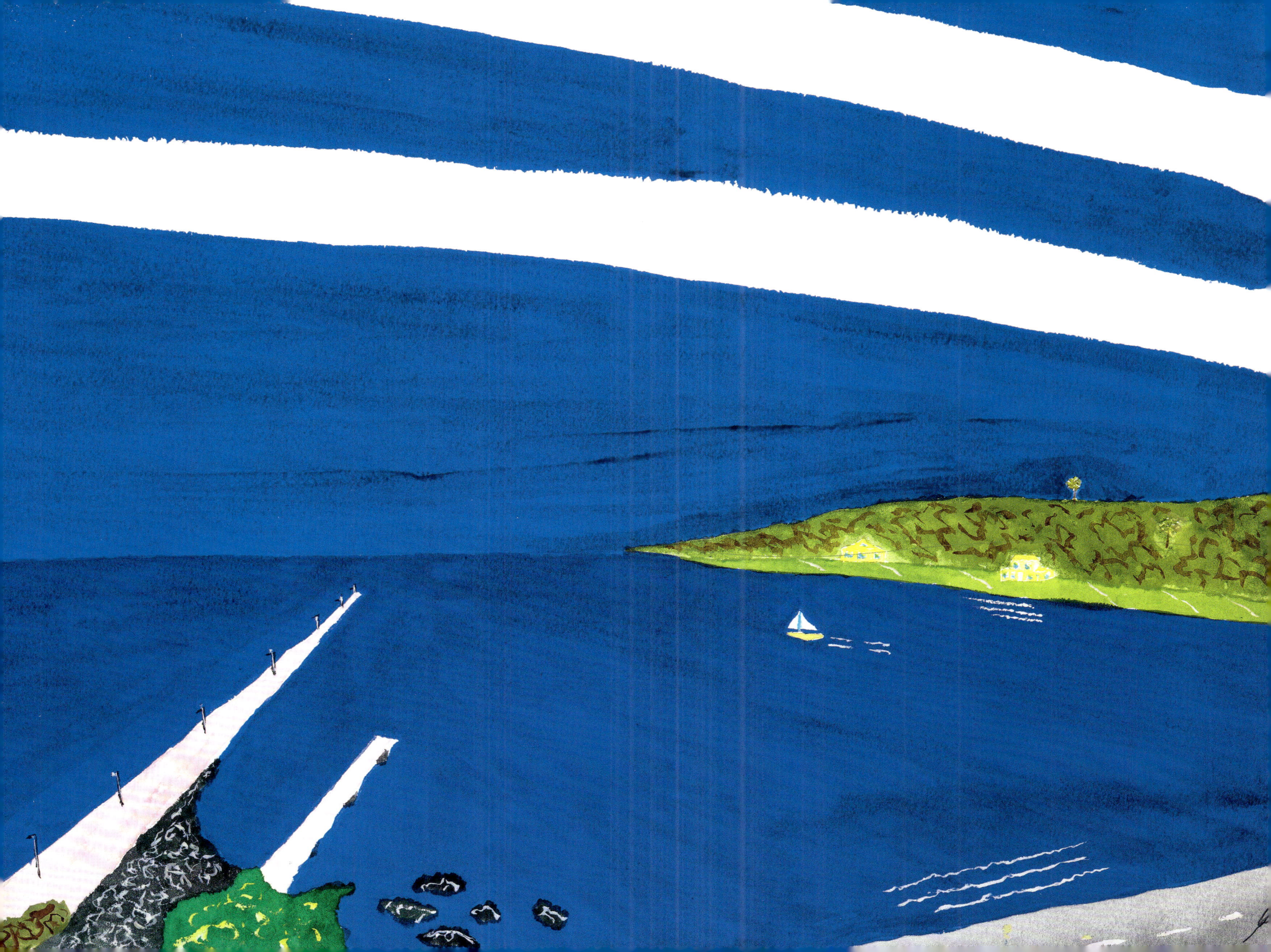

Flights of Fancy

A white egret
flutters up
at the end of the path,
a cloud
on the wing,
a whisper
thanking a breeze –
what do you see
except a flicker of light,
the sky's
silver wrinkle,
the escape
of a whitecap?

The bird
trembles into flight,
then angles
away,
and you are left,
watching the horizon,
on which a tree
has bedded down.

A to Z

An old man,
wrinkled
and smiling,
looks up
from his newspaper
when he least
expects it,
only to see
a young lady
with a plumeria blossom
in her brown hair,
offering him
a glance,
to which his young-again
eyes
cannot stand
to bid farewell.

A Reckoning

The old dog,
the hibiscus,
the lawn,
the waves,
the doves
that peck
at leftovers,
all hug each other
on a warm day
in April,
when the sky
is a vacant blue,
and only
the soft fingertips
of the grass
make sense.

House in Līhu'e, Kaua'i

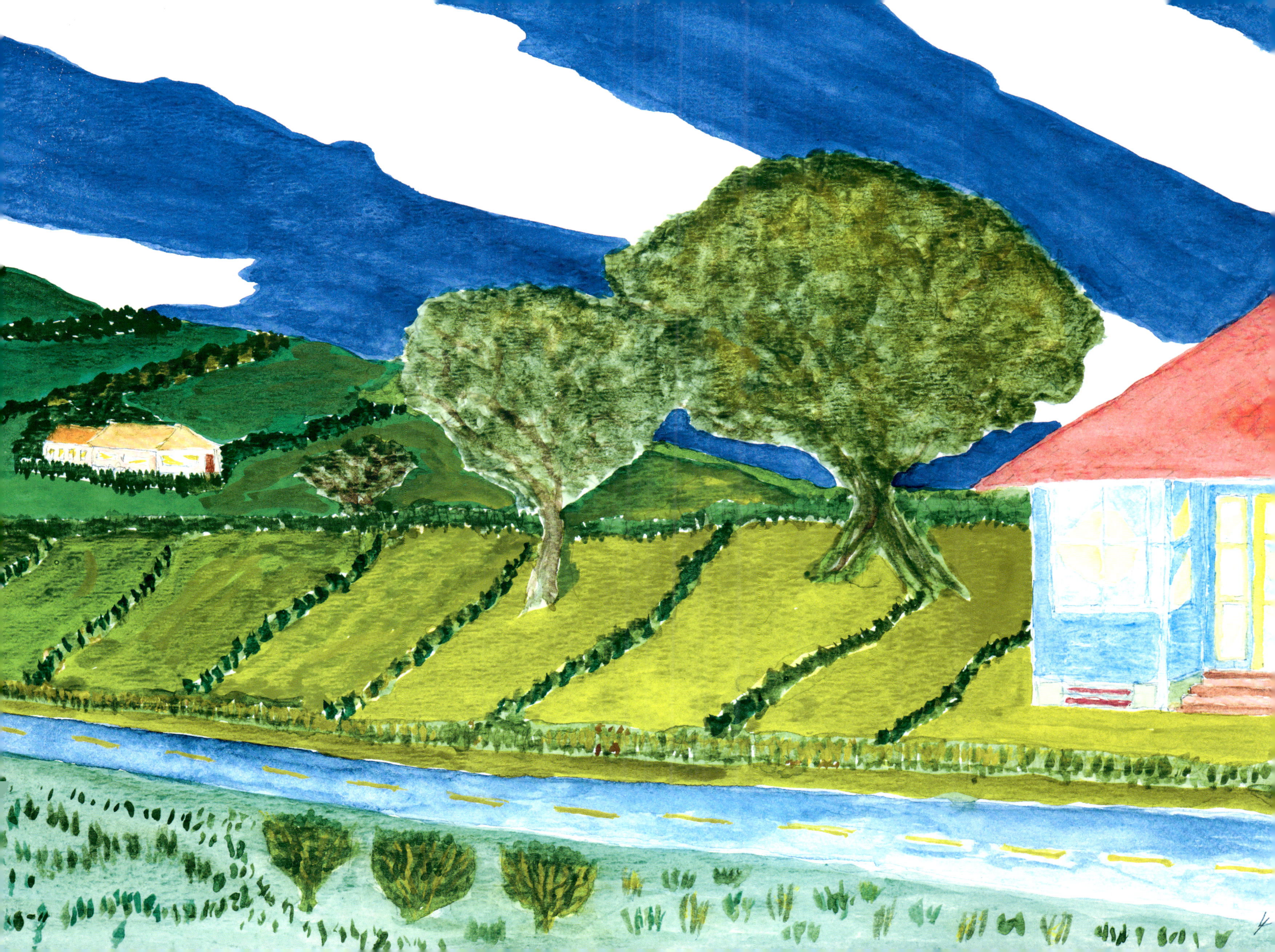

After Easter

Four nēnē geese
cross the road,
trundling forth
on a Sunday morning,
announcing the good news
of a quiet homecoming,
until one honks,
as they reach
the high grass,
where breezes
sing hymns,
and a potluck supper
is served.

Kōloa Road, Kaua'i

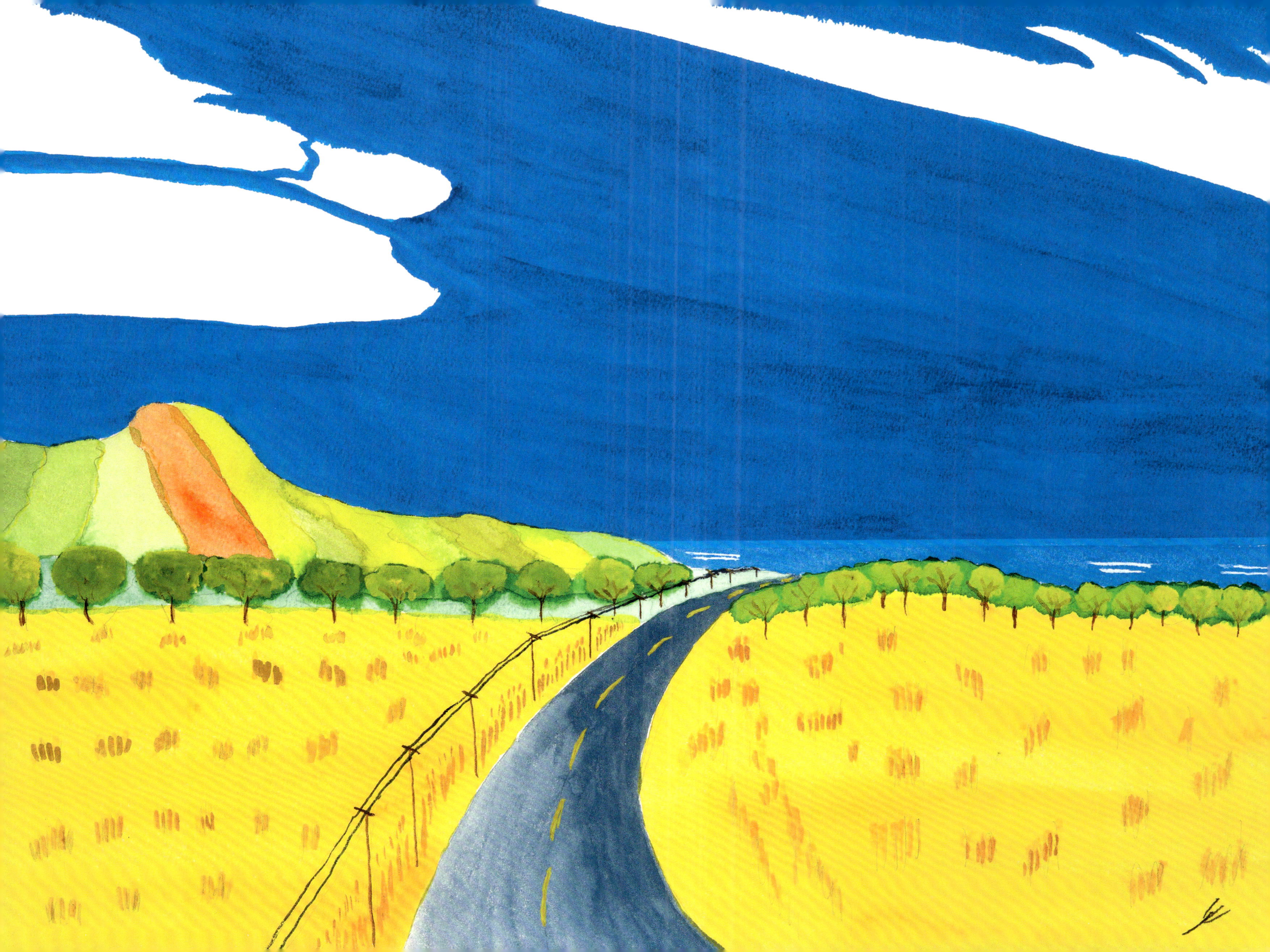

Smooth Sailing

High clouds,
wide-hipped
and bright-eyed,
float
across the sky,
flirting
here and there
with a lonely island,
which begs them
to settle down.

Shedding tears,
they set out again,
unfurling
their white skirts
and dancing
with winds,
while islands
watch them
recede
over the ocean,
where they lavish
their shadows
on waves
that have never
counted
on stay-at-home
lovers.

Northeast Shore, Kaua'i

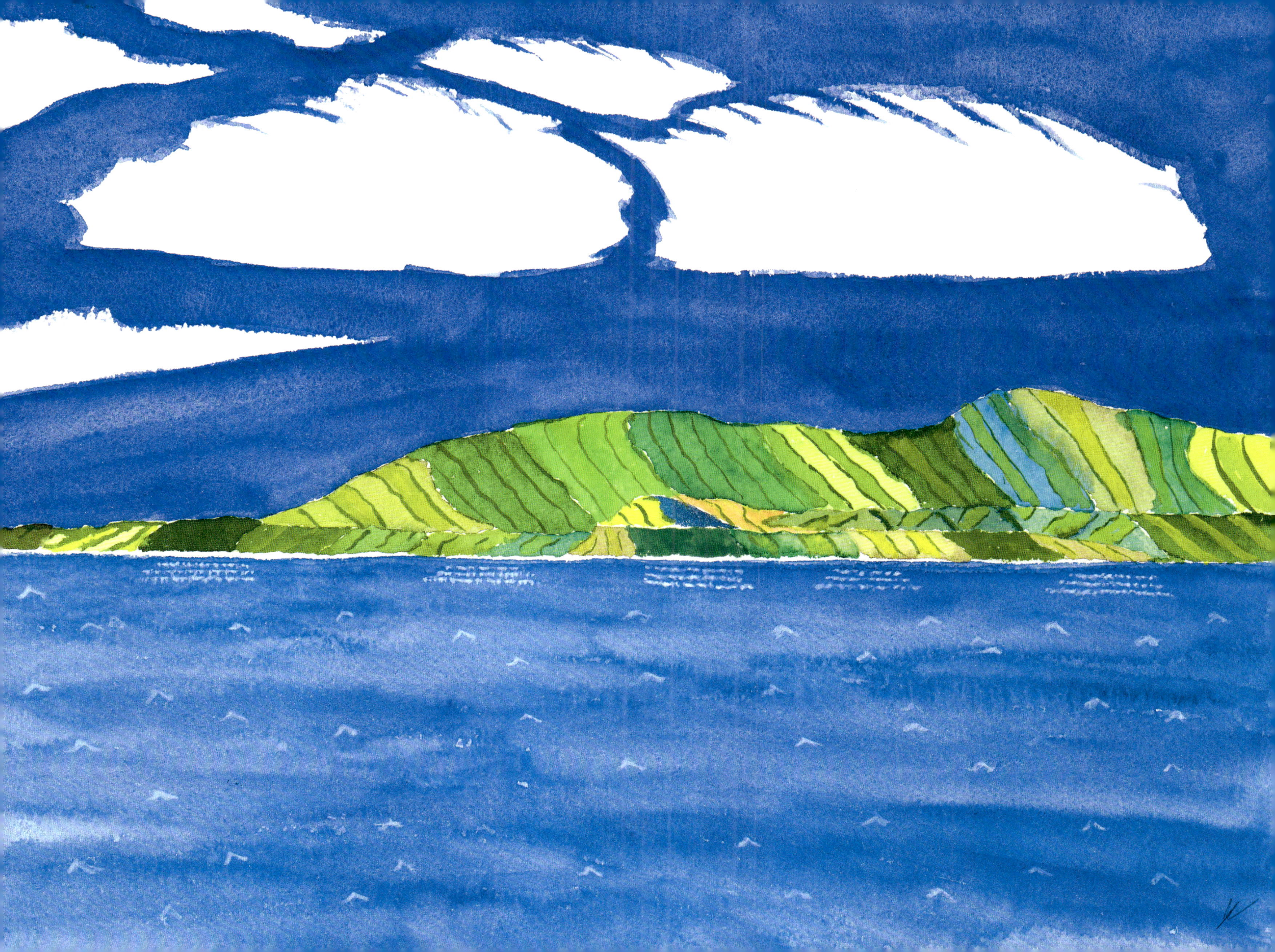

Familiar Territory

Friends
sleep
under the stars,
in a grassy park
beside the ocean,
not remembering
that their predecessors
did the same
two hundred years ago –
the surf
still prattles,
while the palm trees
shake out their manes,
and breezes
rustle
among the bushes,
as the earth
and the stars
exchange their news,
and the latest dreamers
imagine
waking up
to a new day's
laughter.

Brennecke's Beach in March, Kaua'i

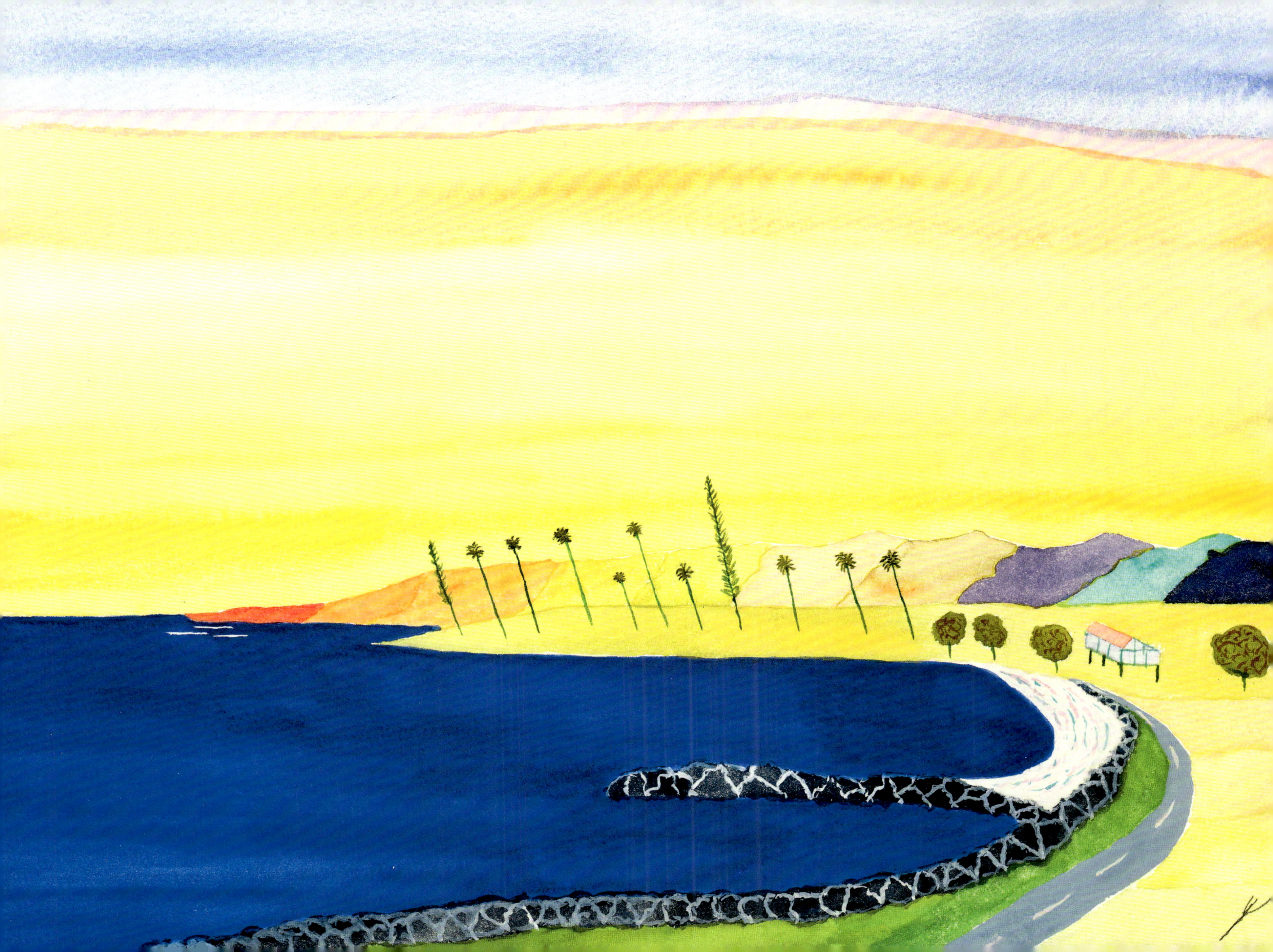

Hawai'i

Sad land,
happy land,
land blessed
by enigmas,
you welcome
the sunlight-clad
rain,
the currents
that nibble at reefs,
the mountains
that crown themselves
with rainbows,
the long valleys
where gods and men
vanish,
the cloud banks
that ripen
and drift,
the sunny beaches
that whisper
to restless
waves.

The sky and the sea
hug
their wandering child,
a stranger to every language,
except the whistling
of the palm fronds,
which know how to laugh,
even in the midst
of a winter rain.

Colorful East Shore, Kaua'i

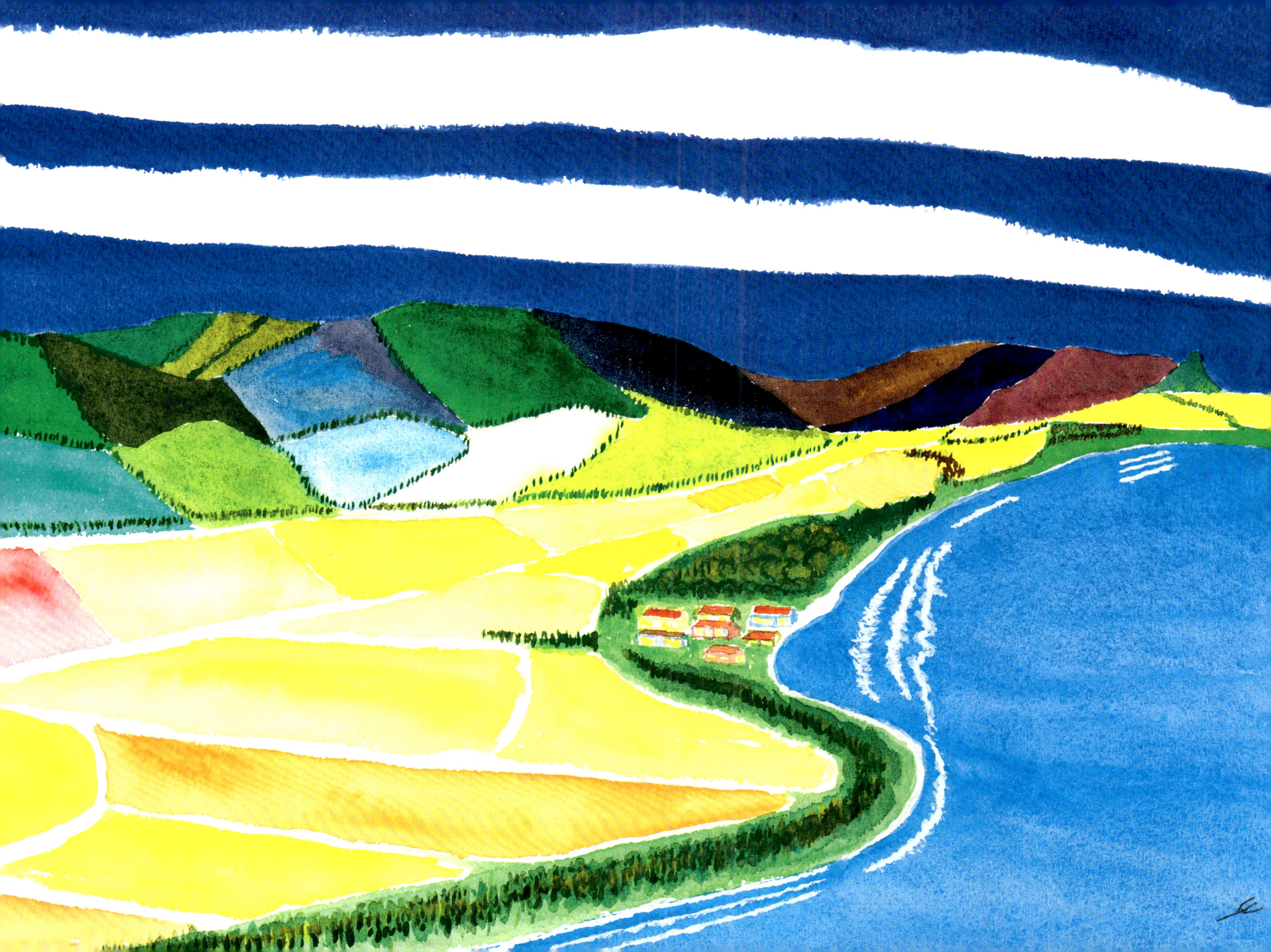

Setting Out in Spring

A small house
near the harbor
oversees
an unruly garden,
where plumeria trees
and hibiscus bushes
guard
Hawaiian moonvines
and bougainvillea –
a tangerine house,
set back
from a muttering road,
rests in the shade
of a warehouse-besieged
palm tree,
and when the tradewinds
kick up their heels,
a jasmine-clad fence
lends its perfume
to a wave-sprouting
ocean.

Bougainvillea, Po'ipū, Kaua'i

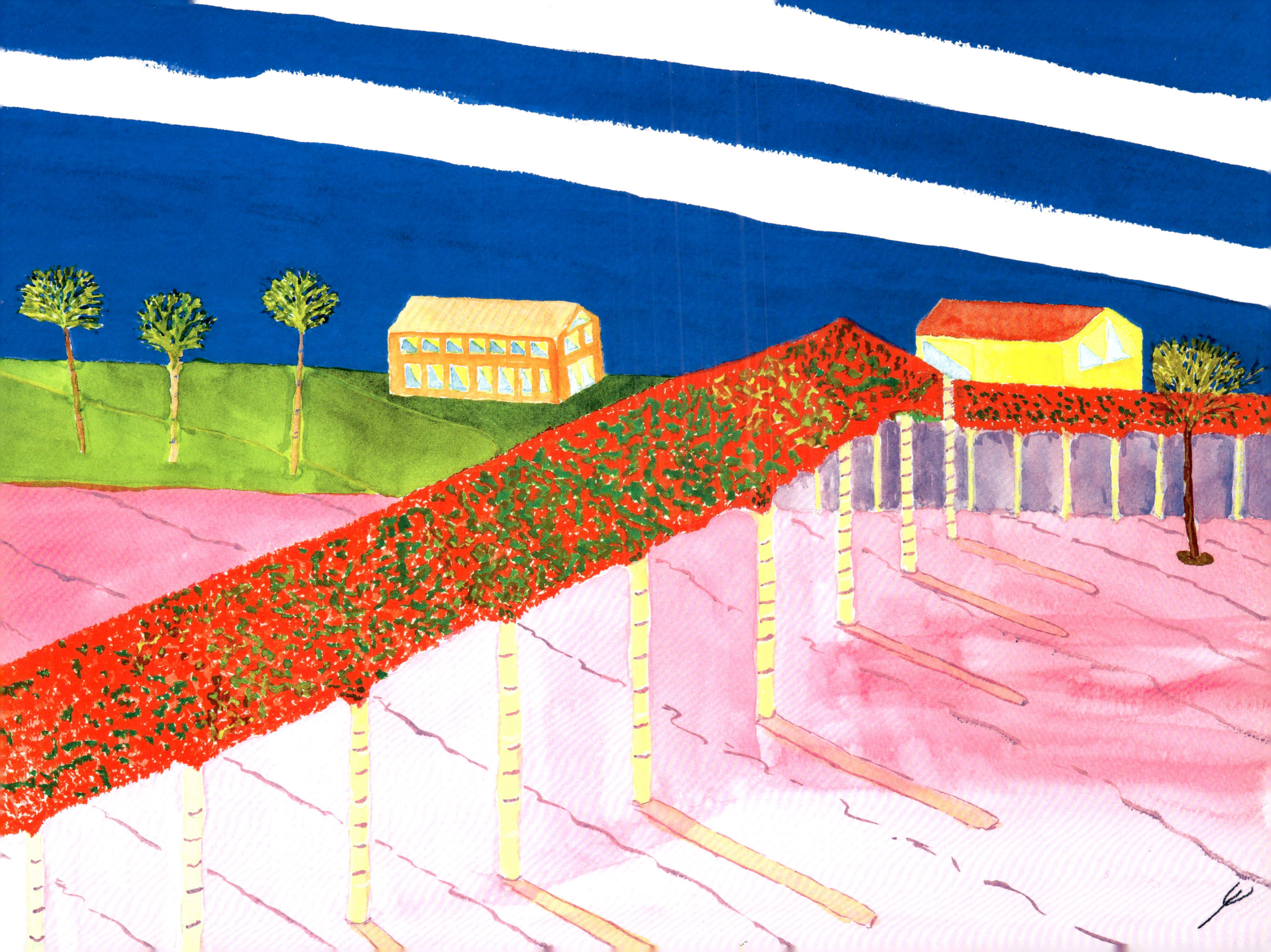

Finding My Way Home

Western light
at dusk
comes calling
when I least
expect it –
my father's light,
that promise
of tomorrow,
always
surprises me,
when it beds down
at the end
of my street –
I tried to tell him,
"Look, even now,
there's light in the sky,"
but I could not deny
that I was telling myself
that the light
would never fade –
who was right,
myself or I,
as I gazed out
at the butterscotch
afterglow?

The light
still comes calling,
night after night,
but will not answer
my question –
all it asks of me
is that I open
my door,
and make room
for its untiring
smile.

Waimea River Bridge, Kaua'i

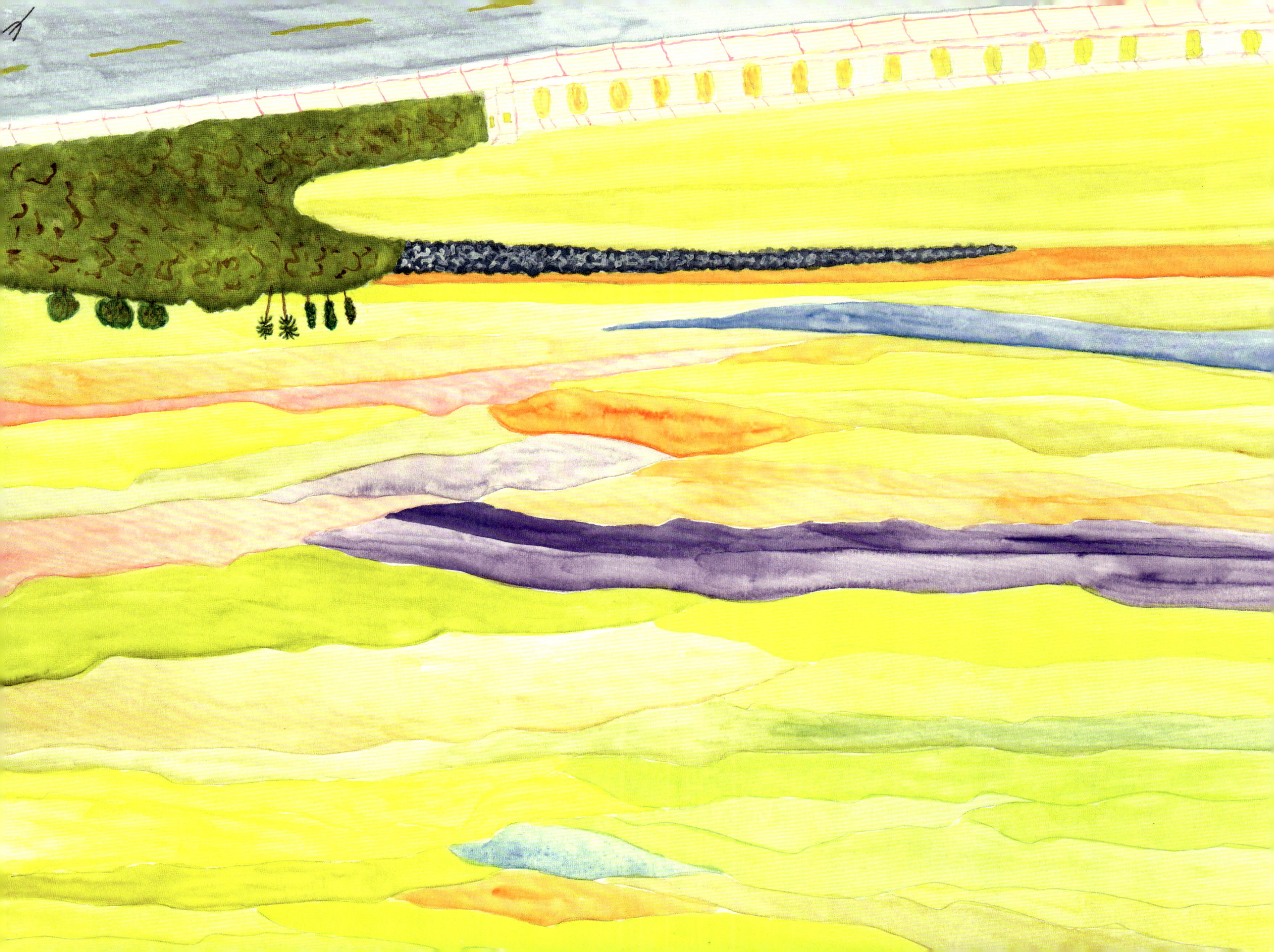